Patches of Godlight

Patches of Godlight

The
Pattern of Thought of
C. S. Lewis

Robert Houston Smith

University of Georgia Press

Athens

Copyright © 1981 by the University of Georgia Press
Athens 30602

All rights reserved

Set in 10 on 12 point Mergenthaler Palatino type
Designed by Gary Gore
Printed in the United States of America

Library of Congress Cataloging in Publication Data

Smith, Robert Houston.
    Patches of Godlight: The Pattern of Thought of C. S. Lewis
    Bibliography.
    Includes index.
    1. Lewis, Clive Staples, 1898–1963.   I. Title.
BX5199.L53S64   230   80–14132
ISBN 0–8203–0528–6

for
Geri and Vanessa—
two important women in my life

Contents

Any patch of sunlight in a wood will show you something about the sun which you could never get from reading books on astronomy. These pure and spontaneous pleasures are "patches of God-light" in the woods of our experience.

Letters to Malcolm

Preface

EVER SINCE Chad Walsh's pioneering essay and subsequent book entitled *C. S. Lewis, Apostle to the Skeptics* appeared in 1946, Lewis has been the subject of many studies, both scholarly and popular. His orthodox Christian belief has often been described, and there has been continuing fascination with his gentle, self-effacing personality, his picturesque Oxonian environs, and his bright circle of literary friends. Indeed, some studies have already begun to re-tread ground that has earlier been well explored, and it may be assumed that so long as Lewis remains popular there will always be a fresh crop of articles and books intended to help novices find their way through the Christian thought which suffuses his voluminous work, fiction and nonfiction alike.

Even the most perceptive scholarly investigations have, however, seldom, if ever, given more than passing attention to the pattern of Lewis's thought in its fullness—his underlying philosophy of religion, as it may be distinguished from his traditional Christian orientation on the one hand and his literary affinities on the other. Yet that world view lay at the heart of all that Lewis thought and wrote. It was not only vast and comprehensive; it had an elegance and richness of detail that has seldom been equalled in the history of Western thought. Perhaps the oversight has arisen from the fact that so few persons today are at home in the thought-world from which that pattern emerged. One who wishes to comprehend Lewis's way of looking at reality must first learn, among other things, the topography of Platonism, Neoplatonism, medieval cosmology and Renaissance imagery; otherwise, regardless of how well he understands Lewis's Christianity or his literary affinities, he will find that Lewis partially eludes him. It is my hope that this work will help to fill this gap in the understanding of Lewis's thought.

The task is not an easy one. Lewis's world view was so much a seamless robe that there is no obvious starting-point or ending. One cannot comprehend any single aspect of his thought in its fullness without knowledge of all the other interlocking parts of the scheme. Still, one must commence and end somewhere. The task is made both easier and more difficult because of Lewis's immense literary production, which ran to some ten thousand published pages. Fortunately the interpreter has a great advantage in the fact that Lewis's thought appeared almost full-blown in the earliest Christian writings that came from his pen. With only a few exceptions one may refer to his early or late works alike for the explication of any given subject without risking significant wrenching of his meaning. Prior to his commitment to Christianity he built his intellectual edifice slowly and precisely, like a master architect; when it was completed in the early 1930s, he inhabited it confidently for more than thirty years, with only an occasional fit of discontent. By almost any standards it was a splendid structure, well worth a lifetime of habitation.

A book of this size has necessary limitations. On matters of Western cultural background I have been obliged to generalize broadly, and in dealing with philosophical positions and problems I have had to focus largely on those matters which interested Lewis rather than attempting a balanced overview. I have tried to let Lewis speak on his own behalf throughout by using quotations liberally, but have had to forego the use of many relevant illustrative passages or relegate them to notes. The same constraints have prompted me to omit virtually all mention of the secondary literature on Lewis; the notes do contain, however, copious references to Lewis's own writings. The reader who wishes to delve into secondary sources on Lewis will find much helpful material in J. R. Christopher and Joan K. Ostling's *C. S. Lewis: An Annotated Check List*. When quoting, I have retained Lewis's British orthography but have changed, when necessary, the kinds of quotation marks in order to obtain consistency of format. Although he was generally a careful grammarian, Lewis was not always judicious in his punctuation; for the most part I have left his punctuation as it appears in his works, but in a very few instances I have altered a carelessness or a typographical error that might otherwise cause a passage to be misread. I have frequently begun or concluded my quotations from Lewis in midparagraph or even midsentence, as need demanded, but always taken care that the passage quoted represents Lewis's meaning correctly; in a few cases I have not attempted to preserve Lewis's paragraphing in a quotation, so that the flow of thought would not be interrupted.

Unquestionably something of Lewis himself will become lost in a study such as this. Call it what you will—flavor, style, charm, vigor, beauty—it has in measure been analyzed away, or at least blunted. There is no substitute for reading the man himself, particularly since he wrote with a flair so dramatically and distinctively his own. Lewis might well have been speaking of himself when he wrote, "The great man, just because of his greatness, is much more intelligible than his modern commentator." [1] He was not, of course, entirely correct in enunciating this principle; otherwise he would hardly have written his illuminating essays on Dante, Spenser, Donne, and other men of letters. My justification for writing this book is the hope that what I say will prompt the reader to turn back to Lewis's own works, there to revel in the variegated garments with which this indefatigable imagist clothes the body of his thought.

R.H.S.

Lewis's Christian Objectivism

There are a dozen views about everything until you know
the answer. Then there's never more than one.

That Hideous Strength

*T*HROUGHOUT his mature life, C. S. Lewis insisted that
his theology contained nothing but basic Christianity. He modestly presented himself as being only a front-line Christian sol-
dier. He did not purport to draw up the articles of war or the
battle plans, but only to carry out the orders that came to him
from a higher power. He reminded his readers that he was not a
theologian, but simply a lay defender of the faith. He was
guided by the creeds of orthodox Christianity, by the mainstream of theological explication within the church, and by conventional Christian practices. Neither a biblical literalist nor a
modernist, he took the Bible largely at its face value, stressing its
profound insight into the central matters pertaining to God and
man. In personal conduct he was a pietist who sought to conduct himself unobtrusively after the model of Christ.

There is, however, much more to the thought of Lewis than
this conventional Christian pietism. Undergirding, enriching,
and occasionally overshadowing his traditional belief is a comprehensive religious philosophy that is both consistent and
elegant. If traditional Christianity is the heart of Lewis's
thought, this philosophical frame of reference is its head; yet it is
not a coldly cerebral construct, but a vibrant fabric that encompasses intellect, feeling, metaphysics, aesthetics, and ethics. At
its core is the conviction that everything in the universe is a

manifestation of a single reality. Jews, Christians, and others have called it God, but it has gone by many religious and philosophical designations throughout history. By its very nature this reality is good, timeless, immutable, and incomparably magnificent. It underlies all lesser realities, and therefore is of supreme importance. All valid thought and activity must necessarily be consonant with this absolute.

Characteristically, Lewis did not claim to have devised this world view himself, even though the varied expression which it finds in his writings may sometimes be said to be distinctively his. He noted with satisfaction that he stood in a venerable heritage that began in paganism, came to fruition in earliest Christianity, and was elaborated further during the next thousand years. He did not make this assertion solely on historical grounds, though he was sure there were such, but also on the philosophical ground that if reality is one, there can be but one correct way of structuring human life and society around it. All other religious and philosophical positions necessarily contain inconsistencies and other imperfections which are bound to manifest themselves to any who attempt to live by them. Thus Lewis regarded himself as a latter-day exponent of a metaphysics that has stood at the center of human thought through the centuries. Only within the past two hundred years, he argued, has the civilized world departed massively from the normative philosophical and religious perspective of the ages, and that late development, he was sure, is an awesome sign of impending doom for civilization.

Lewis found the earliest, and most definitive, philosophical enunciation of this view of reality in the writings of Plato. As a schoolboy he began to read some of the Platonic dialogues in Greek,[1] and while a student at Oxford he deepened his understanding of Platonic thought. Many years later he declared that he loved Plato before he knew St. Augustine,[2] and when listing thinkers with whom he felt a strong sense of kinship he generally mentioned Plato.[3] His grasp of Platonism went far beyond that of a dilettante. At the beginning of his career in 1924–25 he taught philosophy at Oxford, and his lectures of that year show

2

careful attention to various philosophical problems posed by Plato's world view.[4]

Lewis had by no means completed his insight into Plato at this time; he tended to dwell on some of the weaknesses in Plato's thought that are most obvious, such as the regimentation prescribed for the ideal state in the *Republic*. In his verse-fantasy *Dymer*, published when he was twenty-eight and not yet a committed Christian, he alluded to Plato as the fashioner of a government against which the romantic soul must inevitably rebel. Although there is a certain orderly beauty to such a state, life there is monotonous.

> At Dymer's birth no comets scared the nation,
> The public crèche engulfed him with the rest,
> And twenty separate Boards of Education
> Closed round him. He passed through every test,
> Was vaccinated, numbered, washed and dressed,
> Proctored, inspected, whipt, examined weekly,
> And for some nineteen years he bore it meekly.
>
> (Canto I, stanza 6)

We need go no further, for we realize that the lifeless state in which Dymer lives is all too patently a projection of Lewis's own often unhappy (and perhaps exaggerated) memories of life in English schools. Dymer's city is not a real city at all, but a classroom. Lewis has done little more than to construct a straw Platonic city and then grimly proceed to knock down his invention.

Still, there was a deep-rooted affinity for Platonism within him. Some years earlier, when he was a bare twenty years old, he had made his first foray into publishing with *Spirits in Bondage*. Embedded within that work we find an awareness of higher realities that is essentially Platonic, indeed Neoplatonic.

> Atoms dead could never thus
> Stir the human heart of us
> Unless the beauty that we see
> The veil of endless beauty be,

3

Filled full of spirits that have trod
Far hence along the heavenly sod
And seen the bright footprints of God. (P. 74)

It was about this time, while studying at Oxford, that Lewis met Owen Barfield, who considerably expanded Lewis's intellectual horizon and his critical faculties. Barfield had a knack for sensing the deeper values of philosophical systems. Many years later Lewis recalled that once when he and Barfield were lunching in Lewis's room, he happened to refer to philosophy as a "subject." "It wasn't a *subject* to Plato," said Barfield, "it was a way." [5]

In 1929, at the age of thirty-one, Lewis became a theist. A year later he attempted his first novel, which he entitled *The Moving Image*. Of this work he wrote to his friend Arthur Greeves: "By the way, about the 'Moving Image' I should warn you that there is going to be a great deal of conversation: in fact it is to be almost a Platonic dialogue in a fantastic setting with story intermixed. If you take *The Symposium, Phantastes, Tristram Shandy* and stir them all up together you will have the recipe." [6] In the novel Lewis experimented with Socratic dialogue, of which he was much enamored. He did not finish the work, and all trace of it has been lost. Although he remained highly appreciative of Plato's earlier and more vigorous dialogues, he did not again attempt a slavish imitation of that form. Much later, echoes of the dialogues were to appear in such diverse writings as *The Screwtape Letters*, the apologetic books, and the discussions between Ransom and the Green Lady in *Perelandra*.

With his discovery of Charles Williams's *The Place of the Lion* in 1936 and his subsequent, frequent contacts with Williams at Oxford during 1939–45, Lewis came to a richer awareness of the potential relevance of Platonism for his Christian world view. He was much taken with Williams's stress upon the orderliness of the realm of the absolute, and shared with Williams a fascination with the occult. Here, at last, his earlier love of Platonic thought and the influence of Barfield came to fruition. Williams was the catalyst, but the reaction could never have taken place had it not been nurtured in Lewis's mind. Lewis enfolded

4

Platonism into his Christianity, not simply as an intellectual system but as a satisfying window upon reality. This new dimension of his thought can be detected in *Out of the Silent Planet* (1938), and even more in *Perelandra* (1944) and *That Hideous Strength* (1946). It also figures in the Narnian tales, the first of which was begun in 1939.

Platonism, as the mature Lewis perceived it, was a philosophical embodiment of the same absolute truth that was to be found in Christianity. Reality was all that was good in the universe, a magnificent continuum that began with unadulterated reality itself and, in decreasing measure, extended down to the most imperfect manifestations of reality. Plato knew full well that the absolute could not be described literally or accurately with words, and when he made the attempt he was obliged to resort to deceptively simple words and images such as τὸ καλόν (the Good), τὸ κάλλος (the Beautiful), τὸ ἕν (the One), τὸ ὄν (Being) and τὸ θεῖον (the Divine). As the aged Diotima, Socrates' legendary teacher, describes reality in the *Symposium*:

> In the first place, it is everlasting, never coming into existence or perishing, never increasing or diminishing; secondly, it is not beautiful here and ugly there, not beautiful now and then, not beautiful in one respect and ugly in another, not beautiful in one place and ugly in another; again, this beauty will not manifest itself in the shape of, say, face or hands or any bodily thing at all, or in verbal form, or in factual knowledge. It does not reside in any living creature, or in earth, heaven or anywhere else. It is by itself and with itself, in utter simplicity. Whereas all the multitude of beautiful things partake of it and are coming to be and perishing, it does not grow either greater or less, and is affected by nothing.[7]

The ultimate thus does not depend upon the experiential world for its existence, but rather gives rise to the multitudinous phenomena of the universe. Only at the end of this passage does Plato make an assertion that Lewis, as a Christian, could not accept. Plato's ultimate reality, however good and beautiful, was not sentient, active, or personal as was the Christian deity. Still, there was vast ground for agreement between Christianity and Platonism regarding the absolute, and Lewis was prepared to accept the Platonic viewpoint to the extent that this agreement existed. Not only should reality not be thought of as multiple, but it should also, by virtue of its perfection, be the focus of attention for all right-thinking persons.

The nature of right thinking was one of Lewis's lifelong preoccupations. He was profoundly impressed by Plato's conviction that questions about reality can be approached, at least in the initial or lower stages of inquiry, through reasoned argumentation. Reality, being itself orderly and beautiful, must be rational; otherwise it would contravene its very nature. Lewis makes the validity of reason a cornerstone of his apologetic writings; once that validity is established he moves to a closely reasoned argument for the validity of theism as a philosophical position, and from theism he moves on to other rational arguments. Reliance upon reason was not simply a forensic device; it was an integral part of Lewis's philosophy of religion.

Interestingly enough, Lewis was also immensely attracted by another aspect of Plato's thought, the mystical. The dialogues that he found most congenial to his way of thinking were those in which a religious or mystical element was prominent: the *Phaedo*, the *Timaeus*, the *Phaedrus*, and, above all, the *Symposium*. In the latter, as the quotation cited above shows, philosophy imperceptibly shades into something akin to a mystery religion, complete with its revelation of the deity as the culmination of a lengthy spiritual journey. Whether consciously or unconsciously Lewis identified himself with that school of Platonic scholarship which sees Plato as essentially a religious mystagogue.[8] Plato's vision of the absolute was not something to be analyzed, but an experience to be apprehended intuitively; it was a personal experience. "To die," he told his Oxford students, "without having read the *Symposium* would be ridiculous—it would be like never having bathed in the sea, never having drunk wine, never having been in love." [9] Or again: "If the average student wants to find out something about Platonism, the very last thing he thinks of doing is to take a translation of Plato off the library shelf and read the *Symposium*. He would rather read some dreary modern book ten times as long, all about 'isms' and influences, and only once in twelve pages telling him what Plato actually said." [10] The very setting of the *Symposium* is a heady combination of the physical pleasure of banqueting and the intellectual joy of bright discourse, a gathering of half a dozen men of diverse backgrounds and learning—a kind of meeting such as the Inklings sometimes had in Oxford. The theme of the evening's conversation is love, a topic admirably suited to Plato's exposition of the mystical philosophy of the Good. Lewis reveled in Plato's insight into the *mysterium tremendum* that was reality, and in his own writings found no better devices than Plato's: reason, myth, symbol, and analogy. And, like Plato, he found no inherent contradiction between reason and mysticism. Both were valid paths to God; where reason faltered for lack of data, mysticism could carry the devotee to higher realms, but at last both paths faded into insignificance in the blinding light of the absolute itself.

Platonism was an intensely satisfying aesthetic experience for Lewis. It postulated a cosmology in which all things in the universe were viewed as having a proper rank and function. It was a system that tried to leave out no known phenomenon. It demanded more than intellectual assent; it assumed personal involvement on the part of each initiate into the mysteries of reality. [11] And it promised the initiate something that few philosophies since Plato's time have ever provided: a sense of being in the presence of that which gives beauty and joy to life. This Lewis felt with his whole being. He loved the comprehensiveness of Plato's scheme of things, from the pedestrian aspects of daily experience to the soaring heights of the absolute. The very philosophical system itself was a supreme work of art. In Plato's hands the chosen vehicle of expression, the dialogue, became a superbly aesthetic expression. Plato's ascent to the ultimate, Lewis perceived, was itself a work of art. One who ascends to the realm of the absolute is not only safe from the perturbations of everyday existence but also a joyful participant in a dimension that is infinitely more beautiful and satisfying to the soul than the phenomenal world can ever be. For Lewis, as for

Plato, the aesthetic was an inextricable element of reality itself. Lewis ignored—with some justification, no doubt—those passages in the *Republic* in which Plato seems to deny that aesthetics is a legitimate consideration of philosophy. He evidently recognized that Plato was far more an aesthete than his castigations of the arts might suggest.

Now, if reality is one and is both good and beautiful, then it follows that Plato assumed that there was only one possible right way for everything to be. There are universal verities that, on a small scale, faithfully reproduce the verities of the absolute itself—as, for instance, when arithmetical calculations express unchanging universal truths. The phenomenal world and all human experience contain reflections, echoes, or other imperfect copies of the unitary reality. Reality must stand objectively outside the individual person. Human minds do not make reality, but reality makes possible human minds—as well as everything else that exists. Reality makes possible all rational thought, all moral rightness in the world, and all beauty. Furthermore, the truth that is manifested at one level can be expected to be manifested at other levels as well, though in different garb.

With such concepts Lewis could in principle agree. He discussed the parallelism of manifestations of reality on different levels under the rubric of "transposition." When, he said, we find that a small system duplicates a larger one in some significant way, we may assume that the lesser system is based on the greater one. "Transposition occurs whenever the higher reproduces itself in the lower," he wrote.[12] Transposition is, in some ways, a form of symbolism; yet Lewis pointed out that it is more than that. It is a distinctive way in which reality manifests itself. Since there is only one reality, it is inconceivable that reality should not be reflected all along the continuum of being. Lewis's discussion of transposition took place within the context of a sermon at Oxford, but the concept is present elsewhere in his writings. In his fiction there are numerous instances of things that, on a small scale, suggest larger cosmic realities. Like Plato, Lewis sometimes dealt with small, easily comprehensible matters in the hope that they would suggest larger truths. It is this cosmic principle of transposition that constituted the philosophical justification for Plato's and Lewis's extensive use of myth and analogy. Cosmic truth extends—or at least may extend—to the content of fiction, and good fiction will, both thinkers agreed, imitate larger realities.

Lewis ignored many aspects of Plato's thought entirely, as he also did certain problems that are heatedly debated among Platonic scholars. He displayed no interest in the chronology of the dialogues or in the question of the extent to which Plato may have represented Socrates accurately. He did not ask whether the dialogues were meant to communicate all of Plato's teachings or only those matters about which Plato was willing to speak publicly. He largely ignored the mathematical rigors that Plato found to be so essential to the education of the philosopher.[13] He rarely undertook a critique of the detailed argument of any of the dialogues, preferring rather to try to see what Plato was driving at in a larger way, and he never supposed that the validity of any of Plato's insights rests upon the particular line of argumentation that Plato advances. He never bothered to sort out Plato's views on the place of women in the order of reality, although it is possible that he assumed (perhaps under the influence of the apostle Paul) that males have an inherently dominant role in life.[14] He deplored what he took to be Plato's tolerance of pederasty, but he did not belabor the matter. Once past the youthful period reflected in *Dymer*, he did not flail Plato for the regimentation proposed in his ideal state. Perhaps most noticeably of all he ignored the formal doctrine of the Forms that is found in Plato's earlier dialogues. Lewis accepted the insight that underlay the Forms, but correctly sensed that the validity of the concept was not dependent upon Plato's specific explication; and, indeed, Plato himself seems in his later dialogues to have regarded his earlier labored efforts as somewhat futile. Although he toyed with notions related to the Forms in *Perelandra*, he introduced nothing into his novels that is comparable to the extensive utilization of the Platonic Forms that he found in Charles Williams's *The Place of the Lion*. He had occasion to mention the Forms even less in his nonfiction.[15] Sometimes the amount of emphasis

Lewis gave to aspects of Platonism was influenced by his knowledge of the subsequent history of Neoplatonism and medieval Christian Platonism.

Only rarely did the mature Lewis express hostile feelings toward Plato. The most notable (and amusing) instance of such negativism appears in a letter he wrote to Barfield in 1939. "My distrust," he grumbled, "of all lexicons and translations is increasing. Also of Plato—and of the human mind." As if this were not enough, he went on to foresee "no future for poetry" and anticlimactically added that a planned walking tour he was to take would be a ghastly failure and his braces were in a frightful condition.[16] These last grumpish complaints reveal that he did not really expect Barfield to take his sweeping pronouncements seriously. Lewis's occasional expression of disagreement with Plato tended to be on specific points in his dialogues, such as the precise nature of the rungs of the ladder of ascent toward reality postulated in the *Symposium*,[17] rather than on the basic philosophical stance. Even though disputation with others was a lifelong habit that prompted him to challenge friends and enemies alike, Lewis never vented upon Plato vituperation of the sort that reflects deep animosity.

Lewis had no difficulty in finding important affinities between Platonic thought and Christianity. He spoke of "the Jewish, Platonic, Christian fashion" of understanding reality, implying, seemingly, that the three are essentially in agreement.[18] Upon one occasion he asserted: "We do of course find in Plato a clear Theology of Creation in the Judaic and Christian sense; the whole universe—the very conditions of time and space under which it exists—are produced by the will of a perfect, timeless, unconditioned God who is above and outside all that He makes. But this is an amazing leap (though not made without the help of Him who is the Father of lights) by an overwhelming theological genius; it is not ordinary Pagan religion." [19]

When he was aware of a conflict between Platonism and Christianity, Lewis always permitted Christianity to dominate—at least, superficially. When he was not conscious of any essential difference between the two systems, he sometimes unwittingly permitted Platonic elements to slip into the foreground, perhaps because they provided an aesthetic dimension that Christianity tended to lack. His affection for Platonism continued throughout his life, although from the mid-1950s onward it seems to have waned slightly as he became less confident of mankind's ability to comprehend reality. This loss of confidence may be detected in *Till We Have Faces* and *A Grief Observed*; nevertheless, it is worth noting that Lewis's most warmly appreciative comments about Plato appear in his late book *Reflections on the Psalms*.

Not surprisingly, Lewis argued that the Jewish-Platonic-Christian tradition to which he committed himself stands squarely in the mainstream of the history of ideas, even when it has gone by other names. He found that most of the world's religions have presupposed the existence of another and more important dimension to reality than the phenomenal world. He felt a degree of kinship with supernaturalism wherever it was to be found; indeed, by his own admission he was fascinated all his life by such extremes of supernaturalism as the occult and even sheer magic.[20] The term *supernaturalism* might, accordingly, be used to categorize Lewis's philosophy of religion. Certainly Lewis used that and cognate words with approbation many times in his writings. In its most basic sense the term refers to a belief in an unseen but superior power that is active in the universe. It is a truism that, as Lewis says, "Christianity claims to be telling us about another world, about something behind the world we can touch and hear and see."[21] Lewis employed the term prominently in defining his Christian position in the early chapters of *Miracles*. Yet the very associations of the word with magic and other forms of the occult (as when one speaks of "supernatural goings-on") tend to make it less serviceable than it might otherwise be, even though Lewis would not necessarily object to magical connotations to a moderate extent. More significantly, the term does not in itself connote any element of rationalism; that fact alone would make it only partly satisfactory as the primary designation for his philosophy of religion.

What, then, shall we call Lewis's way of viewing reality? It would be very easy to speak of his Christian Platonism. Lewis was certainly as much of a Christian Platonist (or, more properly, a Platonistic Christian) as Clement of Alexandria or Origen had been during the second and third centuries. One might also recognize Lewis as an absolutist, for he was indeed that. To the extent that absolutism might be said to be the antithesis of relativism or subjectivism, the term would have merit; for Lewis was deeply opposed to all philosophical viewpoints that held that truth was only relative or personal. "In all the things which I have written and thought I have always stuck to traditional, dogmatic positions. . . . The world of dogmatic Christianity is a place in which thousands of people of quite different types keep on saying the same thing, and the world of 'broad-mindedness' and watered-down 'religion' is a world where a small number of people (all of the same type) say totally different things and change their minds every few minutes." [22] Yet for a variety of reasons neither of these labels is entirely satisfactory.

The term best suited to describe Lewis's philosophy of religion is *objectivism*. A great many times in his writings Lewis used the words *object* and *objective* when elucidating the philosophical dimensions of his thought, and always favorably. "Unless," he once wrote, "we return to the crude and nursery-like belief in objective values, we perish." [23] He spoke favorably of objective thinking and regarded reality as objective. What he meant by *object* was not some material thing but the real in contrast with the imaginary or phenomenal. He emphatically rejected any philosophy that asserted that the absolute resides only within the mind. Reality, he insisted, is a dimension that exists outside ourselves, unchanging and independent of any external factors. It is the ground of all other, lesser being. Lewis did not deny the importance of the thinking and feeling person, but he insisted that the individual person has no meaning apart from an assumed metaphysical basis of the phenomenal world. In his autobiography he discussed objective reality in terms of his youthful love of "Northernness."

> Only when your whole attention and desire are
> fixed on something else—whether a distant
> mountain, or the past, or the gods of Asgard—does the
> "thrill" arise. It is a by-product. Its very existence
> presupposes that you desire not it but something other

and outer. If by any perverse askesis or the use of any drug it could be produced from within, it would at once be seen to be of no value. For take away the object, and what, after all, would be left?—a whirl of images, a fluttering sensation in the diaphragm, a momentary abstraction. And who could want that? This, I say, is the first and deadly error, which appears on every level of life and is equally deadly on all, turning religion into a self-caressing luxury and love into auto-eroticism. And the second error is, having thus falsely made a state of mind your aim, to attempt to produce it. From the fading of the Northernness I ought to have drawn the conclusion that the Object, the Desirable, was further away, more external, less subjective, than even such a comparatively public and external thing as a system of mythology.[24]

Objectivism sees—to use one of Lewis's own analogies—the phenomenal world as standing in relation to absolute reality somewhat as the figure of Hamlet stands vis-à-vis Shakespeare.[25] Hamlet is contained within Shakespeare as a person may be said to be related to God. Each has its own existence, but the distance between the creator and the creature is infinitely great. God is the ultimate Object insofar as he is absolute, perfect, and immutable—and that toward which human beings instinctively are drawn. Lewis's thought in this regard closely approximates Plato's; the chief difference is that for Plato the ultimate object is not a personal deity but the impersonal principle of the good.

Lewis's objectivism was thus essentially a theistic philosophy.[26] To that philosophy Lewis added the specific content of the Christian faith, so that God is perceived to be the kind of deity proclaimed in Christianity. It is therefore necessary to speak not simply of objectivism, but of Christian objectivism, if we wish to indicate Lewis's particular position. The two words do not designate distinct systems of thought, but a merging into a monolithic whole of two historically discrete ways of thinking.

Running through much of Lewis's writing, like a persistent countermelody, is the belief that the greatest danger to human beings is that of losing sight of objective value, of degenerating into self-centered creatures wallowing in subjectivism, making gods of the appetites and irrational preferences and even mere whims.[27] Under the same anathema Lewis also placed individualism, so far as it involves the disregard of the cosmic order of things. The individualist falsely supposes, he complained, that he can lift himself by his bootstraps, create marvelous things, and be master of his destiny. All such thought, he insisted, is sheer delusion, the imagination run amok. A person can find true individuation only to the extent that he attunes himself to the objective reality that underlies his very being.

Lewis left no facet of Christian objectivism unexamined. Although he devoted much attention to metaphysical considerations, he did not neglect values. We have already noted that he regarded morality as being based on objective values that can be perceived and be effectively utilized in daily life. In aesthetics there is likewise objective truth. In addition to personal preference, and indeed rising above it, is the objective beauty that should be the most important concern of the artist. In an imaginative dialogue in *The Great Divorce* Lewis has a heavenly spirit say to an artist of limited vision whose subjectivism has landed him in Hell, "When you painted on earth—at least in your earlier days—it was because you caught glimpses of Heaven in the earthly landscape. The success of your painting was that it enabled others to see the glimpses too." The sole legitimate function of the artist is to see glimpses of reality, not to express himself, or to paint for money, fame, or vanity's sake. Lewis did not mean that the artist has to paint with photographic literalism. He had the heavenly spirit speak favorably of the time when the fallen artist, then just beginning his career, had properly been concerned more with what he saw (that is, the objective reality) than with how he painted (that is, subjectivism). "Light itself," the spirit declares, "was your first love: you loved paint only as a means of telling about light." [28] Objectivism is, in fact, better served by the inner eye than the outer.

Objectivism is relevant to literature as well. Lewis essentially agreed with Plato that fiction and nonfiction alike are to be judged by the extent to which they say something valid about reality. He thus harbored a dislike for literary criticism that was based upon subjectivism. In his classic essay *The Personal Heresy in Criticism* he argued that there can be risk of misinterpretation if a critic assumes that there is an intimate connection between a work of literature and the life of its author. Although literature (above all poetry, but in measure other kinds of writing as well) may reveal something personal about the author, it generally will not and should not do so. An author who is worth his salt "is not a man who asks me to look at *him*," he wrote. "He is a man who says 'look at that' and points; the more I follow the pointing of his finger the less I can possibly see of him." The author thus transforms an experience that is initially private and personal into one that is "public, common, impersonal, objective." [29] We find in a work concepts, ideas, and reflections on feelings experienced by the writer, but not the person of the writer himself. Consistent with this viewpoint, Lewis shrank in alarm from tendencies toward a cult of personality that he saw developing among some of his admirers—a cult that his death has intensified.

Admittedly Lewis came close to departing from his own critical principle in his autobiography. *Surprised by Joy* invites the reader to look at Lewis intimately, and links his writings closely with his own personal development, as if the author intended that his personality—at least, so far as he chose to reveal it—be used in the understanding of his writings. Now, it may be that Lewis was tacitly confessing in this book that he had overstated the case against personal heresy, or it may be that he simply fell victim to the vanity that comes upon many a distinguished person at the end of his career; yet the work may not, upon close examination, violate Lewis's earlier convictions at all. It can be argued that in *Surprised by Joy* Lewis was primarily functioning as an exponent of Christianity, not of himself; he was serving, as he had so often done before, as an intellectual evangelist. Although the autobiography may not have been consciously apologetic, it was a work of spiritual encouragement of the same *genre* as Augustine's *Confessions*. [30] Lewis was not so much concerned to give autobiographical information per se or clues to his writings (and when he does so he is not always accurate) [31] as to proclaim what God had done in leading him to Christianity. That this is the case is strongly suggested by the fact that once he recorded his conversion to Christianity, he abruptly brought the autobiography to a close.

Subjectivism is not the only threat that Lewis saw to objectivism. Plato's own pupil Aristotle was responsible in the third century B.C. for effecting some shifts in emphasis that have had lasting results in the history of ideas. Lewis was too knowledgeable in the history of philosophy to accept some of the popular notions of the differences between the thought of the two philosophers, and with no small justification perceived Aristotle to be more a continuator of the Platonic tradition than an opponent. With regard to cosmology, among other things, such is certainly the case; Aristotle largely accepted Plato's teachings, adding to them only his Prime Mover as a means of attempting to bridge the gap between the phenomenal world and the realm of the absolute, thereby coming closer to the enunciation of a diety than had Plato. In metaphysics he modified the difficult doctrine of the Forms, but did not reject the concept outright. In ethics he accepted the doctrine of universal mores, but cast it in a form that, as Lewis was quick to point out, was consistent with Platonism. For Lewis, Aristotle merited a place near Plato in the ranks of the intellectual heroes of civilization. "To lose what I owe to Plato and Aristotle," he once declared, "would be like the amputation of a limb." [32]

While not oblivious to these affinities, Lewis sensed in Aristotle an essentially different approach to reality from that of Platonism. Aristotle focused his attention on the material world, whereas Plato had looked beyond. He was sobersided, in contract to Plato's imaginativeness. He lacked those qualities which Lewis found so praiseworthy in Plato: an awe in the presence of reality, a mystical bent, an internalized aesthetic sense. He was wise, but he could never guide Lewis toward the absolute. From him one could learn the rules of logic, but from Plato one could learn about the goal of human striving. Lewis respected Aristotle's rationality, but scientific observation was not for him. And thus in the final analysis he was obliged to relegate Aristotle to a place inferior to Plato's. In *The Great Divorce* the street in Hell down which Lewis imagined that he was walking was lined with "dingy lodging houses, small tobacconists, hoardings from which posters hung in rags, windowless warehouses, goods stations without trains, and bookshops of the sort that sell *The Works of Aristotle.*" [33]

He was inclined, then, to reject the medieval nominalist position, which was heavily Aristotelian, in favor of the "realist" position which was Platonic. Basically, however, Lewis did not greatly care for the medieval formulation of the Platonic-Aristotelian controversy, and he himself seldom used the term *realist* except in the inverted modern sense of that term—as, for instance, when he described Trollope's fiction as "work of an unusually solid, realistic, and humdrum kind.[34]

Lewis considered and dismissed numerous other world views—other "isms," he scornfully called them—that constituted, in his judgment, perversions of the proper understanding of reality. One such was materialism.[35] He inveighed against the Epicurean philosopher Lucretius for his unabashed advocacy of such a point of view. Lucretius argued for a deterministic view of the universe; he denied that religion had any metaphysical basis, and he praised nature. He found no reason to suppose that the soul was immortal, and looked to no realm beyond the present world. All this was anathema to Lewis, who attacked not only materialism (which he regarded as being a more widespread philosophy in the twentieth century than in Lucretius's day) but naturalism as well, deeming both to be utterly, and dangerously, opposed to supernaturalism. "The Naturalist believes that a great process, or 'becoming,' exists 'on its own' in space and time, and that nothing else exists—what we call particular things and events being only the parts into which we analyze the great process or the shapes which that process takes at given moments and given points in space. This single, total reality he calls Nature. The Supernaturalist believes that one Thing exists on its own and has produced the framework of space and time and the procession of systematically connected events which fill them." [36] This description forms part of an extended refutation of naturalism in the opening chapters of *Miracles.* Linking naturalism with determinism, Lewis attempted to show the logical inconsistencies of the position. Whether or not he described naturalism accurately is debatable; certainly many scientists would not accept his description.

Not surprisingly, Lewis tended to be hostile to experimentation and "scientism," by which he meant false science masquerading as humanitarianism. Of the latter we shall have more to say in chapter 8. Experimentation Lewis regarded as the dangerous tool of relativists, naturalists, and determinists. The chief activity of the evil organization N.I.C.E. in *That Hideous Strength* is scientific, or pseudo-scientific, experimentation, including the vivisection of animals—a practice that Lewis deplored.[37] In *The Magician's Nephew* the wicked Uncle Andrew's preoccupation is with experimentation, a practice that in his hands is nothing but black magic. In *The Silver Chair* Eustace Scrubb and Jill Pole are pupils in a school called Experiment House, which is a hotbed of progressive education. Lewis could not, to be sure, object to experimentation under certain circumstances; what he found objectionable was the materialistic, progressivistic view of the universe that endless experimentation seemed to imply.

Also falling beneath his withering glance was the theory of emergent evolution, which had grown apace since the time of Darwin in the mid-nineteenth century.[38] More than once his writings show the frustration and despair that this view produced in him.

> By universal evolutionism I mean the belief that the very formula of universal process is from imperfect to perfect, from small beginnings to great endings, from the rudimentary to the elaborate: the belief which makes people find it natural to think that morality springs from savage taboos, adult sentiment from infantile sexual maladjustments, thought from instinct, mind from matter, organic from inorganic, cosmos from chaos. This is perhaps the deepest habit of mind in the contemporary world. It seems to me immensely unplausible, because it makes the general course of nature so very unlike those parts of nature we can observe.[39]

From Lewis's point of view, the theory of evolution is inherently implausible because it sees the higher as emerging from the lower. From the lifeless sea comes life, from the amoeba evolves the starfish, from the fish emerges mankind. Regardless of what the inductive evidence suggests, deduction obliges the thinking person to reject such a preposterous notion. To be sure, the evolutionary process that Darwin observed did take place, but not in the mindless way that the evolutionists suppose; it occurred because there was a divine mind shaping matter. Left to its own devices, nature will inevitably grow disorderly and run down.

> In the world I know, the perfect produces the imperfect, which again becomes perfect—egg leads to bird and bird to egg—in endless succession. If there ever was a life which sprang of its own accord out of a purely inorganic universe, or a civilization which raised itself by its own shoulder-straps out of pure savagery, then this event was totally unlike the beginnings of every subsequent life and every subsequent civilization. The thing may have happened; but all its plausibility is gone. On any view, the first beginning must have been outside the ordinary processes of nature. . . . You have to go outside the sequence of engines, into the world of men, to find the real originator of the Rocket. Is it not equally reasonable to look outside Nature for the real Originator of the natural order? [40]

This line of reasoning, so characteristic of Lewis, is both Platonic and Christian. It is found in a variety of forms throughout Lewis's writings. It is at once a rational deduction and an article of belief. "We must insist from the beginning," wrote Lewis, "that we believe, as firmly as does any savage or theosophist, in a spirit-world which can, and does, invade the natural or phenomenal universe." [41] This conviction is a foundation-stone of Lewis's Christian objectivism.

To the list of proscribed philosophies Lewis adds, upon occasion, other "isms," some ancient and some largely modern formulations.[42] It is to be expected that he opposed agnosticism, atheism, and nihilism. Hedonism likewise fell under the ban, as did utilitarianism and pragmatism. So, too, did skepticism, even though Lewis always retained a high respect for the honest skeptic; some of Lewis's most likable characters—McPhee in *That Hideous Strength*, for example, and Trumpkin the red dwarf in *Prince Caspian*—are good-hearted skeptics, much like Lewis's old teacher Kirkpatick.[43] To the extent that all such philosophies are opposed to objectivism, Lewis was prepared with a firm, sometimes vehement, and often simplistic rejection.

There is no gainsaying that in philosophical matters Lewis had a penchant for dichotomization. On the one hand lay his Christian objectivism, a way of looking out upon the universe which he believed to be the mainstream of civilized thought and the only viable world view. On the other lay a grab-bag of all opposing philosophical positions. What the latter had in common was their rejection of the idea of a supernatural or objective reality in the universe. Lewis did not hesitate to label these two major opposing systems with a variety of terms such as objectivism versus subjectivism, supernaturalism versus naturalism, and Christianity versus materialism. The banners may change, but it is the same battle that is being fought again and again in the minds of men.[44] Although Lewis would doubtless have argued that this dichotomy has warrant, the evident delight with which he arrayed the forces against one another suggests that he had been more than a little influenced by the dualistic picture of the confrontation between the hosts of God and the minions of Satan that is painted in Christian apocalyptic tradition.[45] Repeatedly in his novels he carries out the same black-and-white scenario: On the one side are those who live in devout service to a supernatural reality, and on the other are assorted skeptics, pragmatists, materialists, blasphemers, schemers, and clods. It is a picture which accords with Lewis's conviction that erroneous thinking can never have the same status as right thinking.

By now it will be apparent that C. S. Lewis is one of those thinkers who tend to use nomenclature rather casually. Occasionally, when discussing a term in Christian theology—say, *love* or *law*—he can labor mightily to explicate the full meaning of the word; of that fact his *Four Loves* is ample witness. Otherwise he shows hardly any interest in technical terminology.[46] Materialism, naturalism, and determinism can, under his pen, subtly coalesce, separate, and merge again. This attitude is one that was engendered from the reading of ancient philosophers more than medieval or later thinkers. Neither the ancient Greeks nor Lewis felt the need to restrict philosophical discourse to a set of carefully defined terms. Plato never settled upon a single, sufficient name for the absolute; Lewis never selected a single term to designate the philosophy of religion around which his life revolved. Both thinkers knew well enough the impossibility of language's circumscribing reality, and preferred to seek out as many ways of verbalizing about matters of ultimate concern as they could. Even when he toyed, somewhat uncharacteristically, with words such as *Sehnsucht* and *joy* in *Surprised by Joy*, Lewis cannot properly be said to have been attempting to introduce a technical philosophical vocabulary; [47] such terms cannot bear too much freight, and have in fact already begun to suffer overinterpretation at the hands of some commentators on Lewis.

In the next chapter we shall discuss the ancient, medieval, and Renaissance antecedents of Lewis's thought in some detail; for the present it will suffice to attempt to place Lewis's Christian objectivism within the broader context of his own time. Were we to judge from what he himself implies, we would see Lewis as an isolated figure in the twentieth century, a lone representative of a philosophical absolutism that had gradually disappeared during the past two centuries with the rise of modern thought. But the situation is otherwise. Although it is true enough that the Platonic, objectivist way of viewing reality is no longer the sea in which most persons swim, Lewis was hardly so isolated as he sometimes thought. Although generally on the decline, supernaturalism was far from dead.

As Lewis was growing up in the early years of the twentieth century, the dominant British philosophical tradition was, as he learned well enough, idealism.[48] That philosophy itself was an offshoot of the Platonic tradition. Its early development can be traced through Locke, Berkeley, and Leibniz. As formulated by Bishop Berkeley in the eighteenth century, idealism was intended as a bulwark against the heresies of materialism, skepticism, and atheism, "isms" that Lewis himself disliked heartily. Berkeley's model of the universe began with God, the infinite intelligence; it provided for unchanging ideas, much like those postulated by Plato, and for finite human minds as well. It contained a hierarchical structure of reality from the most real to the largely illusory. Berkeley, and Leibniz as well, believed that their philosophical systems broadly supported traditional theism and many other religious affirmations. Subsequently Kant, Hegel, and other thinkers gave new directions to idealism, but all of them tended to give to the mind a position of importance: first the human mind, with its ability to interpret the data of the senses and to engage in deduction, and then a deduced divine mind, in which all reality exists. Some idealistic thought inclined in the direction of pantheism, the belief that the divine mind must in some sense be present in all phenomenal things.

Lewis encountered idealism largely through British philosophers, who had begun expounding that philosophy a half-century before he came upon the scene. At Oxford, Thomas Hill Green, F. H. Bradley, and others had asserted that idealism was an antidote for the poisons of positivism, utilitarianism, and social individualism, among other world views. By the 1880s these thinkers had been joined by men such as Edward Caird, Bernard Bosanquet, and Andrew Seth, all of whom, though differing on some matters, agreed that something more than the world of nature must be postulated, namely, a spiritual reality which itself stood outside nature. That reality is unitary and infinite, and gives meaning to the descending orders of reality beneath it. British idealism reached its peak of popularity during the years prior to World War I. By this time the philosophical stance of the Oxford idealists had filtered down to the middle class in the form of popular idealism, according to which belief in spiritual values, ethical standards ("high ideals") and a transcendent mind (God) were paramount.

Lewis found much in philosophical idealism that attracted him. He read Bishop Berkeley while a student at Oxford, and found him, far from being the silly old man that some thought him to be, actually "a very interesting fellow." [49] Kant as well as the French philosopher Henri Bergson he perceived as being on his side, even though he did not bother to master the thought of either. He was finally obliged to reject idealism because, although it provided a desirable emphasis upon the priority of mind over matter, it failed to provide a deity that had any significance except as an intellectual construct. Recalling his Oxford years, he later wrote:

> There were in those days all sorts of blankets, insulators, and insurances which enabled one to get all the conveniences of Theism, without believing in God. The English Hegelians, writers like T. H. Green, Bradley, and Bosanquet (then mighty names), dealt in precisely such wares. The Absolute Mind—better still, the Absolute—was impersonal, or it knew itself (but not us?) only in us, and it was so absolute that it wasn't really much more like a mind than anything else. . . . The emotion that went with all this was certainly religious. But this was a religion that cost nothing. We could talk religiously about the Absolute: but there was no danger of Its doing anything about us.

In spite of the fact that idealism could not offer a personal God, Lewis found something to commend. "There was one really wholesome element in it. The Absolute was 'there,' and that 'there' contained the reconciliation of all contraries, the transcendence of all finitude, the hidden glory which was the only perfectly real thing there is. In fact, it had much of the quality of Heaven. . . . What I learned from the Idealists (and still most strongly hold) is this maxim: it is more important that Heaven should exist than that any of us should reach it." [50] There was, in fact, more than simply this one insight that Lewis found attractive. Nevertheless, idealism was not the end of the journey for him; from there he progressed to a brief pantheistic stage, then to theism, and finally to Christianity. [51]

If he was influenced by the prevailing philosophical climate of his youth, Lewis was also receptive to some aspects of the wave of thought that succeeded idealism. By the time he entered Oxford, absolute idealism had already been given severe philosophical blows by an emerging school of realism, the pioneers of which had been Bertrand Russell, Alfred North Whitehead, and G. E. Moore. Whitehead boldly declared that all philosophy was but a series of footnotes to Plato. The newcomers took their departure from the absoluteness of mathematics and deductive logic, and went on in various ways to postulate the existence of such Platonic entities as universal realities and an absolute good that differs from all other entities and is not itself a part of the natural order. By the early 1920s many philosophers had deserted idealism in favor of this realism, and a rich array of books had been published that enunciated the philosophy. Lewis acknowledged that one of these, Samuel Alexander's *Space, Time and Deity*, exerted a strong influence upon him.[52] The early fascination of these realists with metaphysical absolutes soon faded; by the 1930s the movement had begun to bifurcate into schools of linguistic analysis and logical positivism, with a consequent loss of most of the earlier Platonic and absolutist elements.

What of Lewis's place in modern theology? There is no question but that he was most at home with traditional theological formulations. He could quote with far more knowledge and enthusiasm from a seventeenth-century divine than from a twentieth-century theologian. He found it difficult to suppose that recent theologians could have as clear a view of the proper order of things as had earlier Christian thinkers. He was not, however, entirely unfamiliar with the resurgence of the Platonic tradition that occurred in British theology early in the twentieth century. As a scholar he was well acquainted with the Cambridge Platonists of the seventeenth century; now there came a brief and limited revival of this mystical tradition by thinkers such as Baron von Hügel, Evelyn Underhill, and William R. Inge. Dean Inge purveyed a Platonism that was heavily aesthetic but not lacking in metaphysical concerns. He protested against the pell-mell rush of society into pragmatism, humanitarianism, and progressivism, and even attacked such traditional concepts as democracy and patriotism as being lying spirits of the present age. Although Lewis was favorably inclined toward some of the ideas of the latter-day English Platonist Christians, his occasional comments suggest that he found them more fascinating than determinative for his philosophy of religion.

Lewis had some knowledge of modern non-Anglican theologians, but he made no attempt to read systematically or extensively in their works. He sampled Søren Kierkegaard, but gave up the effort because he sensed too great a philosophical incompatibility. He rarely mentioned any recent theologian in his own theological writings, even when their pronouncements would have accorded well with his own views.[53] This broad indifference to modern theology may have stemmed, in part, from his desire to avoid the imbroglio of current trends; certainly he avoided, throughout his life, as much disputation with fellow Christians as he possibly could. It may also have arisen out of the conviction that "what's good is not new, and what's new is not good" in theology. And it may be yet more, for Lewis always displayed a strong tendency to pursue his own course of analysis without resorting to the documentation, debate with fellow thinkers, and pedantry that lesser minds found so stimulating. He was usually confident that his insights would provide significant clues to the understanding of the issue under discussion. In his writings on English literature he displayed much the same disinterest, or apparent disinterest, in the work of other scholars that can be seen in his theological writings.

In spite of this unconcern with contemporary theological trends, Lewis was in no small measure a participant in the theological climate of his time. He began his religious writing in the mid-1930s, in a period of deepening disillusionment with traditional religious institutions, with the possibility of a Christian kingdom of God on earth, with the naive optimism about the perfectability of man. In Europe political instability was giving rise to totalitarian governments; in the United States the social gospel, which had dominated Christian thought for several decades, had collapsed; in England, which felt the new theological mood somewhat less acutely, the British empire had passed its zenith and was already commencing a decline that was to accelerate throughout Lewis's life, and soon the European political ills would touch England itself. It was a time when one would expect not a fresh burst of optimism and humanism but a retrenchment into more traditional Christian attitudes toward human nature and society, and that was in fact what happened.

The times were catching up with Lewis's own proclivities. In response to the growing loss of innocence, thinkers like Karl Barth in Switzerland and Reinhold Niebuhr in the United States began to write in a new vein. Although differing in many ways, they tended to urge a reaffirmation of traditional Christian doctrines, and stressed the transcendence and judgment of God. They sensed a depth to evil that liberal theologians of earlier decades had often denied. They questioned the naive assumptions of humanity's endless progress. This kind of thinking produced, among other theological movements, Neo-orthodoxy, a theology that was in its outlines not greatly uncongenial to Lewis's own thought, except in its insistence upon the total depravity of man and a corresponding distrust of reason.[54] It was no coincidence that some of the classic Christian thinkers whose writings began to be reexamined were ones whom Lewis also read with particular interest: Tertullian, Origen, and—above all—Augustine.

Although the writings of Barth, Niebuhr, and other proponents of orthodoxy came to be known in Britain, England itself produced relatively few important exponents of this new wave of thought. Nevertheless, the mood was felt there and the writings of continental and American theologians were widely read. These developments cannot have escaped Lewis. Although he never became a neo-orthodox theologian himself, he was in sympathy with much of the trend, for it meant the rejection of secularism, materialism, scientism, liberalism, and the raft of other modern views which Lewis disliked. One can read many pages of the writings of David R. Davies, an English counterpart to Niebuhr, without finding any statement that Lewis would have disputed; indeed, there is a fervor and sharp intolerance of divergent views that is akin to Lewis's. To be sure, there are some differences. Among other things Davies was, like Niebuhr, far more politically oriented than Lewis—a heritage from liberal theology. When Niebuhr and Davies spoke of Christian realism they had in mind less the medieval meaning of realism than a common-sense realism, the sort of thing that Lewis meant when he discussed a phase of "popular realism" through which he went before moving to idealism. Interesting as they are, these evidences of the affinities of Lewis's thought with broader aesthetic trends are only incidental to our concerns.

Having sketched here the framework of Lewis's vast and orderly philosophy of religion, in the chapters that follow we shall examine the abundant detail with which Lewis explicated his thought.

The Old Western Model of Reality

I have made no serious effort to hide the fact that the old
Model delights me as I believe it delighted our ancestors.

The Discarded Image

"THE educated man," Lewis wrote, "habitually, almost
without noticing it, sees the present as something that grows
out of a long perspective of centuries." [1] The past that was most
important to him was that between the rise of the Hebrew and
Greek cultures and the emergence of the modern scientific
world in the eighteenth century. All that he wrote was directed
toward helping the modern inquirer perceive the truth and
importance of a world view that had once held vast sway in the
West but was now everywhere in retreat. His studies in literature deal, in a scholarly way, with much of the same material
that his religious writings treat argumentatively and imaginatively. In his literary criticism he refers to this world view with as
much dispassion as possible, whereas in his apologetic and
fictional writings he becomes one of the makers of that very
body of literature himself—a medieval-Renaissance thinker,
propounding with all the fervor and skill he can muster a cause
that he fears may already be lost.

Preoccupied as he was with the philosophy, theology, and
literature of the West during the first seventeen centuries after
Christ, Lewis was inevitably impressed by the magnificent
world view of that tradition. Although he could have derived his
philosophy of religion solely from Plato's dialogues and the
basic documents of early Christianity, he had neither the desire

nor the need to do so. One of the factors contributing to his conversion to Christianity had been his discovery that most of the thinkers throughout history whom he most admired were "in the pack"—persons who believed in the existence of an objective supernatural reality beyond the phenomenal dimension.[2] It was not that Lewis simply wished to retreat into the safety of the majority opinion of the prescientific era; on the contrary, his personal inclination was to avoid whatever the majority of persons thought or did and to strike out in directions of his own. Rather he was convinced that, even though individual persons might err in their judgments, mankind as a whole was capable of deducing or intuiting ideas that in some measure reflected metaphysical reality. He felt compelled to take seriously the wisdom of the centuries that recognized a supernatural reality in, or more properly beyond, the universe.

Traditional Western wisdom was not, he conceded, infallible; its cosmology was not literally true, nor was its ethical system so absolute as its advocates had supposed. Nevertheless, the centuries-old objectivism of the Christian world view in the West was, so far as it went, a valid insight into the nature of reality. Lewis was explicit in rejecting the "chronological snobbery" of those persons who suppose that whatever is old is to be discredited,[3] and emphatic in pointing to the essential harmony of the various strains of Platonic and Christian thought that coalesced in the Middle Ages and continued, with fresh increments, into the Renaissance. That massive, harmonious entity, expressed in countless works of art and literature that differed from each other in details but not in their essential view of reality, he referred to simply as the Model. Around the Model revolved, in one way or another, almost all of the Old Western Culture.

The heady amalgam of Platonic and Christian thought attracted numerous rich embellishments during late antiquity, the Middle Ages, and the Renaissance: pagan mythology, Gnostic speculations, Ptolemaic geography, stoicism, Aristotelian thought, bits of other philosophies, assorted superstitions, artistic flourishes—all were brought together into a system of comprehensiveness and dazzling beauty. For Lewis this aesthetic dimension was of no minor significance; it was to provide many a bright image for the pages of his fiction. Indeed, without the elaborations of Plotinus, Dante, Spenser, and others he might never have hit upon a viable framework for his Narnian tales or his planetary romances, and in any case would not have had a storehouse of imaginative details with which to enliven his novels. When his readers assume, as they apparently sometimes do, that all of the mythological and cosmological details of his fiction stem from the author's own imagination, they are but confirming the fact that the Model, after reigning over Western thought for two millennia, is now all but forgotten.

Lewis never attempted to conceal his dependence upon the Model, yet he did not take the trouble to describe his perception of this venerable Western tradition in print until near the end of his life, when he prepared the manuscript of *The Discarded Image*. Subtitled *An Introduction to Medieval and Renaissance Literature*, the book was based upon lectures that he had delivered many times at Oxford. It traced the development of the mainstream of Christian-Platonic tradition from antiquity through the Middle Ages and Renaissance. It was here that Lewis introduced the term *Model* to refer to this old Western world view. He was particularly interested in cosmological aspects of the Model, but he discussed other dimensions of it as well. Although *The Discarded Image* is one of the "literary" works that scholars interested in Lewis's religious thought have tended to ignore, it is, in fact, an essential companion for the study of Lewis's philosophy of religion and his fiction. We shall have more to say about the book when we discuss Lewis's cosmology in the next chapter; for the present it will help to guide us through the intricate paths of the developing Western tradition. But it will not be our only guide, for there are many facets of that history that Lewis does not attempt to treat. To have a fuller picture we shall have to fill some of the gaps.

Lewis's historical sketch begins, for all practical purposes, with the first century B.C., but it is better for us to commence several centuries earlier. During the centuries following Plato's death the Academy in Athens declined; Plato's successors during the first several hundred years, largely known to us only by name, moved first toward emphasis upon mathematics, then toward skepticism, and then in the direction of a synthesis of Platonic thought and other philosophical systems. Nevertheless, Platonism did not die. During the Hellenistic period, the cosmopolitan city of Alexandria in Egypt became the center of renewed interest in Plato's dialogues, and there were numerous attempts by thinkers in Alexandria to incorporate Platonic thought into various philosophical and religious systems. Although much of this effort was doubtless intellectually pedestrian, it is clear that these thinkers, along with some others elsewhere in the Greek-speaking sphere, helped to bring Platonism into the main current of Hellenistic thought. Polytheism, though still alive, was increasingly unsatisfactory to intellectuals in that international age, as were the traditional practices of image-making and temple worship. Platonism, with its emphasis upon a single ultimate reality that transcended all physical manifestations, had immense appeal for intellectual persons. Such persons also tended to like the concepts of a hierarchy of being and of a mystical ascent toward the absolute. Platonism was a philosophy well suited to the conceptual undergirding of the mystery religions that were growing in popularity throughout this period.

By the first century B.C. Platonism was being assimilated into Judaism in Alexandria and doubtless elsewhere. Philo Judaeus drew heavily upon an already hellenized form of Platonism for his interpretation of the text of the Hebrew Torah. During this same period, some Roman men of letters who had philosophical inclinations began independently to incorporate Platonic elements into their thought, along with imaginative metaphysical notions, all of which would eventually find their way into the Model with the passing centuries. It is here that Lewis picks up the story of the formation of the Model.[4] He notes that in the first century B.C. Cicero wrote his own *Republic*, fashioned after Plato's dialogue by that name, in which he described an alleged dream of Scipio Africanus Minor, who appears as one of the speakers in the dialogue. This *Somnium Scipionis*, as it is called, assumes the existence of a single ultimate reality, a hierarchical universe, the immortality of the soul of the noble person, and the relative insignificance of the physical world. Approximately a hundred years later Lucan and Statius wrote the *Pharsalia* and the *Thebaid*, respectively; in these works one finds a cosmology that is reminiscent of the *Somnium Scipionis*, but with some new details. Lewis draws attention to Apuleius's *De deo Socratis* in the second century A.D., in which there is a discussion of daemons that takes its departure from Plato's dialogues but goes on to a cosmology of creatures having natures midway between the gods and human beings that vastly amplified Plato's own beliefs and anticipates medieval cosmology.

It will be noticed that as yet there is no Model, but only some of the components of the Model that was to develop. These ancient writers did not take over Platonism in its entirety; indeed, they could not do so, for they probably had not read the dialogues at first hand. Platonism had been transmitted to them largely through intermediaries, and it was already intermingled with many other concepts. The writers did not have a unified world view, even though some details in their works were similar. They shared the broad assumption that there exists a single supernatural reality beyond the phenomenal world, but they showed no interest in the doctrine of the forms, questions about the place of reason and many other matters that concerned Plato. They often became fascinated with odd cosmological minutiae, some borrowed from Plato and some from popular traditions. Yet the first steps had been taken toward the development of the Model.

To continue tracing this history we must temporarily leave *The Discarded Image* and pick up the history of earliest Christianity. The assimilation of Platonism to Christianity began almost as soon as there was a Christian community. The affinities between the two world views were strong from the beginning. Jesus himself may never have heard of Plato, yet he shared with him a concern for the transcendental and a disinterest in the material and ephemeral. He advanced no metaphysical system as such, yet his understanding of the perfection, immutability, beauty, and joy of the Kingdom of Heaven was a counterpart to Plato's doctrine of the Good and the Forms. Jesus' rapturous contemplation of God as the ultimate reality is akin to the most mystical of Plato's descriptions of the ecstasy of those who descry the good as the culmination of their philosophical pilgrimage. Like Plato, but in an unsystematized way, Jesus assumed that heavenly perfection should be mirrored in earthly institutions and in the life of individual persons; both are in essential agreement about the transpositions that take place from higher to lower levels of reality. In his cautions about the dangers of self-indulgence, Jesus spoke much as Plato does. To be sure, there are differences between the two thinkers. Jesus' God is far more personal than Plato's Good could ever be. Jesus saw a magnitude to evil that Plato did not perceive, and the intensity of his eschatological picture was far greater than anything in the dialogues. He displayed no concern for epistemological issues, and did not accord to reason the place that Plato gave it; indeed, Jesus was basically anti-intellectual, whereas Plato was openly intellectual. Still, the differences were not entirely irreconcilable, and most Christians were to perceive the areas of agreement as being greater than those of disagreement.

Some elements of popular Platonism can be detected in the letters of the apostle Paul. The most notably Platonic work in the New Testament is, however, the Epistle to the Hebrews, probably written near the end of the first century. Here, to a remarkable extent, is set forth in careful detail a world view that postulates two realms, the perishable and the imperishable. Much less self-consciously Platonic, yet perhaps more profoundly akin to Platonism in its way of viewing reality, is the Gospel of John. In that mystical work Jesus mediates to man a perfect, heavenly realm in which the believer can participate by believing in Jesus as the Christ. A similar view is expressed in the three brief epistles in the New Testament that go by the names of First, Second, and Third John.

Although he did not discuss the affinities between Platonism and the New Testament in *The Discarded Image*, Lewis occasionally mentioned points of similarity elsewhere in his writings.[5] When he found some aspect of Platonic thought or the Model that had New Testament warrant, such as the hierarchical order of the universe implied in several of the Pauline epistles, he seized upon it enthusiastically. Inasmuch as he believed that

33

there was only one correct way of viewing reality, he was never surprised to encounter a truth—literal or figurative—in a multiplicity of places. Indeed, he expressed more than once the conviction that it is the recurrence of certain ideas in various cultural traditions, whether through direct historical contacts or independently, that tends to demonstrate the universal truth of those ideas. Still, he held Christianity to be the repository of the fullest measure of divine truth.

The church's tradition constituted yet another medium of divine revelation; hence Lewis had a theological interest in the post-biblical development of Platonic Christianity as well as a broader literary concern. The development, which spanned more than a thousand years, saw the emergence of the full-blown medieval and Renaissance Model, which was conceptually convoluted and teeming with liveliness. The earliest post-biblical Christian writers who presupposed the essential correctness of Platonic absolutism were the second-century apologists Athenagoras, Justin Martyr, and Mincius Felix. It was, however, with the content of Alexandrian theology that the most important enunciation of a Platonic Christianity took place, above all in the thought of Origen and Clement of Alexandria.

By no means all theologians of this period were so convinced that Plato was a valid tutor unto Christ. Platonism in Christianity might well have languished had it not been for a development that took place outside Christian circles. As the aged Origen lay dying, a young pagan named Plotinus began writing treatises on Platonism that were to revitalize the spent and sterile Platonic Academy. Although a gifted metaphysician, Plotinus was anything but a cold scholar. His writings restored to Platonism a fervor that had been lacking for many centuries. He was intoxicated with the absolute, and his writings were redolent with intense longing for union with the Good. Yet he tolerated no shallow intimacy with the ultimate; his God is infinitely remote from the imperfect phenomenal world, and he is reluctant to say anything positive about the deity. God is not even being itself; at most God is a source or ground of being. One ascends to the Good not through progressive knowledge but through the stripping away of all false notions about reality, through a *via negativa*. Yet what lies at the end of that way is infinitely worth the trouble. And, curiously enough, Plotinus found room for aesthetics, ethics, and personal devotion within his philosophy; it is not surprising that he has been called a religious person of the highest order. His wide-reaching net also encompasses an elaborate cosmology in which there is an almost endless hierarchy of created orders in the universe. Whether Plotinus was but systematizing and making public what the Academy had taught through the centuries, or altering Platonism into a new phenomenon (perhaps in part under the growing influence of Christianity) has long been debated among scholars. The important thing is that he gave to Platonism a distinctive interpretation, commonly called Neoplatonism, that was to exert an extensive influence upon Christianity during the formative period of the Model.

Lewis had no small measure of affinity for Plotinus. Although never adopting that thinker's philosophy, he was attracted to many of the same aspects of Platonism that interested Plotinus. Neither he nor Plotinus cared much for Plato's doctrine of the Forms, yet both were immensely attracted by the concept of supernatural entities that impinged upon human existence; for Plotinus there was an endless parade of Forms emanating from the absolute, whereas for Lewis it was often sufficient to speak of heavenly realities or angelic beings. Still, Lewis knew that the apostle Paul had listed supernatural beings in a hierarchical arrangement, and that fact was enough to give him warrant to introduce a modified hierarchy of celestial beings in some of his fiction. He sensed in Plotinus's hierarchy of being not simply a philosophical scheme but an aesthetic insight of stunning magnificence. He either did not know about or had no concern for Plotinus's other interests, such as government, which received scant attention in the philosopher's magnum opus, *The Enneads*. Both thinkers could, however, agree with Plato's essential conviction that the content of education should reflect the existence of an objective reality underlying the universe.

In view of the numerous bonds of understanding between Lewis and Plotinus, it is notable that Lewis was never greatly inclined to speak favorably of Plotinus. To be sure, when comparing Christian doctrine and philosophy he relatively seldom spoke favorably of any philosopher save for Plato himself. Furthermore, he objected that Plotinus tends to float off into ethereal regions.[6] His protests have a rather hollow sound; the objection may be valid enough, but Lewis himself was at times answerable to the same charge. His derogatory comments are, however, relatively few and brief, and they usually appear in connection with some issue on which Lewis believed that Christianity offered a better answer than did Neoplatonism.

For the next several centuries Neoplatonism was widely influential in both pagan and Christian circles. Its fate in pagan tradition is largely irrelevant for our purposes, since after the total triumph of Christianity in the sixth century paganism was no longer a viable philosophical option. Christian and non-Christian writings alike often have so similar a Neoplatonic cast that scholars are not always sure whether a Neoplatonist or a Christian wrote them. Lewis singles out several thinkers of this seminal period, when the Model was in the process of formation.[7] The earliest is Chalcidius, writing in the early fourth century, whose translation of the first half of Plato's *Timaeus* into Latin became the sole direct contact most Christian thinkers of the Middle Ages had with the Platonic dialogues. Lewis also devotes attention to Macrobius, who wrote around A.D. 400, Dionysius the Areopagite a century later, and Boethius, whose *De consolatione philosophiae* in the early sixth century became one of the most widely read books in Christendom during the next thousand years.[8]

By the latter part of the sixth century, Lewis avers, the essential characteristics of the medieval frame of mind had come into being. Platonism was an integral part of the medieval world view. But it was not a pure Platonism, based on first-hand, accurate knowledge of the writings of Plato himself. The medieval thinkers received a diffused Platonism consisting of Neoplatonic elements and scraps of assorted other traditions.[9] Almost no one read Plato himself, yet Platonism was everywhere in the intellectual climate of Christendom. From the sixth century until the twelfth there were no fresh investigations into Plato's dialogues, but only the reading of Boethius, the moral writings of Cicero, Statius, Claudian, and a few others, and Apuleius's essay on the god of Socrates. [10] By the twelfth century even so learned a scholar as Abelard knew of Greek philosophy only through the fathers of the church, some of the orations of Cicero, a couple of Aristotle's treatises, the Latin translation of the first half of the *Timaeus*, the treatises of Pseudo-Dionysius, Boethius's *De consolatione philosophiae*, and a few late Neoplatonic essays. It was inevitable that Platonism should have a different form and function within medieval thought than it had originally had.

During the late Middle Ages the most vigorous promulgation of Christian Platonism took place in a circle of thinkers at Chartres, among whom the best known was perhaps Bernard of Chartres, whom John of Salisbury described as "the most consummate Platonist of our age." Also to be noted among the late medieval Platonist Christians is Bernard of Tours, also known as Bernardus Silvestris. [11] Lewis, who prefers to refer to him by the latter name, was fascinated with his cosmological speculations. These are to be found in a remarkable treatise, written partly in prose and partly in poetry, called *De mundi universitate*, which deals largely with cosmology. Here the later Neoplatonic cosmological extravagances found a cordial home, along with statements that intermingle medieval magic and doubtless the author's own speculations as well; for the most part, however, the author did not invent his cosmological concepts but gave vigorous and imaginative form to those in his milieu. The work allegorically explicates the cosmological origin of the Earth and the universe. Bernard begins with Nous, that divine intellect which stands intermediate between God and Soul. Nous separates matter into four categories and creates the material world. At Nous's bidding, Urania (astrology) and Physis (the physical world), aided by Nature, shape human beings out of the four elements of matter, and thus a microcosm comes into being. Bernard's dependence upon Plato's *Timaeus* is plain enough, even though his presentation does not purport to depart from orthodox Christianity. Although curious from a modern point of view, the treatise constitutes a serious attempt on the part of the author to fashion a Christian cosmology that was consonant with philosophy.

In its most elaborate late-medieval form, the Model was magnificently unified, orderly, comprehensive, and beautiful.[12] Working on the assumption that Apuleius had enunciated centuries earlier, medieval thinkers filled every nook and cranny of the universe with life. There were no empty or unexplained parts of God's creation. Vast and complex though the universe was perceived to be, it nevertheless had been reduced to a comprehensible scheme. The *via negativa* of the Neoplatonic metaphysicians gave way to a positive, if naive, understanding of reality. How literally did the medieval thinkers believe in the Model? Not so much as we might suppose, suggested Lewis.[13] They knew that it was, after all, only a Model, and possibly replaceable; but the Model satisfied an immense longing for a system of reality that left nothing unaccounted for, even if high imagination had to be employed. Theologians—especially the brighter ones—knew that many aspects of the Model were speculative, and hence they seem not to have taken it quite so literally as did persons in the arts. Lewis observes, "Not only epistemologically but also emotionally the Model probably meant less to the great thinkers than to the poets. . . . Delight in the Medieval Model is expressed by Dante or Jean de Meung rather than by Albertus and Aquinas."[14] One particular group of medieval thinkers, the experts in the spiritual life, ignored the Model almost completely. This, says Lewis, is partly because the spiritual treatises are entirely practical, like medical books. It must be remembered, however, that Lewis is concerned primarily with cosmological aspects of Platonic Christianity when discussing the Model. In its totality, Christian supernaturalism or objectivism is more than cosmology, and even those who rejected the cosmology of the Model during the Middle Ages stood generally within the Platonist-Christian frame of reference.

As the Middle Ages drew to a close, the Model received what Lewis perceived to be its finest expression in Dante's epic theological poem, *The Divine Comedy*. Dante achieved a synthesis of religion and cosmology that the medieval thinkers, for all their efforts, had not previously been able to devise. Said Lewis:

> Their cosmology and their religion were not such easy
> bedfellows as might be supposed. At first we may fail to

notice this, for the cosmology appears to us, in its firmly theistic basis and its ready welcome to the supernatural, to be eminently religious. And so in one sense it is. But it is not eminently Christian. The Pagan elements embedded in it involved a conception of God, and of man's place in the universe, which, if not in logical contradiction to Christianity, were subtly out of harmony with it. There was no direct "conflict between religion and science" of the nineteenth-century type; but there was an incompatibility of temperament. Delighted contemplation of the Model and intense religious feeling of a specifically Christian character are seldom fused except in the work of Dante.[15]

The Divine Comedy presupposed virtually the entire Model, while at the same time embellishing it with Dante's own fertile genius. Its most notable feature is its elaborate cosmology, which places the Earth at the center and surrounds it with nine concentric circles representing the seven planets (including the moon and the sun), the stellatum (stars) and, at greatest distance, the Empyrean realm of Heaven. There are, however, many other Platonic elements in the work, pertaining particularly to nature, reason, and morality. Dante's images for ultimate reality (God) were akin to Plato's. Although Lewis himself could refer to Dante's thought as "Christian-Aristotelian theology,"[16] the major Aristotelian component was the Primum Mobile, mediating between the absolute and the created universe. Basically Dante's world view was the Platonic-Christian one of the Middle Ages.

The Renaissance saw a great new surge of interest in Platonism. During the fifteenth century manuscripts of Plato's dialogues began to be ferreted out of obscurity, with the result that what Plato actually wrote could be studied for the first time in many centuries. Although it is customary for the Renaissance to be seen as a marked departure from the Middle Ages, Lewis preferred to stress the continuity of cultural tradition from the one period to the other.[17] Certainly Platonic tradition had not been lost during the Middle Ages; its affinity for Christianity had been too great for such a separation to have taken place. It is true, however, that the

Renaissance interest in man, invention, and individual achievement planted the seeds that would grow into a new secularism with the passing centuries.

Lewis was well acquainted with some of the major Italian Platonists of the Renaissance. Among these were Marsilio Ficino, Nicolas de Cusa, and Pico della Mirandola, all of whom he mentions knowledgeably, upon occasion, in his writings. Although he found much that attracted him in the thought of the Platonists of the Italian Renaissance, he tended to reject the humanistic, theosophical orientation that he found there.[18] Nevertheless, the aesthetic and mystical aspects of Neoplatonism that recurred in Renaissance expressions of the Model seldom failed to evoke at least a partially positive response from Lewis, as we find in his poem "On a Theme from Nicolas of Cusa":

> When soul and body feed, one sees
> Their differing physiologies.
> Firmness of apple, fluted shape
> Of celery, or tight-skinned grape
> I grind and mangle when I eat,
> Then in dark, salt, internal heat,
> Annihilate their natures by
> The very act that makes them I.
>
> But when the soul partakes of good
> Or truth, which are her savoury food,
> By some far subtler chemistry
> It is not they that change, but she,
> Who feels them enter with the state
> Of conquerors her opened gate,
> Or, mirror-like, digests their ray
> By turning luminous as they.[19]

Lewis's own lifelong fascination with the occult made him, to an extent greater than he usually cared to admit, a bedfellow of the Florentine Platonists, with their belief that the myths and symbols of the pagan past were veiled expressions of the same truth that is in Christianity.[20]

It was the English Platonists that Lewis knew best. His studies of Spenser have found a secure niche in the history of modern scholarship. Spenser was very much a Platonist—just as he was also an Elizabethan and a Calvinistic Christian. Avoiding some of the excesses of the Italian Platonists, he drew heavily upon the medieval Model for his world view. His abundant use of allegory was not itself Platonic, but by the sixteenth century allegory had evolved into a frequent handmaid of Platonism and Christianity. Spenser's Platonism was not derived from Plato's dialogues directly but, like the Platonism of the Model, was mediated and interpreted by Neoplatonism. Although he accepted the fundamental Platonic conviction that there is a heavenly pattern, or Form, for the universe and each phenomenal thing in it, Spenser did not develop a comprehensive Platonic cosmology; nor was he obliged to do so, for the Model was still a living part of the intellectual trappings of the Elizabethan world. Most of what he knew about Neoplatonism had, in fact, been gleaned from the Model, rather than from the direct reading of Neoplatonist writings.[21] By this time the Model had been enriched in countless small ways through Renaissance accretions; it was a vessel veritably bursting with concepts plucked from centuries of development in the Western world. As Lewis's *Spenser's Images of Life* shows, the Platonism in *The Faerie Queene* is both diffuse and complex. The school of thought to which Spenser belonged, Lewis points out, felt that in the long run everything must be reconcilable. There was no belief, however pagan or bizarre it might seem, that could not somehow be accommodated if only it were rightly understood.[22] This assumption is one that had been characteristic of the Platonic strain in Western thought from the beginning.

By the seventeenth century the scientific inadequacy of the medieval Model was becoming increasingly apparent, yet imaginative writers—above all, poets—continued to make use of it, presumably because it afforded values that the emerging scientific approach to cosmology did not have. The English writer of greatest interest to Lewis during this century was John Milton. As Lewis's casual references to Milton's writings in *The Discarded Image* attest, Milton knew the Model well and drew heavily upon it. Yet he differed from that earlier grand cosmological scenarist,

Dante, in his avoidance of cosmological precision—a practice, Lewis believes, that indicates that Milton did not wish to present a cosmology that was any more obviously out of step with modern science than necessary.[23] Thus already one can see the dissolution of the once-absolute beginning to take place. For all this, Milton managed not to depart from orthodox Christian doctrine as it had been expounded by an earlier Platonic Christian, Augustine.[24]

Milton was not the only English writer of that century to find values in Platonic Christianity; there was John Donne early in the century, and then the Cambridge Platonists, among whom was Henry More. These latter derived their Platonism largely from the Renaissance form of that philosophy which, being heavily Neoplatonic, had a mystical cast. They stressed the place of reason in religion and deplored all ecclesiastical authoritarianism; the universe, they held, is an orderly place, the structure and laws of which are accessible to sensitive persons. Lewis had much in common with these thinkers, though he seldom acknowledged the bond. His lack of reference to others who had influenced him or who shared with him important presuppositions should not be taken to be the result of ignorance or hostility on his part; by now we have become accustomed to seeing how relatively infrequently, other than in his autobiography, Lewis mentions thinkers whose philosophies or scholarly insights moved in the same direction as his own. Even when he was not a lonely trailblazer, Lewis liked to imagine himself to be one: a man of independent mind, willing to sit at the feet of only a few of the brightest intellectual lights.

Looking back over the two thousand years between the time of Plato and that of Milton, Lewis was profoundly impressed with the essential continuity of Western culture. In his address "De Descriptione Temporum" he argued vigorously that the traditional divisions of history into Antiquity, the Dark Ages, the Middle Ages, the Renaissance, and the Modern era are inadequate, inasmuch as they introduce into Western history discontinuities that do not in fact exist. He discerned an essential continuity from Plato's time well into the seventeenth century and beyond, into the more obviously transitional eighteenth century. Throughout these two millennia, he insisted, people tended to think in ways that were more alike than different. They shared an essentially supernaturalist, i.e., objectivist, view of processes. To the extent that ancient Hebrew religion found its way into Christianity, it, too, may be said to participate in that very same culture; certainly it was structured around a supernaturalist understanding of reality. Thus he was convinced, as he asserted elsewhere, that "all that was best in Judaism and Platonism survives in Christianity." [25]

But the seeds of dissolution had been sown, and the eighteenth and nineteenth centuries saw them sprout and grow rankly. Lewis dourly surveyed that development:

> The sciences then began to advance with a firmer and more rapid tread. To that advance nearly all the later, and (in my mind) vaster, changes can be traced. But the effects were delayed. The sciences long remained like a lion-cub whose gambols delighted its master in private; it had not yet tasted man's blood. All through the eighteenth century the tone of the common mind remained ethical, rhetorical, juristic, rather than scientific, so that Johnson could truly say, "the knowledge of external nature, and the sciences which that knowledge requires or includes, are not the great or the frequent business of the human mind." It is easy to see why. Science was not yet the business of Man because Man had not yet become the business of science. It dealt chiefly with the inanimate; and it threw off few technological by-products. When Watt makes his engine, when Darwin starts monkeying with the ancestry of Man, and Freud with his soul, and the economists with all that is his, then indeed the lion will have got out of his cage. Its liberated presence in our midst will become one of the most important factors in everyone's daily life. But not yet; not in the seventeenth century. It is by these steps that I have come to regard as

the greatest of all divisions in the history of the West that which divides the present from, say, the age of Jane Austen and Scott.[26]

By the eighteenth century he found little to interest him. It is noteworthy that in one of his longer lists of writers whose works displayed "an almost unvarying *something*"—by which he meant the supernaturalism of Platonic Christianity—very few of the persons listed (such as Dante, Bunyan, Hooker, François de Sales, Edmund Spenser, Izaak Walton, Blaise Pascal, Samuel Johnson, Henry Vaughan, George Herbert, Thomas Traherne, Jeremy Taylor, William Law, Joseph Butler, Philip Sidney) [27] lived as late as the eighteenth century. "The list," he said, "is almost endless," but end it did by the eighteenth century.

The disastrous cultural change came, then, with the advent of the scientific era. As this new way of looking upon reality came in, the very life was taken out of the cosmos. "The thought of the new scientists . . . by reducing Nature to her mathematical elements . . . substituted a mechanical for a genial or animistic conception of the universe. The world was emptied, first of her indwelling spirits, then of her occult sympathies and antipathies, finally of her colours, smells and tastes. . . . Man with his new powers became rich like Midas but all that he touched had gone dead and cold." [28] Lewis discussed key aspects of the nineteenth- and twentieth-century mood: a change in political assumptions, an entirely new way of perceiving art, a severance of former ties with the Western religious past, and, last but certainly not least, a dramatically altered attitude wherein progress was celebrated above permanence, and all that was old was treated pejoratively. The result of these trends, which Lewis regarded as thoroughly regressive, is that human beings have cut themselves off from a sustaining tradition. They have thrown out the old Model as being outmoded, but the impersonal, mechanistic model that they have substituted has neither philosophical warrant nor the power to captivate the imagination of aesthetically sensitive persons.

The developments in the last two centuries have not been entirely in one direction. The romantics made a valiant, if inadequate, attempt to find a viable tradition. By virtue of his own love of nature Lewis could not help but find romantic thought attractive. As much as any nineteenth-century romantic Lewis loved to describe the wild sweetness of isolated mountain fastnesses, and in some measure romanticism provided useful imagery for the hierarchy of reality. In his autobiography he confessed to being something of a romantic,[29] and *The Pilgrim's Regress* had as its subtitle *An Allegorical Apology for Christianity, Reason, and Romanticism*. What he meant by *romanticism* in that work was an experience "of intense longing" for an ever-receding, ever-mysterious objective reality that is nothing less than the absolute itself, God.[30] He found value in Coleridge, Shelley, and Wordsworth, but the incompleteness of their world view prompted him to reject romanticism as a substitute for the vanished Model. Romanticism was a "desperate attempt" to bridge a gulf between the objective reality and rootless mankind,[31] but because it remained largely in the outer court of feeling and aesthetics rather than keeping focus on objective reality itself, the attempt was ultimately unsuccessful.

Being cut off from their roots in the "Old Western Culture," as Lewis calls it, English philosophers and writers of the Victorian era held little interest for Lewis. Only a few such persons won Lewis's praise, whether on literary or philosophical grounds. Among the fortunate few was George MacDonald, Scottish divine and author whose mystical novels *Lilith* and *Phantastes* stimulated the imagination of the young Lewis. MacDonald was not a Platonist as such, though he was a thoroughgoing supernaturalist who perceived life to consist of a religio-philosophical quest not unlike the Platonic ascent to the Good. What particularly fascinated Lewis was the way in which MacDonald communicated an essentially Christian message through the medium of magic, imaginary worlds, and symbolism. In *The Great Divorce* Lewis presents MacDonald as the purveyor of heavenly truth whose only possible error while on earth was belief in the ultimate redemption of all mankind. Other nineteenth-century thinkers whose works show Platonic influence, such as the theologian Friederich Schleiermacher and poet-philosopher Matthew Arnold, should have seemed fairly congenial to Lewis; yet these men, in Lewis's eyes, had abandoned too much of the Old Western Culture to qualify as standing within the tradition of the Model.

Lewis himself stood unblushingly on the side of the old tradition. In his inaugural address at Cambridge he declared: "I myself belong far more to that Old Western order than to yours. . . . I read as a native texts that you must read as foreigners. . . . It is my settled conviction that in order to read Old Western literature aright you must suspend most of the responses and unlearn most of the habits you have acquired in reading modern literature. . . . Speaking not only for myself but for all other Old Western men whom you meet, I would say, use your specimens while you can. There are not going to be many more dinosaurs." [32] For a self-styled dinosaur, Lewis proved to be immensely popular with readers. Within his lifetime millions of copies of his books were sold, and they continue to be in vogue. He himself was quite nonplussed by his fame, for it did not accord well with his own self-image of a last, lonely prophetic voice ringing out in the twilight of Western civilization. What gave him his popularity, however, was chiefly his charm as a storyteller and his advocacy of traditional Christian doctrine, rather than his championing of the Model or Old Western Culture in general. So far as the latter are concerned, Lewis remains indeed a dinosaur.

Some readers may have lingering doubts about the seriousness with which Lewis took his world view, but there is no reason to doubt that Lewis was very earnest indeed. He was not, of course, literal-minded about it; he was fully aware that the landscape of Malacandra and the person of Screwtape were the products of his own inventiveness. Yet he would not have us dismiss his (or the medieval world's) imagery as being insignificant or harmlessly amusing. There are, he never tired of iterating, certain things that can be said better—and perhaps solely—by images. Although the structure and details of the old Model may be shown by modern astronomy and physics not to be literally true, the Model may succeed in communicating something significant about the universe that modern models cannot do. The sum is more than its parts.

Lewis argues this and related matters in his epilogue to *The*

Discarded Image. He points out that in the mid-twentieth century we are less inclined to be dogmatic, progressivist, and evolutionist in our thinking about the universe than our nineteenth-century forebears were. "It would therefore be subtly misleading to say 'The medievals thought the universe to be like that, but we know it to be like this.' Part of what we now know is that we cannot, in the old sense, 'know what the universe is like' and that no model we build will be, in that old sense, 'like' it." [33] He disallowed any claim that the scientific model is necessarily superior to the old one. He did not suppose for a moment that the Model would suffice as a working tool for twentieth-century life, but he believed that it has an important use that the current world view has lost: the capacity for firing the imagination, for giving to the person who perceives its structure and beauty a sense of having a place within the cosmos. In its closed system there were no loose ends, and there was no projection of an infinite, impersonal, dehumanized universe. One did not need to take the Model literally in order to take its values seriously.

So thoroughgoing was Lewis's commitment to the Platonic-Christian view of reality expressed in the Model that we find that outlook in his broader speculations about culture. He was fully prepared to assume that the values that resided in the Old Western Culture were ones which had existed ever since civilization itself began, and perhaps before. Plato was not the first to live under the aegis of the supernatural, to accept the existence of an objective reality beyond the phenomenal world; neither did a sense of moral rightness begin with the Christian church. Such basic elements were a part of an Old Human Culture which stretches back to time immemorial. [34] Historically and archaeologically there is evidence to support Lewis's assumption that human beings have been religious beings since the very distant past; indeed, Lewis himself dips into historical anthropology briefly in the first chapter of *The Problem of Pain*; yet in the main the hypothesis lies beyond full proof. Possibly because he sensed this, he also experimented with an outright fictional device in his planetary romances. There he described a time in the remote past when the planets of the solar system had communication with one another, were peopled by a single kind of spiritual beings, the eldils, and employed a single language called Old Solar. He did not describe the situation in detail, but it would seem that the Old Solar Culture would be analogous to the Old Human Culture that he postulates for our own Earth. Both of these cultures are but devices whereby he can extend the values of the Old Western Culture to other times and places.

Thus far in our discussion of the Old Western Culture and the Model of reality that was its foundation we have dealt with general considerations. In chapter 4 we shall discuss in detail the cosmology of the Model. Now, however, we must turn to a consideration of the most important aspect of Christian objectivism, that of the ultimate reality which Christians call God.

3

Reality and God

"Of course I realise it's all rather too vague for you to put into words. . . ."

"On the contrary, it is words that are vague. The reason why the thing can't be expressed is that it's too *definite* for language."

Perelandra

*T*HE Old Western tradition that Lewis champions asks us to turn our common sense upside down and believe that there is a reality of inestimable importance that lies beyond the phenomenal world. That reality Plato called, as we have seen, by various names: the Good, the One, the Beautiful, and very Being itself. Sometimes, resorting to religious language, he referred to it as "the divine." Christians called that same reality "God," and declared that God was one and good, and the source of all being and all beauty. Lewis did not suppose that one must choose between Platonism and Christianity, but rather that the two views of reality are or can be complementary. Still, there were some potential differences between the two views, as his own writings subtly, and sometimes unintentionally, indicate.

The Platonic picture of the absolute, in spite of occasional mystical flights that can be found in the dialogues, tended to emphasize transcendence. For the most part Plato spoke about ultimate reality as having no personality and no regard for the lesser realities in the scale of being. He did provide for a demiurge to mediate between the perfect and the earthly spheres, but that power was distinct from the Good itself, and was never thoroughly integrated into the Platonic world view. In Neoplatonic writings there is a marked tendency for the ultimate to be understood as being so utterly remote that it is beyond all human comprehension. Plotinus asserted that God could not even be described as τὸ ὄν, pure being; the most that he was willing to concede is that God is the ground of all being. What God himself is no one can possibly say.

The documents of earliest Christianity reveal quite a different emphasis by Jesus and his disciples. Although grand and exalted, the God of the earliest Christians was an immanent deity, replete with emotions and other anthropomorphic qualities. He was vigorous and active, and had regard for the well-being of each believer and for mankind as a whole. He was seen as breaking into the earthly sphere repeatedly to give new laws, to give succor, or to right some wrong. Jesus taught his hearers to call this absolute reality "Father" and to pray to God, trusting that he would hear the petition. He did not cringe at anthropomorphism in his allusions to God. Although many sayings attributed to him do indeed presuppose that God is transcendent, he did not allow transcendence to separate the perfect God from the imperfect world. Subsequent to Jesus' lifetime Christians affirmed that Jesus himself, as the Christ, was the supreme instance of the immanence of God.

Lewis attempted to present both the transcendence and the immanence of God. When composing his fiction, however, he generally stressed transcendence—and not surprisingly, in view of his Platonic bent. Characteristically, in his trio of planetary romances he directly alludes to God only a few times, and then as "Maleldil's Father," who is so remote that Lewis is unwilling to say anything whatever about him. He shows the same tendency in the Narnian stories, where God is the "Emperor-Beyond-the-Sea" [1] whose will the great lion Aslan carries out, but who is never described and never appears in the action of the tales. Between this unapproachable God and the phenomenal world there is a vast gap. God is, in this sense, wholly other.

However averse to speaking directly of God in his fiction,

Lewis had no hesitation about pointing to him through analogy, symbol, and metaphor. His language for making statements about God was frequently that of images. For some of these he was, in measure, indebted to Plato; for others, the Model; for yet others, the imaginativeness of more recent thinkers. Tracing the sources of his symbols held only slight interest for him; what was important was that the images be deeply rooted in reality. They did not belong to any one person or school of thought but were, he believed, spontaneous and inherently appropriate ones for the elucidation of reality. Perhaps if we could look deeply enough into his early life we would find that most of the images had been his own discovery long before he encountered them in literature. When he found that thinkers such as Rudolph Otto, George MacDonald, Charles Wiliams, and Edwin Bevan [2] had independently found such imagery to be fundamental in religious experience, he was immensely encouraged.

The most broadly transcendental of all of Lewis's symbols was that of remoteness or awesomeness. Lewis frequently employed this concept in his planetary romances, where one finds that there always seems to be some reality higher than the reader can possibly imagine or the author can even describe. The absolute recedes forever into the distance; it is often alluring, occasionally threatening, and always overwhelming. One such instance of combined remoteness and awesomeness appears in Lewis's description of the visit of Glund, the celestial intelligence of the planet Jupiter, to earth. "Kingship and power and festal pomp and courtesy shot from him as sparks fly from an anvil. The pealing of bells, the blowing of trumpets, the spreading out of banners, are means used on earth to make a faint symbol of his quality. It was like a long sunlit wave, creamy-crested and arched with emerald, that comes on nine feet tall, with roaring and with terror and unquenchable laughter. It was like the first beginning of music in the halls of some King so high and at some festival so solemn that a tremor akin to fear runs through young hearts when they hear it." Sensing, perhaps, that this rather labored description has failed to communicate the ineffable glory and remoteness of Glund by comparison with all that is human, Lewis boldly forged ahead to assert that even this inexpressible cosmic grandeur was not that of God himself, but only of one of God's created beings. Indeed, the great Glund is many degrees down in the hierarchy of being. "This was great Glund-Oyarsa, King of Kings, through whom the joy of creation principally blows across these fields of Arbol [the solar system], known to men in old times as Jove and under that name, by fatal but not inexplicable misprision, confused with his Maker—so little did they dream by how many degrees the stair even of created being rises above him." [3] It was Lewis's intention that the reader be left totally unable to perceive even the slightest bit of the grandeur of God himself. Both Maleldil and his Father are infinitely remote from humankind. It is this assumed remoteness that makes the celestial hierarchy necessary, for otherwise there would be no contact at all between absolute reality and the phenomenal world.

Lewis liked to emphasize that if God is indeed as transcendent as Christian supernaturalism has traditionally declared him to be, he is far too "other" for human beings to treat him patronizingly or casually. Since human rationality, valid though it is, remains limited, the rationality of God must infinitely exceed that of persons. Thus the acts of God in the world must at times appear to human reason as being unpredictable, unsettling, dangerous, and even monstrous. When the planetary intelligences of Mars and Venus attempt to materialize before Ransom in the final great scene in *Perelandra*, they are so essentially different from human beings and superior to them that Ransom can only perceive them as horrible apparitions. "A tornado of sheer monstrosities seemed to be pouring over Ransom. Darting pillars filled with eyes, lightning pulsations of flame, talons and beaks and billowy masses of what suggested snow, volleyed through cubes and heptagons into an infinite black void. 'Stop it . . . stop it,' he yelled, and the scene cleared." [4] Thus Lewis attempted to suggest the utter transcendence of celestial beings.

Such experiences of that which is totally above and beyond human comprehension can be deeply disturbing, and that is precisely what Lewis hopes that they may be. He was stern in his condemnation of persons who claim to believe in God yet who demonstrate no fear of the Lord. His autobiography reveals his own profound anxieties as, in his youth, he began to consider the possibility of believing in God. How much easier life would be, he declared, if there were indeed no God with whom one had to reckon! [5] As he wrote in *Miracles*, "There comes a moment when the children who have been playing at burglars hush suddenly: was that a *real* footstep in the hall?" [6] The malefactors in *That Hideous Strength* find themselves in precisely this sort of predicament. They have attempted to play God and to invoke divine powers to further their cause, and as a result they are inundated and ultimately destroyed by those powers. Lewis pictures the dismay of dabblers in religion who unexpectedly encounter God: "We never meant it to come to *that!* . . . One may be in for *anything*." [7] What one is "in for" may be delightful or it may be horrible, but it is always out of the ordinary. It is this conviction that lies at the heart of Lewis's argument that it is possible for God to perform miracles in our world. Once, he insists, one really believes in God, one must concede that no possibility of divine intervention in the world is too gross, too trivial, too implausible, or too absurd.

Lewis was quite cognizant of the fact that in Christian thought the monstrous has generally been attributed to Satan rather than to God. [8] He agreed that the Devil is characterized by monstrous qualities such as bestiality, cruelty, vanity, deception, and a host of other evils. [9] In *The Last Battle* he portrays the false god Tash as such a being: ugly beyond comparison, rapacious, witless, and sluggish. The true deity has none of the characteristics of Tash, but is kind and just. Lewis's concern seems to be to point out that although the wisdom of God sometimes appears arbitrary and even cruel to human beings, it stems in fact from higher realities than man can conceive. Thus when God wreaks bloody vengeance upon the people of N.I.C.E. in *That Hideous Strength*, there is some divine wisdom that warrants the slaughter. Sometimes Lewis suggested that monstrousness is a false human perception of what is, in fact, a benevolent deity. Such may, in part, be the case with Ungit in *Till We Have Faces*. [10]

Closely related, but more specific as a form of remoteness, is the imagery of height. The assumption that that which is physically higher is also of greater inherent importance conceptually or spiritually appears to be deeply ingrained in human thought. Certainly Lewis made the fullest possible symbolic use of height in his fiction. The paradise where the deity Aslan dwells is a land of supernaturally lofty mountains that are utterly inaccessible to the creatures of Narnia except when they are summoned there after death or for a special divine mission. At the end of their pilgrimage toward Aslan's country, Edmond, Eustace, and Lucy get a glimpse of the mountainous paradise before the vision fades: "What they saw—eastward, beyond the sun—was a range of mountains. It was so high that either they never saw the top of it or they forgot it. None of them remembers seeing any sky in that direction. And the mountains must really have been outside the world. For any mountains even a quarter of a twentieth of that height ought to have had ice and snow on them. But these were warm and green and full of forests and waterfalls however high you looked." [11] In *The Last Battle* the Narnians who enter Aslan's realm after the great eschatological upheaval find themselves climbing ever upward, with an over-widening perspective on reality. At times the climb is vertiginous:

> For now they saw before them Caldron Pool and beyond the Pool, the high unclimbable cliffs and, pouring down the cliffs, thousands of tons of water every second, flashing like diamonds in some places and dark, glassy green in others, the Great Waterfall; and already the thunder of it was in their ears.
> "Don't stop! Further up and further in," called Farsight, tilting his flight a little upwards. . . .
> Jewel reached the foot of the Waterfall first, but Tirian was only just behind him. Jill was last, so she could see the whole thing better than the others. She saw something white moving steadily up the face of the Waterfall. That white thing was the Unicorn. You couldn't tell whether he was swimming or climbing, but he moved on, higher and higher. [12]

Their supernatural energy never flagging, the joyful Narnians swim straight up the waterfall and continue their ascent.

Beauty is a close concommitant of height in Lewis's thought. When the reader obtains a close view of the beckoning heights of Aslan's country, the scene is one of nearly indescribable delight. Typical of several such passages in the Narnian tales is one that appears in *The Silver Chair*. "They saw smooth turf, smoother and brighter than Jill had ever seen before, and blue sky, and, darting to and fro, things so bright that they might have been jewels or huge butterflies." Jill feels fright at this unexpected vista, yet Lewis pointedly mentions that "she had been longing for something like this." [13] He may well be speaking very personally here, for he himself had always longed for the sight of such a paradise, which for him symbolized reality itself. In his autobiography he admits that landscape exerted a powerful influence upon his imaginative processes during his youth.

> Hitherto my feelings for nature had been too narrowly romantic. I attended almost entirely to what I thought awe-inspiring, or wild, or eerie, and above all to distance. Hence mountains and clouds were my special delight; the sky was, and still is, to me one of the principal elements in any landscape, and long before I had seen them all named and sorted out in *Modern Painters* I was very attentive to the different qualities, and different heights, of the cirrus, the cumulus, and the raincloud. As for the Earth, the country I grew up in had everything to encourage a romantic bent, had indeed done so ever since I first looked at the unattainable Green Hills through the nursery window. [14]

This delight in the imagined wilds of distant landscape was attested by his brother Warren. [15] Although he possessed, as his diaries as a young man show, a certain gift for the description of scenery, he was interested in topography not for its own sake, but as a mystical guide to higher realities. [16] In this matter, perhaps more than any other, he was very much a romantic. His romanticism was as sturdy a sort as he could make it to be. In his poem "To Roy Campbell" he wrote:

> In England the romantic stream flows not
> From waterish Rousseau but from manly Scott,
> A right branch on the old European tree
> Of valour, truth, freedom, and courtesy,
> . . . .
> It flows, I say, from Scott; from Coleridge too.
> A bore? A sponge? A laudanum-addict? True;
> Yet Newman in that ruinous master saw
> One who restored our faculty for awe,
> Who re-discovered the soul's depth and height,
> Who pricked with needles of the eternal light
> An England at that time half numbed to death
> With Paley's, Bentham's, Malthus' wintry breath. [17]

One notes in these few lines the terms "awe," "depth and height" and "light," all of which are symbolic of the experience of God in the thought of Lewis as well as being frequent romantic images.

Although he went far beyond romanticism in his philosophy of religion, Lewis never disowned the romantic streak within him. Unlike many romantics, however, he was unwilling to remain at a strictly aesthetic level of appreciation of the natural world. Indeed, although he had certain aesthetic interests, he never evidenced more than a pedestrian insight or critical competence in matters of painting, architecture, sculpture, and music. [18] His keen eye for landscape was intimately linked with metaphysical and imaginative preoccupations. At times he came close to the enunciation of a philosophy of the description of landscape in literature. To be properly stimulating to the mind, he said, a fictional landscape must have both geographical plausibility within the framework of the story and a dimension of cosmic distance. In an essay on William Morris's fiction he wrote:

> Other stories have only scenery: his have geography. He is not concerned with "painting" landscapes; he tells

you the lie of the land, and then you paint the landscapes for yourself. To a reader long fed on the almost botanical and entomological niceties of much modern fiction—where, indeed, we mostly skip if the characters go through a jungle—the effect is at first very pale and cold, but also very fresh and spacious. We begin to relish what my friend called the "Northernness." No mountains in literature are as far away as distant mountains in Morris. The world of his imagining is as windy, as tangible, as resonant and three-dimensional, as that of Scott or Homer.[19]

In his own fiction he forewent, for the most part, the element of coldness as an image of landscape, presumably because that quality conveyed too negative a picture of reality; otherwise he retained much of his youthful enthusiasm for the mystery and joy of distant landscapes and sudden glimpses of beauty. For him, as one would expect by virtue of his objective philosophy, there is no true art apart from beauty. "The great use of the idyllic in literature," he wrote, "is to find and illustrate the good."[20]

This combination of beauty and higher realities is one of the most constant features of Lewis's fiction. As the voyagers approach Aslan's country in *The Voyage of the Dawn Treader*, they are bombarded with varied images of visual and olfactory delight. The water beneath them is said to grow sweeter at the same time that the air is growing clearer and the sun brighter. The children encounter, as they drift along, a carpet of preternaturally white lilies that grow as far as the eye can see and that exude a heavy, heady fragrance. Similarly, the pristine planet Perelandra (Venus), as yet unsullied by the Devil, is redolent with exotically delightful sights, sounds, smells, tastes, and textures. Again, in the heavenly Narnia that supplants the old Narnia at the end of *The Last Battle*, Lewis does everything possible to suggest aesthetic pleasures.

> They stood on grass, the deep blue sky was overhead, and the air which blew gently on their faces was that of a day in early summer. Not far away from them rose a

grove of trees, thickly leaved, but under every leaf there peeped out the gold or faint yellow or purple or glowing red of fruits such as no one has seen in our world. . . .

Everyone raised his hand to pick the fruit he best liked the look of, and then everyone paused for a second. This fruit was so beautiful that each felt, "It can't be meant for me . . . surely we're not allowed to pluck it."

"It's all right," said Peter. "I know what we're all thinking. But I'm sure, quite sure, we needn't. I've a feeling we've got to the country where everything is allowed."

"Here goes, then!" said Eustace. And they all began to eat.

What was the fruit like? Unfortunately no one can describe a taste. All I can say is that, compared with those fruits, the freshest grapefruit you've ever eaten was dull, and the juciest orange was dry, and the most melting pear was hard and woody, and the sweetest wild strawberry was sour. And there were no seeds or stones, and no wasps.[21]

Convinced though he was that reality is beautiful, Lewis never fully succumbed to the romantic notion that through beauty one comes to know God, and he carefully avoided suggesting that the experience of earthly beauty is a sufficient encounter with God. All earthly beauty is but an imperfect mirror of the absolute beauty of the Creator.

It will be noticed that the descriptions of beauty that we have cited from Lewis's writings have all been those of landscape. Lewis did give some descriptions of personal beauty, such as that of the magnificent lion-redeemer Aslan; but these are infrequent and relatively brief. There is no doubt that in his fiction he found that he could suggest absolute beauty better by means of land-scape than through persons.[22] The elaborate mystical journey that Ransom makes in the closing pages of *Perelandra*, from the planet Venus toward ever purer reaches of reality, consists en-tirely of changing scenes. At the culmination Ransom finds him-self not in the presence of a divine person but in a place of "simplicity beyond all comprehension." [23] Lewis is not far here from the spirit of Plotinus's *via negativa*, nor for that matter from some oriental philosophies.

Similarly, as the saved Narnians journey inward and upward from the entrance of the heavenly Narnia at the end of the great eschatological drama in *The Last Battle*, they pass through ever-increasing delights of vista, and the reader is led to expect that they will soon see God. But nothing of the sort happens. To be sure, Aslan is there, and as they look upon him he "no longer looked to them like a lion" [24]—presumably an allusion to his taking on of a heavenly form, either that of the resurrected Christ or some indescribable new appearance—yet he, too, is but a dweller in the heavenly realm that is reality; he does not swallow up all landscapes of delight and all individual personalities into himself. The pilgrims in *The Voyage of the Dawn Treader* are seeking not so much Aslan as Aslan's country; the very imagery of journeying tends to suggest a place, rather than a person, at the end. Even young John in Lewis's early *The Pilgrim's Regress* tends to seek a distant, alluring land rather than God. To be sure, Lewis implies that at the heart of the heavenly realm the journeyer will find God; but that final stage of the pilgrimage is left shrouded in the mist.

Another prominent image for absolute reality in Lewis's writing is that of firmness and weight. Lewis never tired of repeating that reality must be vastly solider than anything we experience in our world. He liked to point out the falsity of the popular notion that God and the supernatural are vague simply because they do not present themselves to the five senses. That popular assumption, he insisted, has things quite topsy-turvy. In *The Great Divorce* he forcefully used this idea of the increasing firmness and weightiness of things as one ascends the ladder of reality. When assorted dwellers in Hell visit the fringes of Heaven they experience an intensification of their tactile and visual perceptions. Lewis, who as narrator is among the travelers who make this trip, notices that his fellow visitors, who had seemed to be normal and solid while still in the nether regions, appear to be quite ghostlike in the fresh, clear regions of Heaven.

My attention was caught by my fellow-passengers, who

were still grouped about in the neighbourhood of the omnibus, though beginning, some of them, to walk forward into the landscape with hesitating steps. I gasped when I saw them. Now that they were in the light, they were transparent—fully transparent when they stood between me and it, smudgy and imperfectly opaque when they stood in the shadow of some tree. They were in fact ghosts: man-shaped stains on the brightness of that air. One could attend to them or ignore them at will as you do with the dirt on a window pane. I noticed that the grass did not bend under their feet: even the dew drops were not disturbed. [25]

In his preface to this work Lewis acknowledges that he first got the idea of the solidity of the real, in comparison with the insubstantiality of the relatively unreal, from the reading of an American science fiction story several years earlier. Yet he surely is being too modest, for the same imagery had occurred to him as a young man. [26]

In the planetary romances Lewis used similar imagery. In *Out of the Silent Planet*, published three years before *The Great Divorce*, he introduced his readers to eldils, who are angelic beings. In good Platonic fashion, and probably with much delight, he again turned the common-sense perception of reality upside down. To human beings an eldil is a thin, half-real body of wraithlike appearance that can go through walls and rocks; to himself, he is most solid, and walls and rocks are like clouds. [27] Since the eldils are, as he constructed his story, higher than humans in the cosmic hierarchy of being, it is human perception that is to be regarded as distorted, not the eldils'. He continues this imagery in the second novel in the series. Upon awakening after his first night on Perelandra, Ransom "saw reality, and thought it was a dream." Later he learns that "only Maleldil sees any creature as it really is. . . . You have never seen more than an appearance of anything." [28]

Lewis did not confine his use of the imagery of the solidity of reality to his fiction. In *Miracles* he declares:

The ultimate spiritual reality is not vaguer, more inert, more transparent than the images [in the Old Testament], but more positive, more dynamic, more opaque. Confusion between Spirit and soul (or "ghost") has here done much harm. Ghosts must be pictured, if we are to picture them at all, as shadowy and tenuous, for ghosts are half-men, one element abstracted from a creature that ought to have flesh. But Spirit, if pictured at all, must be pictured in the very opposite way. Neither God nor even the gods are "shadowy" in traditional imagination: even the human dead, when glorified in Christ, cease to be "ghosts" and become "saints." The difference of atmosphere which even now surrounds the words "I saw a ghost" and the words "I saw a saint"—all the pallor and insubstantiality of the one, all the gold and blue of the other—contains more wisdom than whole libraries of "religion." If we must have a mental picture to symbolise Spirit, we should represent it as something *heavier* than matter.[29]

Referring to ultimate reality, he says in the same work:

God is basic Fact or Actuality, the source of all other facthood. At all costs therefore He must not be thought of as a featureless generality. If He exists at all, He is the most concrete thing there is, the most individual, "organised and minutely articulated." He is unspeakable not by being indefinite but by being too definite for the unavoidable vagueness of language. . . . Grammatically the things we say of Him are "metaphorical": but in a deeper sense it is our physical and psychic energies that are mere "metaphors" of the real Life which is God.[30]

We shall have more to say about this understanding of the place of imaginative thought, including myth, in chapter 6.

Another major image of reality in Lewis's works is that of

spatial magnitude. The concept is related to the imagery of remoteness, height, and solidity. Lewis liked to think of reality as infinitely large. His most emphatic statement of the analogy appears in *The Great Divorce*. When, as narrator, he descends from the autobus that has brought his group from Hell to Heaven he experiences something new: "I had the sense of being in a larger space, perhaps even a larger *sort* of space, than I had ever known before: as if the sky were further off and the extent of the green plain wider than they could be on this little ball of earth. I had got 'out' in some sense which made the Solar System itself seem an indoor affair." [31] In a similar vein *The Last Battle* has the saved Narnians experience larger and larger space as they travel farther into the new, heavenly Narnia. When they first enter the new Narnia, it seems to be contained within the twelve- by six-foot stable where Tashlan had been worshipped, yet once inside they realize that they are in a whole landscape. At Aslan's urging they move westward in the phantasmagoric terrain. Although a great many creatures are moving in the same direction, the country proves to be amply wide enough for all. After half an hour, "or it might have been half a hundred years later, for time there is not like time here" they come to a special garden, strikingly like the one that Digory and Polly had visited in the old Narnia on the day of creation. As she looks at it, Lucy, who is especially perceptive of heavenly realities, sees that the garden is larger than it at first appeared to be.

> Lucy looked hard at the garden and saw that it was not really a garden at all but a whole world, with its own rivers and woods and sea and mountains. But they were not strange: she knew them all.
>
> "I see," she said. "This is still Narnia, and, more real and more beautiful than the Narnia down below, just as *it* was more real and more beautiful than the Narnia outside the Stable door! I see . . . world within world, Narnia within Narnia. . . ."
>
> "Yes," said Mr. Tumnus, "like an onion: except that as you continue to go in and in, each circle is larger than the last." [32]

The picture is that of an infinite number of circles, each larger and more patently real than the previous, and each—by virtue of transposition—embracing all that was true and valid in the lower order of reality.

The concept of a paradoxical reversal of the space of the universe, so that as one enters ever-decreasing concentric spheres, space expands, is one that Lewis borrowed from that most estimable and imaginative adapter of the Model, Dante. As Lewis observed in *The Discarded Image*, Dante boldly turned the cosmos inside out, conceptually speaking, so that the Earth was seen not as the center of the universe but as its rim, the outermost edge where being fades into nonbeing.

> A few astonishing lines from the *Paradiso* (XXVIII, 25 *sq*.) stamp this on the mind forever. There Dante sees God as a point of light. Seven concentric rings of light revolve about that point, and that which is smallest and nearest to it has the swiftest movement. This is the Intelligence of the Primum Mobile, superior to all the rest in love and knowledge. The universe is thus, when our minds are sufficiently freed from the senses, turned inside out. Dante, with incomparably greater power is, however, saying no more than Alanus says when he locates us and our Earth "outside the city wall." [33]

This last allusion is to the Epistle to the Hebrews, which, as we saw in chapter 2, brings together the Hebrew Scripture, Platonism, and Christianity into a remarkable synthesis. The "city" is, of course, Jerusalem, symbolic in this context of heavenly perfection.

Lewis's imagery of the infinite largeness of reality is, in one sense, a denial that reality has any spatiality as such. The higher realm is in some measure accessible from lower ones, though never completely in this life; and lower realms are accessible from the higher, for otherwise there would be no metaphysical basis for the phenomenal world. Movement from one realm to another is sometimes easy, as in the case of mathematical problems and principles. In most cases, however, it is difficult and sometimes unpredictable. One never knows when one will feel a stab of otherworldly joy, sense a universal moral truth, or feel a moment of mystical communion with the transcendent. Lewis represents the problem of access from one dimension to another in his descriptions of various doorways through which people can enter or leave Narnia. In one Narnian story the doorway is the back of a wardrobe, in another it is a gate in a wall, and in another it is a magic ring. Narnia is not, of course, a perfect, heavenly realm, but simply another world; the stories do presuppose, however, that all worlds must be present, unseen, in every world, even though few human beings ever have the ability to move from one dimension to another.

Perhaps the most dramatic illustration of this concept in Lewis's fiction is to be found in the scene in *The Last Battle* in which the band of redeemed Narnians leave the imperfect old Narnia behind and joyfully make their way into the heavenly Narnia through the supernatural doorway of a humble stable. Also entering through the same stable door is a group of dwarfs—not good ones, but bad ones who had joined the enemies of Aslan during the recent eschatological events under their slogan, "The Dwarfs are for the Dwarfs." They are obviously too selfish to participate in Aslan's kingdom; hence, though physically within the heavenly Narnia they remain blind to the wonders around them.

> They were sitting very close together in a little circle facing one another. They never looked round or took any notice of the humans till Lucy and Tirian were almost near enough to touch them. Then the Dwarfs all cocked their heads as if they couldn't see any one but were listening hard and trying to guess by the sound what was happening.
>
> "Look out!" said one of them in a surly voice. "Mind where you're going. Don't walk into our faces!"
>
> "All right!" said Eustace indignantly. "We're not blind. We've got eyes in our heads."
>
> "They must be darn good ones if you can see in here," said the same Dwarf whose name was Diggle.

"In where?" asked Edmund.

"Why you bone-head, in *here* of course," said Diggle. "In this pitch-black, pokey, smelly little hole of a stable."

"Are you blind?" said Tirian.

"Ain't we all blind in the dark!" said Diggle.

"But it isn't dark, you poor stupid Dwarfs," said Lucy. "Can't you see? Look up! Look round! Can't you see the sky and the trees and the flowers? Can't you see *me*? . . . She stooped and picked some wild violets. "Listen, Dwarf," she said. "Even if your eyes are wrong, perhaps your nose is all right: can you smell *that*." She leaned across and held the fresh, damp flowers to Diggle's ugly nose. But she had to jump back quickly in order to avoid a blow from his hard little fist.

"None of that!" he shouted. "How dare you! What do you mean by shoving a lot of filthy stable-litter in my face? There was a thistle in it too." [34]

There are a number of passages elsewhere in Lewis's writings in which the spiritually blind are shown to be living in self-imposed misery.[35] Like the dwarfs, the inhabitants of Hell who visit Heaven in *The Great Divorce* are surly, bitter, and blind to the delightful world that lies in their midst. The theme is indeed an old one: A realm of joy is ever accessible to those who have the spiritual receptors to perceive it. It should be noted that participation in this heavenly reality has nothing as such to do with aesthetic sophistication. The most sensitive patron of the arts might be quite blind spiritually.

Certainly among the great images of reality in Lewis's thought is that of light. Many thinkers in the Platonic and Christian traditions down through the centuries had used light to represent God as the ultimate source of all that is good in the universe. In commenting on Dante's use of this symbol, Lewis plainly declares that "God is, or is like, light, not [only] for the purposes of this bit of poetry but for every devotional, philosophical, and theological purpose imaginable within a Christian, or indeed, a monotheistic, frame of reference." [36] The symbol is, he points out, "almost a part of nature, not of art, for nothing else will do and it is almost dictated, as Dr. Edwyn Bevan has shown, by the shape of the human mind." [37] The imagery is related to that of height, for customarily light does not come from below the observer. To these considerations Lewis adds another: "We cannot see light, though by light we can see things." [38] The ultimate remains, as ever, shielded by its own magnificence, yet it gives meaning to all that is. Plato had said, or implied, much the same thing in his analogy of the cave and elsewhere in his dialogues. The idea is an interesting amalgam of philosophical concepts and speculation about the physics of light.

The most important single image of light is, of course, that of the sun. In the *Republic* Plato used the sun as an analogy of the Good. The figure was especially well suited to that purpose, for the sun's shape is in accord with the Platonic concept of the sphere as the perfect form. As the nourisher of life on Earth, the sun represents cosmic beneficence, and by virtue of its uniqueness within our solar system it has the unity requisite for the Platonic One. Also, whether by curious coincidence or because it signifies a metaphysical truth, the light-waves emanating from the sun are, individually, never diminished as they pass through the vast reaches of space, but only diffused; a particle of light falling on the remotest of planets is as much pure light as it was when it left its parent sun. Furthermore, the heliotropism of many earthly creatures, flora and fauna alike, is reminiscent of Plato's assumption that all sensitive persons naturally turn toward the Good. Yet, just as human beings cannot look directly at the sun without being blinded, so mortals, because of their imperfections, cannot perceive the Good directly, but must circle about it as a moth flutters about a flame—or, to use another simile, must observe it dimly through a smoked glass. Finally, like Plato's absolute, the sun has, for all practical purposes, neither beginning nor end; it does not differ from day to day nor change its apparent orbit. These many similarities make the sun a uniquely appropriate symbol of the Platonic ultimate.

Lewis made much of the imagery of the sun in the first of his planetary romances, *Out of the Silent Planet*. Here, leaving the earthly atmosphere behind, his hero Ransom experiences the sun with an intensity he has never felt on the murky, silent planet

Earth. Although ostensibly describing the light that flooded the spaceship, Lewis was in fact introducing cosmological considerations based upon his recognition of the analogy of the sun to absolute reality. He portrayed the light that Ransom sees as being so bright that when it comes in through only a tiny aperture in the protective shutters over the windows it bathes everything in brilliant, unearthly clarity. Ransom feels a near-supernatural vigor and exhilaration in the presence of the cosmic life-force. Lewis devoted considerable space to a description of the quality and absoluteness of the interplanetary sunlight. He did not, however, choose to imply that the sun is God himself; he allowed it to serve as a momentary God-surrogate for his hero, and to be the first of many lessons about the great hierarchy of being that Ransom was to absorb during his interplanetary adventures.[39]

Lewis explored the ramifications of the symbol of light more subtly and inventively in *The Voyage of the Dawn Treader*. The English children and their Narnian friends journey across the sea toward Aslan's country, sailing eastward as if guided by the dictum *ex oriente lux*. The sun grows larger, the light becomes more intense, the air feels cleaner, and the very water on which the *Dawn Treader* moves takes on the quality of liquid light. The Narnian sun itself is not in Aslan's country, yet it, too, partakes of the characteristics of the absolute. Lewis emphasizes not only the light that the sun gives but the warmth as well. Unlike the warmth of the sun during the voyage to Mars in *Out of the Silent Planet*, which brings physical discomfort as well as contentment to Ransom, this warmth is entirely beneficent.

Elsewhere in his fiction Lewis returned to the imagery of the sun, but in a less sustained way. In *That Hideous Strength*, St. Anne's, the place where the company of true Christians have their headquarters, rests atop the highest hill in the vicinity and is bathed in sunlight, while the town of Edgestow, where the university and the headquarters of the evil N.I.C.E. are situated, is generally befogged. Jane Studdock observes this phenomenon as she nears St. Anne's:

> She looked ahead: surely that bend in the road was more visible than it ought to be in such a fog? Or was it only

that a country fog was different from a town one? Certainly what had been grey was becoming white, almost dazzlingly white. A few yards further and luminous blue was showing overhead, and trees cast shadows (she had not seen a shadow for days), and then all of a sudden the enormous spaces of the sky had become visible and the pale golden sun, and looking back, as she took the turn to the Manor, Jane saw that she was standing on the shore of a little green sun-lit island looking down on a sea of white fog, furrowed and ridged yet level on the whole, which spread as far as she could see. . . . She took a deep breath. It was the *size* of this world above the fog which impressed her. Down in Edgestow all these days one had lived, even when out-of-doors, as if in a room, for only objects close at hand were visible. She felt she had come near to forgetting how big the sky is, how remote the horizon.[40]

Later Jane has experiences which indicate clearly to her that she has come to a place where heavenly realities become manifest on Earth.

Solar imagery sometimes takes indirect form in Lewis's writings, above all in the figure of Aslan. Large, warm, and benevolent, Aslan is himself a sun-deity. His golden mane resembles the rays of the sun. He is immensely beautiful, yet at the same time powerful; his very look can wither if he is provoked. In linking the imagery of the lion and the sun, Lewis was largely following a convention that was widespread in medieval thought; astrologically the sign of the sun was Leo, the lion. There were other connotations of the lion too, such as that of the Lion of Judah in the Old Testament and the commonplace concept of the lion as king of the animal world—for Narnia is, in spite of the presence of some human beings, essentially an animal-land. Occasionally in medieval thought the lion had evil connotations, perhaps because lions were known to be dangerous beasts, even as the generally benevolent sun could also destroy. It is perhaps these dark potentialities for both the lion and the sun that prompted Lewis to emphasize that Aslan was, from a human point of view, unpredictable. More than once Lewis has Narnians remind one another that Aslan is not a tame lion.[41]

In addition to these major images of reality there are various minor ones as well. Lewis sometimes suggested that God is characterized by infinite speed, which in turn, he asserted, was identical with absolute stillness; that imagery appears in *Perelandra* and *Miracles*,[42] but was otherwise not particularly useful to him. It is appropriate to take note of the fact that he did not ascribe temporality to God. We have already seen that he denied to reality any spatial limitations. Time, too, he insisted, is created by God, and not a characteristic of God himself. "In life and art both," he wrote, "as it seems to me, we are always trying to catch in our net of successive moments something that is not successive." [43] That idea is Platonic; the unchanging cannot, by virtue of its very nature, be within time, for that would mean that it would partake of movement, alteration, and fragmentation. To those who would argue that such an assertion is based on an a priori definition of reality, and that timelessness is unknown in the universe, Lewis would reply that timelessness is indeed very well known, and could point to mathematical principles as an illustration. It is on the basis of his conviction that God does not exist within time that he could argue for a modified form of predestination: Man's choices in life are free ones, but God perceives a person's life in its entirety, without the dimension of temporality, and hence can consign a soul to Heaven or to Hell—according to the person's own decisions on Earth—without any injustice whatever.

Such, then, was the nature and intensity of Lewis's preoccupation with the transcendence of God. Yet as a Christian Lewis was also firmly committed to the concept of divine immanence. More than once he had occasion to point out that Platonism, for all its philosophical insights, was deficient in precisely this regard. To be sure, Plato had contemplated the possibility of a thoroughly righteous person's suffering at the hands of unenlightened fellow creatures; but he did not, and could not, conceive of the Jesus Christ of history and faith.[44] In his own attempt to comprehend this aspect of reality, Lewis had recourse less to reason than to Christian orthodoxy. For his verbal expressions of his conviction, he resorted both to theological language and to fictional representations. The latter, because of their novelty, warrant particular attention.

Lewis's most notable representations of divine immanence are Aslan and Maleldil. For all practical purposes each figure is itself God, but the two differ noticeably in function. Maleldil first appears in *Out of the Silent Planet* as the deity of the inhabitants of Malacandra. When Ransom first learns of him he seems to be the deity of that planet alone, but as the other two stories of the trilogy unfold he is shown to have dominion over all of the planets of the solar system, save only for the fallen planet Thulcandra, which is Earth. Maleldil serves a function somewhat like that of a Stoic *logos*; he is a creating, acting, governing deity, a lawgiver, and a strict, though loving, judge. He is, however, neither seen nor heard by Ransom or by most of the creatures on Malacandra, nor is he said to have had any creaturely incarnation on that planet. He does apparently speak to the governing spirit of Malacandra, and in *Perelandra* he is said to speak directly to the two humanoids who inhabit Venus, much as God is said to have talked with Adam and Eve in Eden. The figure functions somewhat as the Holy Spirit does in Christian tradition.

Lewis hints that Maleldil may have had a role, at a distant time in the past, in fashioning the planetary system. He also indicates that Maleldil came to wrestle with evil on Earth—in other words, that he came to Earth in the person of Christ. "In the Fallen World," we learn, "He prepared for Himself a body and was united with the Dust and made it glorious for ever"—that is, became incarnate, died, and was resurrected.[45] For the inhabitants of Earth he serves as a redeemer; the inhabitants of Malacandra and Perelandra had no need for redemption, for they had never fallen into sin. In one passage Lewis even alludes to the Christian Trinity: The young human king of Venus describes his theological education with the words, "I learned . . . about Maleldil and about His Father and the Third One." [46] In spite of Lewis's attempts to link him with Christ, Maleldil remains, by virtue of his nonappearance, more of a transcendent God than a God incarnate.

The Narnian equivalent of Maleldil is the great lion Aslan. In this figure Lewis brings together both the transcendence and the immanence of God. Aslan is at once supernatural and natural, aloof and personal, irenic and active. He does not dwell in Narnia but comes to the land from a great distance (yet still within the Narnian world) when need arises. He creates,[47] enunciates values, comforts, inspires, judges, battles evil, and rescues his followers. In fullfilling these functions he sometimes resembles a good fairy more than a Christian deity, appearing in moments of dire need like a deus ex machina, to right all wrongs. To be sure, he does not always arrive just when the children want him most; but when he does not, it is because he is testing them and helping them to mature. He can be immensely fierce, as lions should be, but his wrath is always just and purposeful.

The success of the figure of Aslan depends in no small measure upon the fact that Lewis modeled him, in a highly imaginative way, upon Christ. He leaves no doubt about it when, in *The Lion, the Witch and the Wardrobe*, he has Aslan die a sacrificial death at the hands of the White Witch, then rise to life again at dawn.[48] For purposes of the story he had to bend Christian doctrine slightly: Aslan dies not for all Narnians' sins but only for those of Edmund, the bad boy of the story; but Lewis certainly intended that Edmund should represent all. Because he rises to assume his former role as reigning deity of Narnia, rather than—as Christian dogma holds—ascending to Heaven to reign, Aslan remains a present, active ruler among his creatures. Hence Lewis has little need to introduce a figure to correspond to the Holy Spirit of Christian doctrine. When Aslan is absent, the children sometimes feel his spirit guiding them, but that presence is more analogous to the "spirit of Christ" felt within the early church than a full-blown concept of a Holy Spirit as it is set forth in the traditional Christian concept of the Trinity.

In Aslan, therefore, Lewis has presented a far completer picture of the Christ of Christian tradition than he has in Maleldil. Even Aslan's wildness and unpredictability—about which we shall have more to say later in this chapter—have a plausible antecedent in the fierceness of some of Jesus's teachings and the unpredictability of divine intervention in the world.[49] In resisting all attempts by human beings to patronize him, Aslan is but mirror-

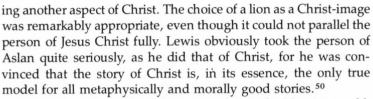

ing another aspect of Christ. The choice of a lion as a Christ-image was remarkably appropriate, even though it could not parallel the person of Jesus Christ fully. Lewis obviously took the person of Aslan quite seriously, as he did that of Christ, for he was convinced that the story of Christ is, in its essence, the only true model for all metaphysically and morally good stories.[50]

Inasmuch as he made Aslan very active in the Narnian world, Lewis was extremely reluctant to assign any role to God ("Aslan's Father" or the "Emperor-Beyond-the-Sea") as distinct from Aslan. Although subject himself to laws of rationality, Aslan can and does do everything that both the transcendent God and the incarnate Christ are said to do in Christian tradition. For Lewis's purposes he is a sufficient God for Narnia. When the children venture eastward beyond Narnia in *The Voyage of the Dawn Treader*, it is Aslan's country that they reach, and Lewis did not choose to postulate anything still remoter and more real than that. When the children enter Aslan's country at the conclusion of *The Last Battle*, it is again the ultimate goal, even though it contains gradations within it that imply an infinite, or nearly infinite, regression. In the latter concept one can detect a Neoplatonic tendency to elevate God beyond all human comprehension. Although the Emperor-Beyond-the-Sea in the Narnian stories is comparable to Maleldil's Father in the planetary romances, he is also comparable to Maleldil himself in his remoteness from the sphere of human action.

Perhaps one reason why Lewis gave Aslan so active a role in the Narnian stories is that Narnia is not a pristine world such as Malacandra and Perelandra are. It is a world in which evil has existed from the day that Narnia was created. Through unfortunate carelessness, children of our own world, who travel magically back in time to other worlds, bring Jadis (the ubiquitous witch) into the scene of the creation of Narnia by Aslan. Jadis remains in Narnia, introducing evil in a variety of diabolical ways.[51] Narnia is therefore in constant need of divine assistance, for the perfect, divine machinery has been tampered with. Malacandra and Perelandra have a much more deistic operation (although Lewis may not quite have noticed that he was proposing something akin to deism); there Maleldil has set everything in motion and, with only an oyarsa and other eldils to attend to the housekeeping, each of the planets continues to function like a beautifully oiled machine. Indeed, it is only when evil is introduced to these planets from Earth that the possibility of a plot for the stories can even arise. It is the presence of evil that makes the fullness of the deity suddenly flame forth.

Christ appears, less directly, in other ways in Lewis's fiction. During the writing of the planetary romances Lewis became increasingly interested in Ransom as a Christ-figure. When the reader first encounters the man in *Out of the Silent Planet* he is an intelligent, genial philologist, but hardly more; indeed, he appears to be rather colorless.[52] One assumes that he is to be the kind of person who, though not interesting himself, tends to have interesting things happen to him. But Lewis needed a figure who could ask questions and be sensitive enough to grasp the meaning of the Malacandrian experience; hence he found himself giving Ransom an increasingly important role. Numerous episodes on the planet expand Ransom's grasp of reality and his philosophical insight. By the end of the novel he is beginning to involve himself in planetary crises.

As *Perelandra* opens, Ransom has been summoned to carry out—though he does not yet know it—a cosmic deed of massive proportions. He must go to Perelandra and try to save the magnificent, unsullied planet from a serpentine temptation that is soon to be attempted upon the two humanoids who inhabit it. That temptation will be to disobey Maleldil and thereby introduce sin to the planet. A vain but malleable scientist from Earth named Weston is the agent Satan intends to use to set Perelandra on the same destructive path he set Earth upon so long ago. As the story unfolds, Ransom begins to grasp the full extent of his involvement with this cosmic crisis, and to perceive the terror and loneliness of his struggle against the wiles of Satan. At first his combat with Weston, whom Satan has possessed, is only verbal; the two men spar with one another on religious and philosophical matters (Lewis makes no distinction between the two), and each attempts to persuade the naive Green Lady of the merit of his world view. When Ransom perceives that this device will not defeat the evil power, he wrestles with the thought that physical combat will be required. Like Christ praying in Gethsemane, Ransom shies away from the thought that he may himself suffer, and perhaps even be killed. His anguished deliberations are subtly guided by a Voice—the voice of Maleldil. "It is not for nothing that you are named Ransom," it points out quietly in his mind, and then it adds, "My name also is Ransom." [53] The allusion is, of course, to Christ as a ransom for mankind of earth; whether or not Lewis is speaking in favor of a ransom theory of the atonement by Christ or simply taking advantage of a fortunate coincidence between a randomly chosen name and a theological doctrine does not greatly matter.

In *That Hideous Strength* Ransom, his victory over Satan on Perelandra a thing of the past, functions as the leader—Pendragon, no less—of a small but dedicated Company of Logres in another cosmic combat with evil, this time on Earth. His role there is suggestive at times of Jesus' role on Earth, though there are many imaginative touches—resplendent robes, the inaccessibility of Ransom from ordinary persons, animals of supernatural intelligence, and the like—that have no correspondence with aspects of the life of Jesus as told in the Gospels. Once more combat ensues, but this time Ransom himself only directs the operations from a distance, rather than undergoing torments by his enemies; once more the power of Satan is defeated and the world is relatively safe, for a time, from new onslaughts of evil. At the end of the novel Ransom is translated to a lesser celestial heaven on Perelandra, there to continue his ascent to the absolute. Throughout the episodes in this third planetary romance there are scattered suggestions of Christ-like qualities or behavior in Ransom, but the imagery is disordered and erratic; obviously it was not a major motif for Lewis in that work.

There is no other notable Christ-imagery in Lewis's fiction, unless perhaps Orual in *Till We Have Faces*. Orual is one of Lewis's most difficult characters. She is very human in her ugliness, her suffering, her jealousy, and her desire to be loved. But she redeems no one, not even herself. Of her Lewis once wrote, "She is in some ways like Christ because every good man or woman is like Christ." [54] He obviously did not regard being "in some ways like Christ" as being a Christ.

When he discussed the person of Christ in his apologetic writings Lewis reverted almost entirely to orthodox Christian doctrine and language, leaving aside Platonism and fanciful representations alike.[55] He also largely abandoned the apologetic device of rational argumentation which served him so well in convincing his readers of the validity of theism. He knew full well that the Christian claim that Jesus was the Christ lies outside all possible rational demonstration.[56] He regarded the Christ-event, as Christian thinkers have traditionally understood it, to be a truth divinely revealed through Scripture and the church. In his autobiography he admits that although he can trace the course of his philosophical and rational progress toward theism, there is a hiatus between his theistic stage of development and his conversion to Christianity.[57] Something other than the strictly rational, unless perhaps on a higher plane of rationality, and something at the same time very personal (perhaps not clearly remembered by Lewis himself), took place in the transition from theism to Christianity. He was later to believe firmly that it was God working through divine processes of his own to bring him to salvation.

Not simply in his representations of Christ but also in some of his discussions of God is Lewis prepared to talk of divine immanence. In his apologetic books and in various other nonfictional writings on Christian subjects, he often fell back upon the traditional understanding of God given in Scripture and creed. Influenced by the language of parts of the Bible itself, he was not at all reluctant to talk of God's activities among men, God's feelings toward his creatures, and God's personal judgment of each soul. In *The Four Loves* he wrote about the nature of divine love; in *Reflections on the Psalms* he talked of God's intervention in the affairs of men; in *Letters to Malcolm* he spoke confidently about an intimate personal relationship between the individual believer and God—although at one point in that work he alluded, in Neoplatonic fashion, to God as "the ground of our being." [58] In *The Case for Christianity* he wrote very much like a traditional exponent of Christianity. He was down-to-earth, homey, conversational; he met the ordinary lay reader on familiar ground:

> Of course God knew what would happen if they

[human beings] used their freedom the wrong way: apparently He thought it worth the risk. Perhaps we feel inclined to disagree with Him. But there is a difficulty about disagreeing with God. He is the source from which all your reasoning power comes; you could not be right and He wrong any more than a stream can rise higher than its own source. . . . If God thinks this state of war in the universe a price worth paying for free will—that is, for making a live world in which creatures can do real good or harm and something of real importance can happen, instead of a toy world which only moves when He pulls the strings—then we may take it it is worth paying.[59]

He wrote in this fashion, upon occasion, without embarrassment. Although he often cautioned that what he said about God in such a vein should not be taken literally, one gets the impression that he did not doubt that what he was saying about God was eminently true and appropriate. His justification for speaking so anthropomorphically lay essentially in the Christian belief in the fatherhood of God and the incarnation of God in Jesus Christ, the supreme instance of God entering the earthly sphere.[60]

Transcendentalism—in the broad, generic sense that we have been using it here—ran deep in Lewis, who was a Platonist and a theist before he was a Christian. That understanding of reality was firmly rooted in both his temperament and his multifaceted rumination upon the nature of things. It also provided almost limitless scope for his rich imaginative powers. More than once as we proceed we shall find ourselves returning to this aspect of Lewis's thought, for it touches every aspect of intellectual activity and human experience embraced within Christian objectivism.

4

Cosmology

Christians . . . live in a graded or hierarchical universe
where there is a place for everything and everything should
be kept in its right place.

"Some Thoughts," in *God in the Dock*

*L*EWIS was almost unique among notable Christian thinkers of the twentieth century in his preoccupation with cosmology. In his autobiography he attempted to explain, or at least
clarify, this fascination.

> The idea of other planets exercised upon me then a
> peculiar, heady attraction, which was quite different
> from any other of my literary interests. Most
> emphatically it was not the romantic spell of *Das Ferne*.
> "Joy" (in my technical sense) never darted from Mars
> or the Moon. This was something coarser and stronger.
> The interest, when the fit was upon me, was ravenous,
> like a lust. This particular coarse strength I have come
> to accept as a mark that the interest which has it is
> psychological, not spiritual; behind such a fierce tang
> there lurks, I suspect, a psychoanalytical explanation. I
> may perhaps add that my own planetary romances
> have been not so much the gratification of that fierce
> curiosity as its exorcism.[1]

His cosmologies were mixtures of commonplace modern science

and high imaginativeness, varying from the relatively cosy cosmos of the Narnian tales to the eerie setting of *The Great Divorce*. In the hands of a less stable person or a hack writer such speculations could easily have become deranged ramblings or drivel; but in his hands cosmology became a work of art and a metaphysical delight. His ingenious explanation of the genesis of his novels may be partly correct, but is by no means the entire story. There was nothing random or casual about his cosmologies. Indeed, they were not multiple at all, in spite of the differences of content that can be found among his fictional works; they were variations upon a single cosmology, that of the Christian-Platonic Model that reached its zenith in the Middle Ages and Renaissance. Extensive cosmological speculation was a part of that Model, and long before the Model took shape Plato had been greatly attracted to cosmological questions. Lewis hardly wrote his novels to rid himself of his interest in such matters; rather, he regarded cosmology as an exceptionally effective way to inform his readers about the kind of objective universe in which he so passionately believed.

As the Model saw it, the universe was indeed a very busy place. Not only was God in Heaven and man on Earth, but there was also an elaborate hierarchy of created beings in Heaven, on Earth, and in the space between. Everything created by God had its proper place within this celestial hierarchy and tended, by its very nature, to stay in its place—or, if momentarily displaced, to return to it. The gradations of reality did not consist of beings unrelated to those of other levels, but of creatures that were in frequent interaction with beings above and below them in the hierarchy. Thus, although the structure of being was perceived by makers of the Model to be static, the universe that stretched beyond the Earth was by no means a lifeless place; rather, it was full of rich movement, color, sound, and sensations. Medieval thinkers did not suppose that God, in his creative power and wisdom, would have left any part of the universe empty of being. The fixed order of the universe was the framework within which there was a ceaseless bustle of activity; everywhere there was life, of all sorts and qualities.

Lewis derived immense enjoyment from conceiving of outer

space as a place filled with vibrancy, "tingling," as he put it, "with anthropomorphic life, dancing, ceremonial, a festival not a machine." [2] He had only scorn and pity for the modern mechanistic view of the universe which, during the past several centuries, has inexorably reduced the world to a gray, empty shell, devoid of souls, colors, smells, tastes, and purpose. His hero Ransom, after experiencing euphoria in the presence of the unadulterated rays of the sun in outer space, finds that his perception of the cosmos has altered. "He wondered how he could ever have thought of planets, even of the Earth, as islands of life and reality floating in a deadly void. Now, with a certainty which never after deserted him, he saw the planets—the 'earths' he called them in his thought—as mere holes or gaps in the living heaven—excluded and rejected wastes of heavy matter and murky air, formed not by addition to, but by subtraction from, the surrounding brightness." [3] In speaking of all planets as "rejected wastes of heavy matter and murky air" Lewis did not actually intend to denigrate the planets as such, for in his fiction he finds all of them, save for Earth, to be pleasant places; rather, he wanted to give new importance to interplanetary space as a part of the cosmos. In this case it is the light of the sun that gives space its liveliness.

Let us sketch, with the help of Lewis's *Discarded Image*, the cosmology of the Model. To begin with, it assumed the validity of a prescientific picture of the universe. [4] The Earth, which was spherical, was thought of as surrounded by a series of transparent globes, each vaster than the previous one. These nested globes separated regions of the heavens, which were called "spheres" or simply "heavens." Each sphere revolved in harmony with the others. Fixed in the surface of each of the first seven globes was a single luminous body that was carried along as the globe moved; these were the planets. Starting from Earth—which was not itself regarded as being one of the planets because it was assumed to be stationary at the center of the concentric spheres—one came first to the orbit of the moon, which the Model took to be dangerous to man. Next came Mercury, to which Medieval thinkers ascribed an assortment of influences upon mankind. Venus, the ancient Aphrodite and

Ishtara, came next. Her influence upon human beings was generally beneficent: she produced beauty and amorousness in individual persons, and fortunate events in history. There followed the sun, the producer of the noblest of metals, gold; he, too, brought about fortunate events. Next was Mars, a maleficent planet named for the ancient god of war, whose metal was iron. The planet next to last was Jupiter, named for the chief of the ancient deities, whose character was serene, cheerful, festive, and magnanimous; he was regarded as the best planet of all. Finally there was Saturn, of melancholy disposition, who was old and sick and produced pestilence, treachery and misfortune; he was the most terrible of the planets. The modern reader is likely to find here an inconsistency within the Model. As Lewis puts it:

> It may well be asked how, in that unfallen translunary world, there come to be such things as "bad" or "maleficial" planets. But they are bad only in relation to us. On the psychological side this answer is implicit in Dante's allocation of blessed souls to their various planets after death. The temperament derived from each planet can be turned either to a good or a bad use. . . . The fault lies not in the influence but in the terrestrial nature which receives it. In a fallen Earth it is permitted by Divine justice that we and our Earth and air respond thus disastrously to influences which are good in themselves. "Bad" influences are those of which our corrupt world can no longer make a good use. [5]

Most users of the Model, of course, never raised this issue at all.

An eighth globe encircled the rest; this was the Stellatum, on whose surface were carried all of the stars. A ninth globe was the Primum Mobile, the sphere that joined the realm of absolute reality to that of the lower eight spheres and the earth. Alone of the globes it carried no luminous body; its existence was inferred by the ancients to explain the motions of all the other globes. This was the highest plane of the temporal and spatial realm;

beyond, vastly larger, was the Empyrean,[6] true Heaven itself, the dwelling place of God.

The Model assumed that the planets move in perfect orbits around the Earth, each higher sphere being the cause of the movement of the next lower one, and all ultimately descending from God through the Primum Mobile. The planets did not, to be sure, move in the same orbits, and philosophers in the tradition of the Model labored mightily to "save the appearances" of the planetary motions—that is, to explain the phenomena without undercutting the Model itself.[7] The Model furthermore portrayed each planet (including, as we have said, the sun and the moon) as the producer of a perfect musical tone that differed from the tone of every other planet, the totality being a full musical scale. The harmonics produced by them became the "music of the spheres." It also tended to personify the planets, with the result that each was understood to be a celestial intelligence that was much below God, yet much above man, in the hierarchy of being. The celestial intelligences were sometimes personified as anthropomorphic figures resting atop their respective spheres; these could, as need arose, be detached from their planets and, decked out in symbols of their natures, manifest themselves separately, even as the ancient gods for whom they were named were once thought to have independence of movement in the heavens and on Earth. It was sometimes held that it was not the celestial intelligences themselves that could descend into the sublunary sphere but earthly duplicates of them. We shall have more to say about this when we speak of Lewis's understanding of the place of paganism in objective truth.

The Model gave particular emphasis, as one might well expect in view of its Christian context, to angels and related supernatural creatures mentioned in the Bible. It placed angels within the planetary spheres, while allowing that they could upon occasion visit the Empyrean and the earthly sphere. At least some kinds of them were, therefore, divine messengers in an important sense, crossing boundaries that ordinarily could not be violated. They were understood to be rational and sinless, except for the fallen angel Satan and those angels who accompanied him in his rebellion against God. The Model distinguished many kinds of angelic beings, frequently dividing them into three classes, each of which contained three species.[8] The first and highest category consisted, in descending order, of Seraphim, Cherubim, and Thrones. These were the creatures closest to reality. They faced God without intermediary, encircling him with their ceaseless dance. The second hierarchy contained Dominions (or Dominations), Powers, and Virtues (in the sense of characteristics). These also stood facing God, but less intimately. The third group consisted of Principalities, Archangels, and Angels. (Lewis notes that the word *angel* is thus both a generic name for all the nine species in the three hierarchies and also a specific name for the lowest species.) These creatures primarily looked toward the Earth and mankind, and were involved in terrestrial activities as the two higher hierarchies were not. As to whether angels were corporeal, some thinkers were inclined to regard them as immaterial; when they "appeared" to human beings it was because they had the power temporarily to put on an illusory body. Others who stood in the tradition of the Model believed, however, that angels were genuinely corporeal, though not necessarily composed of the matter that was found in human bodies.[9]

These facts are, as Lewis aptly observed, only of academic interest until one tries to step inside the medieval mind and learn how such a universe affected those who believed in it. Then the Model springs to life.

> You must go out on a starry night and walk about for half an hour trying to see the sky in terms of the old cosmology. Remember that you now have an absolute Up and Down. The Earth is really the centre, really the lowest place; movement to it from whatever direction is downward movement. As a modern, you located the stars at a great distance. For distance you must now substitute that very special, and far less abstract, sort of distance which we call height; height, which speaks immediately to our muscles and nerves. The Medieval Model is vertiginous. . . . The medieval universe,

while unimaginably large, was also unambiguously finite. And one unexpected result of this is to make the smallness of Earth more vividly felt. . . . Again, because the medieval universe is finite, it has a shape, the perfect spherical shape, containing within itself an ordered variety. Hence to look out on the night sky with modern eyes is like looking out over a sea that fades away into mist, or looking about one in a trackless forest—trees forever and no horizon. To look up at the towering medieval universe is much more like looking at a great building. The "space" of modern astronomy may arouse terror, or bewilderment or vague reverie; the spheres of the old present us with an object in which the mind can rest, overwhelming in its greatness but satisfying in its harmony.[10]

Unlike the mindless, alien space of modern science, the cosmos of the Model had a place for joy, brightness, and values. If he had to choose between the two systems, Lewis would opt for the older view—not because its cosmological details were more accurate (for they are not) but because, as a whole, it conveyed more appropriately what, in his view, reality is.

It is important to realize how small Earth was in this scheme of things. From the vastness of the Empyrean down through a succession of ever smaller planetary globes to the Earth was a journey towards the cosmically insignificant. Contrary to much popular thought about medieval beliefs today, the devisers of the Model did not think of Earth as the most important part of the cosmos; rather they saw it as of relatively minor significance cosmically, the place of least perfection in the entire grand scheme. When Dante wished to portray Hell as even more alienated from God than Earth, he had nowhere else to locate it cosmologically except as the center of the Earth (as distinct from simply being "in the ground"), for there was no place in the universe that was lower.

We must add a few more details to round out the picture of the cosmology of the Model. It is important to note that within the sublunary sphere there were gradations based upon the ancient identification of four basic elements.[11] The globe of the Earth itself was, of course, composed primarily of earth, the heaviest element. Upon the earth rested the second element, water. Above that was the still lighter air. Fire, lightest of all, always flowed, when free, up to the circumference of the natural region, where it formed a sphere just below the orbit of the moon, the point at which all mutability ceased. Amid the four elements on Earth, contingency and fortune held sway, and Satan and his demonic forces continually wrought havoc. According to the Model there were four grades of terrestrial reality: mere existence, of the sort that one observes in nonliving things such as stones; existence with growth, such as occurs in plants; existence and growth with sensation, such as is found among beasts; and, finally, existence with growth, sensation, and reason, which is characteristic of human beings.

In a rather anomalous class were the *longaevi*, as Lewis calls them, creatures whose residence was ambiguous, being in part earth and in part air (or, he might have added, water, or even occasionally—as with the chameleon or the phoenix—fire). [12] Here one finds pans, fauns, satyrs, silvans, nymphs, nereids, hags, goblins, fairies, elves, giants, ettins, bull-beggars (bogies), spirits, witches, tritons, centaurs, dwarfs, incubi—the list is all but endless, and consists of an assortment of faded pagan gods and spirits from many European religious traditions. Although such creatures can be distinguished from one another in various ways, no formal iconography was ever developed within the Model, nor was any fixed list of such personages ever prepared. Generally the *longaevi* were thought of as smaller than human beings—with, of course, the obvious exception of giants, centaurs, and a few others. Some of these creatures are presented as good and kind, whereas others are depicted as evil and dangerous to man; on this matter there was no full agreement among the sources, and some of the *longaevi* can be found to shift from good to bad, or bad to good.

Although there existed some biblical warrant for belief in *longaevi*, Christian doctrine was generally silent about such creatures. Hence thinkers working within the framework of the Model offered various explanations for the origin and cosmological place of the *longaevi:* Sometimes they were taken to be a rational species, alongside men and angels; sometimes they were assumed to be demoted angels; sometimes they were suspected of being a special class of the dead; and sometimes they were regarded as outright devils. Historically there was a trend in the Renaissance away from the medieval acceptance of *longaevi* as instances of the divine and ultimately beneficent filling up of the sublunary region with a delightful array of colorful creatures, toward a fear of *longaevi* as demonic and dangerous to man. In his own fiction Lewis portrayed *longaevi* of both kinds, but gave slight preference to those who were good creations of God.

The *longaevi* were not closely connected with human beings; indeed, they often avoided contact with them.[13] Although not immortal, they were generally—as their name implies—creatures that were long-lived, and by staying deep within the forests, they could usually survive far longer than men. The good ones were sometimes willing to cooperate with human beings, but they maintained their independence vigorously. Hence they stood outside the order of animals that God placed under the dominion of man. So far as ordinary beasts were concerned, man was permitted to use them for his own ends; but if a person attempted to exploit one of the *longaevi* there might be dire consequences. Many of these were assumed to have special powers for manipulating nature, sometimes generalized powers, such as witches and fairies traditionally had, and sometimes quite specific ones, such as unicorns and pans might have. Broadly speaking, they maintained a closer contact with the natural world than man did, and they were governed directly by supernatural powers.

Among human beings, who have more complex mental processes and social structures, the form of government most in accord with reality was monarchy. In the *Republic* Plato had discussed at great length the analogy of earthly government to the structure of reality, and had found the one to be a microcosm of the other. Old Western Culture took monarchy for granted, and found a cosmological place for it. The makers and users of the Model were convinced that monarchy stood within the divine ordering of earthly existence. As God ruled the universe, so an earthly king should govern his people. Not surprisingly, in view of these considerations, Lewis himself had monarchist inclinations, even though his strong individualism led him to champion democracy.[14] His affection for monarchy is apparent in much of his fiction. The medieval thinkers had perceived man as standing in a relationship with animals that was analogous to that of a king and his human subjects. Lewis remained somewhat ambivalent throughout his life about man's relationship with animals. He believed, on the one hand, that animals were, by divine fiat, so far beneath man that human moral considerations did not apply to them, and, on the other, that they merited only the most benevolent of human conduct toward them. It was the former that he stressed in *The Problem of Pain* and the latter in his condemnation of vivisection.

These, then, are the salient features of the cosmology of the Model. We have already mentioned a few of the ways that Lewis was influenced by this tradition in his writings; now we shall want to consider other and more central aspects of his utilization of that cosmology. Not surprisingly, the heaviest utilization appears in his fiction, but it crops out in important ways in his literary and theological essays as well.

The most cosmological of Lewis's fictional writings are the planetary romances. *Out of the Silent Planet* introduces the essentials of the cosmology. The stage on which the action takes place is our own solar system, somewhat modified. Writing as a twentieth-century author who knows that his readers would be largely oriented to the scientific world view, Lewis did not attempt to present the full cosmology of the Model but adapted it in a few necessary ways to present-day astronomy. The Earth is not the geographical center of the cosmology of the trilogy, as it was in the Model; neither do the sun and planets revolve while the Earth stays immobile. As we have seen, only three planets play large roles in the stories: Thulcandra, or Earth; Perelandra, or Venus; and Malacandra, or Mars. Most of the action in the first novel takes place on Malacandra and that in the second on Perelandra, and all of the action in the third is confined to Earth.

In the previous chapter we noted that early in *Out of the Silent Planet* Lewis took occasion to dwell rapturously upon the sun, which he calls "Arbol," as an image of reality. While journeying through the clear reaches of "Deep Heaven" (outer space), Ransom experiences the sun as "a dazzling golden light which completely eclipsed the pale earthlight behind him." [15] It invigorates him physically and mentally, although his companions Weston and Divine, lacking Ransom's capacity for spiritual growth, experience only heightened physical activity. In this regard the spaceship is a miniature Earth where, as on Earth, some persons are relatively unaffected by the presence of reality. Ransom is beginning to perceive reality inwardly, as his faculty for recognizing forms of reality, so long dormant on Earth, slowly awakens and he shakes off erroneous, earthbound ideas.

> Ransom, as time wore on, became aware of another and more spiritual cause for his progressive lightening and exultation of heart. A nightmare, long engendered in the modern mind by the mythology that follows in the wake of science, was falling off him. He had read of "Space": at the back of his thinking for years had lurked the dismal fancy of the black, cold vacuity, the utter deadness, which was supposed to separate the worlds. He had not known how much it affected him till now—now that the very name "Space" seemed a blasphemous libel for this empyrean ocean of radiance in which they swam. He could not call it "dead" ; he felt life pouring into him from it every moment. How indeed should it be otherwise, since out of this ocean the worlds and all their life had come? He had thought it barren: he saw now that it was the womb of worlds, whose blazing and innumerable offspring looked down nightly even upon the earth with so many eyes—and here, with how many more! No: Space was the wrong name. Older thinkers had been wiser when they named it simply the heavens—the heavens which declared the glory—the
>
> > "happy climes that ly
> > Where day never shuts his eye
> > Up in the broad fields of the sky."
>
> He quoted Milton's words to himself lovingly, at this time and often. [16]

Ransom is in the process of liberating himself from the prevailing twentieth-century mood of materialistic science, with its arrogance, its negation of higher values and its essential unimaginativeness. He explicitly rejects the fallacy (which Lewis himself had learned to reject) of chronological snobbery and aligns himself with a cosmology that is at home in traditional Christianity, Platonism, and the Model.

As the spacecraft descends into the atmosphere of Malacandra, the brilliant sunlight of space begins to lessen as planetary vapors begin to obscure the sun.

> It became certain . . . that the light was less overwhelming than it had been at the beginning of the voyage. It became certain to the comparing intellect, but it was difficult to *feel* what was happening as a diminution of light and impossible to think of it as a "darkening" because, while the radiance changed in degree, its unearthly quality had remained exactly the same since the moment he first beheld it. It was not, like fading light upon the Earth, mixed with the increasing moisture and phantom colours of the air. You might halve its intensity, Ransom perceived, and the remaining half you would still be what the whole had been—merely less, not other. Halve it again, and the residue would still be the same. As long as it was at all, it would be itself—out even to that unimagined distance where its last force was spent. [17]

What may appear to be only a physical description proves, in fact, to be a metaphysical assertion that stems from Lewis's imaginative cosmology.

His enthusiasm for solar imagery not withstanding, Lewis did not choose to treat the sun as the supreme deity in his fictional cosmos; having brought his reader to the verge of seeing the sun as a representative of reality, he drops the image and turns to other matters. Eventually, after he has established Ransom on Malacandra, he introduces Maleldil as the effective deity of the planet. Maleldil himself does not appear directly in the story or elsewhere in the trilogy; the highest authority that Ransom encounters is the angelic governor of the planet, Oyarsa. Lewis borrowed the word *oyarsa* from Bernardus Silvestris, where, he notes, it was presumably a corruption of the Greek οὐσιάρχης, a term for a tutelary spirit of a heavenly sphere.[18] Lewis did not attempt to locate the oyarsas precisely in the celestial hierarchy of the model, but they are obviously something like principalities. Save for the "Bent One"—the fallen oyarsa who is to be equated with Satan—they are sinless; they can enter the presence of Maleldil. Yet they can also look downward toward the finite creatures on the planets they govern. They are not infinitely wise,[19] and they vary in intelligence. Still, their knowledge of cosmic matters is vastly superior to that of mortals.

The oyarsas are but the most exalted of a larger class of angelic creatures, the eldils, which we have briefly encountered in the previous chapter. Lewis enjoys describing them, and does so on several occasions. Ransom talks with one of the inhabitants of Malacandra and is told that he must rethink his assumptions about reality.

> "What are *eldila*, and why can I not see them? Have they no bodies? "
>
> "Of course they have bodies. There are a great many bodies you cannot see. Every animal's eyes see some things but not others. . . . Body is movement. If it is at one speed, you smell something; if at another, you hear a sound; if at another you see a sight; if at another, you neither see nor hear nor smell, nor know the body in any way. . . . The swiftest thing that touches our senses is light. We do not truly see light, we only see slower things lit by it, so that for us light is on the edge—the last thing we know before things become too swift for us. But the body of an *eldil* is a movement swift as light; you may say its body is made of light, but not of that which is light for the *eldil*. His 'light' is a swifter movement which for us is nothing at all; and what we call light is for him a thing like water, a visible thing, a thing he can touch and bathe in—even a dark thing when not illumined by the

swifter. And what we call firm things—flesh and earth—seem to him thinner, and harder to see, than our light, and more like clouds, and nearly nothing. To us the *eldil* is a thin, half-real body that can go through walls and rocks: to himself he goes through them because he is solid and firm and they are like cloud. And what is true light to him and fills the heaven, so that he will plunge into the rays of the sun to refresh himself from it, is to us the black nothing in the sky at night. These things are not strange, Small One, though they are beyond our senses." [20]

The description is largely devoid of popular Christian angelology, but is influenced by some of the ideas associated with the Platonic-Christian Model.[21] The imagery of light and speed reappears in connection with reality, and the phenomenal world is said to be far less real than the celestial.

It should be noticed that Lewis was not asserting here that perception is simply relative, or that reality is in the eye of the beholder. The cosmic hierarchy is absolute; it could not be inverted and remain the same.[22] The eldil's perception of reality is qualitatively superior to that of mortals, just as a mortal's perception of reality is superior to that of, say, an ant or an amoeba. It must also be emphasized that Lewis did not intend that his exposition about light and movement be anything more than an imaginative analogy, in spite of the scientific sound of his argument. He doubtless would have granted that even if someone could demonstrate that light and speed do not behave as he claims they do, his basic conception would not thereby be rendered untenable, for ultimately his appeal was to an innate sense of the truth of supernaturalism on the part of his reader. Through the use of imagery, argumentation, and other devices he attempted to lead the reader to the point where, he hoped, the essential truth of the objective understanding of reality would begin to be apparent.

We learn that eldils do not die, do not breathe, do not eat, and do not breed. They move about freely in the Field of Arbol. They are generally prohibited from entering the sublunary miasma—

the region of Earth—where imperfection and sin exist, yet upon occasion it suited Lewis's purpose to have some slight contact between the eldils and the Earth. There is a special group of fallen eldils, led by the Bent One, inhabiting the sphere of Thulcandra; these are prohibited from leaving the sublunary region, lest they contaminate Deep Heaven. In this way Lewis linked his eldils with the Christian tradition about fallen angels. He also, in at least one instance, toyed with the possibility that there might be some creatures with the bodies of eldils that are irrational; these presumably would be confined to the earthy region like the *longaevi*.[23]

In representing the sublunary region as the abode of the Bent One and his minions, Lewis was painting a dark picture indeed of Earth. He calls it "the silent planet" because, being infested with evil, it has been quarantined,[24] lest the evil in it spread to the rest of the dominion of Maleldil and corrupt it. In describing the contrast between the bright and lively realm of Deep Heaven and the darkness and silence of Thulcandra, he once again turned popular notions about reality upside down. Modern man, he argued, has vaunted himself beyond all justification in thinking Earth to be a bright, progressive island within the dreary, black, lifeless reaches of outer space. Thus he followed quite closely the picture of Earth that is found in the Model. As we have noted, Earth was portrayed there in humbling terms; it was "the worst and deadest part of the universe,' 'the lowest story of the house,' the point at which all the light, heat, and movement descending from the nobler spheres finally died out into darkness, coldness, and passivity."[25]

In view of this low estimate of Earth, one is not surprised to find that Lewis also adopted a concept found in some versions of the Model, namely, that although in a phenomenal sense Earth lies at the center of the cosmos, in a conceptual or metaphysical sense it may be said to be situated at the very rim of reality, on the fringes where being fades away into nonbeing. In this philosophical inversion of observable phenomena, God became the center of the universe and could be likened—as indeed Dante does—to a point of light.[26] Thus the Ptolemaic cosmos was transformed into a system that was more conceptually in harmony with the Platonic imagery of the Good as the sun. Lewis was sufficiently attracted by this philosophical inversion of the data of the senses that he declared it to be an understanding of the universe held by Malacandran intellectuals; Ransom recalls that these creatures "have an odd habit, sometimes, of turning the solar system inside out." [27]

Whether perceived in terms of Ptolemaic or inverted geography, Maleldil's dominion is a true οἰκουμένη, a great cosmic household. The planetary intelligences, and in some measure eldils in general, are in contact with one another. The common tongue, Old Solar, illustrates this harmony well. Although he took delight in fabricating words and bits of grammar for this language, Lewis had a far more serious purpose than the customary need science-fiction authors feel for imaginative, plausible detail. Old Solar is not simply a technical convenience for the space-traveler Ransom; it is a direct reflection of Lewis's desire to represent the solar system as a unified, harmonious, interpenetrating, logical reflection of reality. "This was the language spoken before the Fall and beyond the Moon and the meanings were not given to the syllables by chance, or skill, or long tradition, but truly inherent in them as the shape of the great Sun is inherent in the little waterdrop. This was Language herself, as she first sprang at Maleldil's bidding out of the molten quicksilver of the star called Mercury on Earth, but Viritrilbia in Deep Heaven." [28] Lewis was attempting to suggest the cosmic harmony of reality itself, and to make the isolation of Earth from this household of goodness appear all the more painful. The loss of knowledge of Old Solar on Earth, doubtless coupled in his mind with the story of the tower of Babel and the proliferation of languages in Genesis 11, is symbolical of Earth's decline from cosmic perfection under the onslaught of the Bent One.

Lewis returned to this theme in *That Hideous Strength*, where the intellectual and spiritual chaos represented by the N.I.C.E. becomes terrifyingly concrete as the malefactors are beset by incoherence and, in their confusion, perish.[29] Harmony, in Platonic terms, is not simply aesthetic; it is inherent in reality itself, and is by nature good. This Lewis believed, and his conviction extended to all those groups of creatures living by divine truth—the inhabitants of Malacandra, the company of Logres in *That Hideous Strength*, and the church. Only in some of the Narnian stories did he concede that even among initiates into higher realities, practicing the best of good will, personal dislikes and disagreements could erupt and bring about a measure of disunity.[30] As was so often the case, what he believed ought to be weighed more heavily with Lewis than did practical considerations.

In the planetary romances Lewis gave considerable prominence to the pagan gods represented by the planets. Plato himself, while cheerfully paying respect to the traditional deities of Greece, was able to find little place for the gods in his metaphysical system. Fortunately for Lewis, that problem had already been faced by the makers and transmitters of the Model, particularly in the forms that it took in the Renaissance, after the rediscovery of the ancient gods. Lewis's juxtaposition of Mars and Venus in the first two novels of the trilogy is suggestive of speculative thought about those two deities' being opposing yet linked powers. The contrast between the deities of war and love is obvious; what is interesting is the way in which these opposites were reconciled in late forms of the Model. Lewis did not care to exploit the tradition of Mars as a passionate, fierce, rough deity; indeed, he made Malacandra anything but a warlike planet.[31] Venus he did, however, attempt to portray as warmly sensuous.

Among the cosmological motifs that Lewis utilized, none is more entrancing than that of the Great Dance. The concept can be found in Plato and thereafter from time to time in Neoplatonism and various expressions of the Model. It began as a poetic description of the orderly movements of the planets and stars, but it evolved as a metaphor of the harmony of the universe. As the centuries passed, it came to be increasingly mingled with occult thought. Lewis adopted the imagery readily, and more than once referred to it in the planetary romances. The most extensive description of the sacred cosmic dance is to be found in the final, climactic scene in Perelandra, where Ransom witnesses the investiture of the newly designated human king of the planet, Tor-Oyarsa, in the presence of the assembled cosmic dignitaries: the Oyarsa of Malacandra, the Oyarsa of Perelandra (who is in the very process of surrendering her ascendancy over the planet to the new king), countless eldils, and still others. The oyarsas, along with the king and queen and Ransom himself, engage in a solemn litany on the theme of the Great Dance—or the Great Game, as Lewis occasionally calls it. Thereafter follows the dance itself, which Lewis gradually transforms into a cosmic panorama which culminates in a spiritual ecstasy for Ransom that leads to the fringes of very reality itself.[32]

Cosmology in the Narnian tales is less elaborate than in the planetary romances. There is none of the philosophical and aesthetic subtlety of the eldils, and none of the complex interweaving of social aspects of Christian objectivism such as Lewis attempted in *That Hideous Strength*. Nevertheless, only the fabric of the stories differs; the conceptual framework is still that of Christianity, Platonism, and the Model, just as it is in the trilogy. It could hardly be otherwise, for Lewis believed every other model to be flawed. He could not bring himself to forge any imaginative worlds unless he could give his willing assent to their potential existence. What he discovered was that the picture given in the Model was so long forgotten by almost everyone in the twentieth century that he could reintroduce it, in a form that would make it palatable to the modern reader, and most persons would take the picture to be a novel creative effort. Even today Lewis is still credited with far more ingenuity in his cosmological pictures than he actually was obliged to employ. His greatest inventiveness lay in adapting the Model and related traditions to his needs, and in the thoroughness with which he comprehended the objectivism of the Model.

Narnia has no geographical relationship to Earth; in this regard it differs from the precise and relatively plausible relationships of Earth and other planets in the Deep Heaven trilogy. Its time is not precisely synchronous with that of Earth, though both places have irreversible time that runs in the same direction; as a consequence, Earth's time may appear to slow or stop while Narnia's continues, or conceivably vice versa. Although Narnia participates only modestly in the cosmological geography of the Model, the stories presuppose the metaphysical viewpoint of the Model. It is a land analgous to Earth: it is sublunary, a region where evil stalks as well as a place where there is much possibility for good. Certainly the childlike charm of the Narnian tales does not separate them from Old Western Culture, for stories of similar literary and historical naiveté are put to important didactic use in Plato's dialogues and the Bible alike,and are not unfamiliar within the context of the Model.

Lewis indulged himself in imaginative speculation about *longaevi* slightly in the planetary romances and much more extensively in the Narnian tales. He peopled Narnia not only with ordinary animals and human beings, but with talking animals, fauns, centaurs, walking trees, satyrs, dwarfs, unicorns, and giants. Although he ascribed genetic characteristics of behavior to some of these creatures, such as dull-wittedness to giants, he did not devote much attention to the behavioral psychology of these Narnian *longaevi*. There is an indeterminate number of demonic creatures that, from time to time, figure in the stories: ghouls, boggles, ogres, cruels, hags, spectres, incubuses, wraiths, horrors, efreets, sprites, orknies, wooses, ettins, werewolves, and others. In large measure the assorted *longaevi* give a desirable element of the unexpected and the whimsical to the tales, though it is perhaps fortunate for the children who read the books that the demonic beings do not occupy a very large place in most of the episodes. It is noteworthy that many of the *longaevi* have moral qualities associated with them. Dragons, for instance, are assumed to be not only physically terrible and ugly but immoral or amoral as well, as the story of the boy Eustace's being temporarily changed into a dragon indicates.[33] Dwarfs, being so much like humans, have especially complex characteristics that frequently involve them in situations requiring ethical value-judgments: They can be wise and value-oriented, as are Doctor Cornelius and Trumpkin in *Prince Caspian,* or foolish and self-centered, as are the black dwarfs in *The Last Battle.* Often even the ubiquitous talking animals of Narnia are faced with the need for moral decisions, to which they respond in varying ways. Lewis did not lack precedent for placing the creatures in such predicaments, for the Model saw moral analogues in the behavior of animals.[34]

By comparison with the planetary romances, the Narnian

stories are almost devoid of concern with celestial beings of any sort. In *The Voyage of the Dawn Treader* Lewis touched momentarily on the Platonic concept that the heavenly bodies are rational and sentient. To this idea he added the suggestion of free will and the possibility of sinfulness. On an isolated island the children encounter the venerable Ramandu, who serves to enlighten them on certain cosmological matters. He himself was, he tells them, once a star.

> "The days when I was a star had ceased long before any of you knew this world, and all the constellations have changed."
>
> "Golly," said Edmund under his breath. "He's a retired star."
>
> "Aren't you a star any longer?" asked Lucy.
>
> "I am a star at rest, my daughter," answered Ramandu. "When I set for the last time, decrepit and old beyond all that you can reckon, I was carried to this island. I am not so old now as I was then. Every morning a bird brings me a fireberry from the valleys in the Sun, and each fireberry takes away a little of my age. And when I have become as young as the child that was born yesterday, then I shall take my rising again." [35]

Ramandu then mentions that a magician whom the voyagers have earlier encountered on the island of the Dufflepuds—"Duffers," he calls them—is also a fallen star.

> "Is he a retired star, too?" said Lucy.
>
> "Well, not quite the same," said Ramandu. "It was not quite as a rest that he was set to govern the Duffers. You might call it a punishment. He might have shone for thousands of years more in the southern winter sky if all had gone well."
>
> "What did he do, Sir?" asked Caspian.
>
> "My son," said Ramandu, "it is not for you, a son of Adam, to know what faults a star can commit." [36]

The belief that the stars are individual souls is found in Plato's

Timaeus, as is the concept of the reincarnation of souls in new bodies. Lewis was adapting Plato's thought imaginatively, and intermingling with it some bits of other traditions.

Almost everything that the reader learns about the realm above the heavens in the Narnian stories comes through Aslan, whose nature and functions we have already mentioned. To Aslan Lewis ascribed not only the Christ-like functions of lawgiving (or, more precisely, the interpretation of the law of the Emperor-Beyond-the-Sea) and redemption, but creation as well. He is the active agent of God in the world. In *The Magician's Nephew* Lewis graphically describes the very creation of Narnia.[37] Coming late in the Narnian series, the account is notable for its seemingly effortless harmonization with all of the detail of the Narnian world to which Lewis had committed himself in earlier volumes in the series. In that work Lewis introduces two new children, Digory Kirke and Polly Plummer, who discover how to transport themselves to other worlds and other times by means of magic rings. Unpredictably the rings take them, inter alia, to the scene of the creation of Narnia at the word of Aslan. The lion brings Narnia into existence in an extended dramatic episode that owes much to the biblical account of creation yet goes far beyond the scriptural story. He commences creation by singing the celestial lights into being—first the stars, and then the sun.

> A voice had begun to sing. It was very far away and Digory found it hard to decide from what direction it was coming. Sometimes it seemed to come from all directions at once. Sometimes he almost thought it was coming out of the earth beneath him. Its lower notes were deep enough to be the voice of the earth herself. There were no words. There was hardly even a tune. But it was, beyond comparison, the most beautiful noise he had ever heard. It was so beautiful he could hardly bear it. . . .
>
> Then two wonders happened at the same moment. One was that the voice was suddenly joined by other voices; more voices than you could possibly count. They were in harmony with it, but far higher up the scale:

cold, tingling, silvery voices. The second wonder was
that the blackness overhead, all at once, was blazing
with stars. They didn't come out gently one by one, as
they do on a summer evening. One moment there had
been nothing but darkness; next moment a thousand,
thousand points of light leaped out—single stars,
constellations, and planets, brighter and bigger than any
in our world. There were no clouds. The new stars and
the new voices began at exactly the same time. If you
had seen and heard it, as Digory did, you would have
felt quite certain that it was the stars themselves who
were singing, and that it was the First Voice, the deep
one, which had made them appear and made them
sing.[38]

The music is, of course, the Platonic music of the spheres, the
perfect harmony of the tones emitted by the celestial bodies as
they move in their divinely ordained orbits. Thereafter Aslan bids
the ground, still barren of vegetation, to put forth grass, trees,
and flowers. Next he creates animals of all the diverse kinds
known on Earth, and with his staring eyes, his warm breath, and
his utterances he turns some of the animals into talking beasts
and assorted *longaevi*. Lewis did not have Aslan create human
beings; rather, the lion establishes a London cabbie and his wife,
brought from the children's own world, as the progenitors of the
new world: They are Narnia's Adam and Eve, who are to be king
and queen over the animals of Narnia, just as in the biblical story
man is given dominion over the creatures of the Earth.[39] Subsequently there is an account, much modified from the biblical
tradition, of the temptation of Adam and Eve in Eden—a theme
that Lewis had earlier treated at great length, and in a different
manner, in *Perelandra*.

The most sustained cosmological efforts in the Narnian tales
focus upon Aslan's country, which is a heavenly realm. Both the
final chapters of *The Voyage of the Dawn Treader* and the opening
chapters of *The Silver Chair* offer glimpses of that land, as we have
previously had occasion to mention. The contrast between the
purity of the atmosphere in Aslan's country and the thickened,

miasmic vapors of Narnia [40] is particularly redolent of the Model. These glimpses of Aslan's country do not, however, tell us much about Narnian cosmology as such. In the concluding chapters of *The Last Battle* Lewis attempted a more ambitious cosmology that incorporated elements of Platonism, the Bible, and the Model, as well as numerous unifying and enriching details of his own. Consistent with his objectivism, his heavenly realm was not utterly different from the old Narnia, but rather a perfect Narnia. The topography of the Narnian Paradise was very much like that of the earlier Narnia, but all things were transposed into something greater and more wonderful in every way. As he indicated in more than one place in his writings, he was convinced that reality cannot be entirely unlike what we know in our world, since our world must be understood as a reflection, however imperfect, of absolute reality. Using the fictional Narnia he illustrated this philosophical conviction vividly. Thus he intended that the reader understand the Narnian condition as being applicable to our own world and the heavenly realm where God is present. Let us follow his explication.

Evil has become so pervasive that Narnia cannot be saved by any of the customary means, and must pass away. It has been a proving ground for souls, and as such has served a useful function in the divine economy; but now something new must take place in the cosmos. Aslan sets up his supernatural doorway and the saved Narnians enter, while those who have willfully defied Aslan remain outside. As the saved stream into the new Narnia, the old Narnia begins to pass into eternal darkness. It is not mourned for long, because the new Narnia contains all that was good in the former one, and none of the evil. The new Narnia is not a copy of the old; rather, the old was but an imperfect copy of the heavenly Narnia that has always existed. The cosmology of the heavenly Narnia dawns only gradually upon the band of the saved.

> They kept on stopping to look round and to look behind them, partly because it was so beautiful but partly also because there was something about it which they could not understand.

"Peter," said Lucy, "where is this, do you suppose?"

"I don't know," said the High King. "It reminds me of somewhere but I can't give it a name. Could it be somewhere we once stayed for a holiday when we were very, very small?"

"It would have to have been a jolly good holiday," said Eustace. "I bet there isn't a country like this anywhere in *our* world. Look at the colours. You couldn't get a blue like the blue on those mountains in our world."

"Is it not Aslan's country?" said Tirian.

"Not like Aslan's country on top of that mountain beyond the eastern end of the world," said Jill. "I've been there."

"If you ask me," said Edmund, "It's like somewhere in the Narnian world. Look at those mountains ahead—and the big ice-mountains beyond them. Surely they're rather like the mountains we used to see from Narnia, the ones up Westward beyond the Waterfall?"

"Yes, so they are," said Peter. "Only these are bigger."

"I don't think *those* ones are so very like anything in Narnia," said Lucy. "But look there." She pointed southward to their left, and everyone stopped and turned to look. "Those hills," said Lucy, "the nice woody ones and the blue ones behind—aren't they very like the southern border of Narnia?"

"Like!" cried Edmund after a moment's silence. "Why they're exactly like. Look, there's Mount Pire with his forked head, and there's the pass into Archenland and everything!"

"And yet they're not like," said Lucy. "They're different. They have more colours on them and they look further away than I remembered and they're more . . . more . . . oh, I don't know. . . ."

"More like the real thing," said the Lord Digory softly.

Suddenly Farsight the Eagle spread his wings, soared thirty or forty feet up into the air, circled round and then alighted on the ground.

"Kings and Queens," he cried, "we have all been blind. We are only beginning to see where we are. From up there I have seen it all—Ettinsmuir, Beaversdam, the Great River, and Cair Paravel still shining on the edge of the Eastern Sea. Narnia is not dead. This is Narnia."

"But how can it be?" said Peter. "For Aslan told us older ones that we should never return to Narnia, and here we are."

"Yes," said Eustace. "And we saw it all destroyed and the sun put out."

"And it's all so different," said Lucy.

"The Eagle is right," said the Lord Digory. "Listen, Peter. When Aslan said you could never go back to Narnia, he meant the Narnia you were thinking of. But that was not the real Narnia. That had a beginning and an end. It was only a shadow or a copy of the real Narnia, which has always been here and always will be here: just as our own world, England and all, is only a shadow or copy of something in Aslan's real world. You need not mourn over Narnia, Lucy. All of the old Narnia that mattered, all of the dear creatures, have been drawn into the real Narnia through the Door. And of course it is different; as different as a real thing is from a shadow or as waking life is from a dream." . . . He added under his breath, "It's all in Plato, all in Plato." [41]

Lewis follows this dialogue with a discursive explanation of how the sunlit, new Narnia—the eternal, heavenly one—differs from the old Narnia, and for once he deserts his Platonism utterly, and probably through oversight. He suggests that the eternal Narnia is to the old Narnia as an image in a looking-glass is sometimes superior to the real things it reflects. Plato would have looked askance at the analogy, for to him mirror-images were, plausibly enough, less real than the things they mirrored. Even the apostle Paul knew that in a mirror one sees darkly. Perhaps Lewis was, for just a moment, influenced by the romantic aspects of a mirror, the sort of notion found in *Through the Looking Glass*.

He was not yet finished. Were he to have stopped at this point, his cosmology would have sufficed within the framework of Narnian geography, but would not have encompassed the world from which the children came. With characteristic boldness he broadens his vista in the last chapter of the book. As the saved creatures run farther into Aslan's country, going ever higher on the steep slopes, yet never becoming weary or winded, they can discern an ever larger landscape stretching far and wide behind them.

> And Lucy looked this way and that and soon found that a new and beautiful thing had happened to her. Whatever she looked at, however far away it might be, once she had fixed her eyes steadily on it, became quite clear and close as if she were looking through a telescope. She could see the whole southern desert and beyond it the great city of Tashbaan: to eastward she could see Cair Paravel on the edge of the sea and the very window of the room that had once been her own. And far out to sea she could discover the islands, island after island to the end of the world, and, beyond the end, the huge mountain which they had called Aslan's country. But now she saw that it was part of a great chain of mountains which ringed round the whole world. In front of her it seemed to come quite close.[42]

So it turns out that Aslan's country lies not just east of Narnia but all around, a vast encircling range of lofty mountains, like the rim of a bowl with the land and sea of Narnia lying within the bowl.

> Then she looked to her left and saw what she took to be a great bank of brightly-coloured cloud, cut off from them by a gap. But she looked harder and saw that it was not a cloud at all but a real land. And when she had fixed her eyes on one particular spot of it, she at once cried out, "Peter! Edmund! Come and look! Come quickly." And they came and looked, for their eyes also had become like hers.
> "Why!" exclaimed Peter. "It's England. And that's the

house itself—Professor Kirke's old home in the country where all our adventures began!"

"I thought that house had been destroyed," said Edmund.

"So it was," said the Faun. "But you are now looking at the real England within England, the real England just as this is the real Narnia. And in that inner England no good thing is destroyed."

Suddenly they shifted their eyes to another spot, and then Peter and Edmund and Lucy gasped with amazement and shouted out and began waving: for there they saw their own father and mother, waving back at them across the great, deep valley. It was like when you see people waving at you from the deck of a big ship when you are waiting on the quay to meet them.

"How can we get at them?" said Lucy.

"That is easy," said Mr. Tumnus. "That country and this country—all the *real* countries—are only spurs jutting out from the great mountains of Aslan. We have only to walk along the ridge, upward and inward, till it joins on." [43]

Lewis brings not only England and Narnia into juxtaposition but, as his allusion to Professor Kirke's former house indicates, past and present as well. What he was trying to suggest by doing so was that earthly concepts of time and space no longer exist in the heavenly realm; all time and all space, so far as they may worthily participate in the heavenly realities, are eternally present. There is no need to cry over lost moments of happiness or places of value, for in Aslan's country "no good thing is destroyed." The concept is not specifically Platonic, but neither is it contrary to Platonism. Lewis simply extended Plato's concern for the preservation of what is valuable in the human soul to concern for value wherever it may have existed in the universe.

The cosmology that underlies the planetary romances and the Narnian tales can be found elsewhere in Lewis's fiction. The surface changes from time to time, but the structure remains basically the same. In *The Great Divorce* Lewis stresses the differences between the two realms, the real and the phenomenal: One finds a Heaven of bright ghosts and solid things, and a Hell of gray delusions and unsubstantiality. In *The Pilgrim's Regress* reality is represented by lofty western mountains that eventually prove to be identical with eastern mountains (inasmuch as the planet in that story is spherical), just as in *The Chronicles of Narnia* the eastern and western mountains of Aslan's country prove to be part of a single great ring of mountains. As we have tried to show, Lewis would argue that he was not exploiting merely any convenient cosmology in his stories, but the only viable cosmology that there is.

The value that he found in this cosmology is that it gets as close as possible to conveying what reality is, even though no verbalization can hope to describe the absolute. Although the cosmology of the Model came to him fortuitously in his study of the history of Western literature, he never regarded that world view casually. He coupled a penetrating intellectual analysis to his aesthetic delight in the Model. Concerning the place of Mars and Venus in his fiction he wrote: "The characters of the planets, as conceived by medieval astrology, seem to me to have permanent value as spiritual symbols—to provide a *Phänomenologie des Geistes* which is especially worth while in our generation." [44] Again, concerning the sexual distinctions maintained in the Model and in Old Western Culture generally, he observed: "We are dealing with male and female not merely as facts of nature but as the live and awful shadows of realities utterly beyond our control and largely beyond our direct knowledge." [45] Thus when he declared, "I hope no one will think that I am recommending a return to the Medieval Model," [46] he understated his case. What he meant to say was that he did not expect persons living in the twentieth century to return to a literal belief in the Model; what he did hope, however, was that the Model would be perceived as a magnificently tuned instrument for saying something significant about reality. To be sure, abstract theological statements can also say something about reality; if he had not believed this, he would hardly have found value in the creeds of the church. But abstract theological language cannot claim an inherent superiority over mythological and symbolic expressions of belief. We shall have more to say about the place of myth in Lewis's thinking in the next chapter.

Lewis was deeply committed to the concept of a hierarchical universe. Like medieval cosmologists, he wanted to believe that every aspect of existence, from the most exalted to the humblest, has absolute, objective meaning—not simply for him, but for everyone and everything. His fiction was basically not plot-oriented, or even fundamentally adventure-centered; it was primarily expository, focusing on his world view. What he sought to do was to describe the manifestations of a metaphysical reality in varied contexts.[47] Once one understands his frame of reference Lewis becomes intelligible. His stories tend, appropriately, to be rich in settings; he had relatively little interest in characterization.[48] Even his love of courtly manners stemmed in large measure from his conviction that the universe was orderly, decorous, and monarchical, and that the acts of earthly creatures should attempt to reproduce that heavenly reality on Earth.

5

Universal Truths

Unless Reason is an absolute—all is in ruins.

"Is Theology Poetry?" in *They Asked for a Paper*

We are guided by . . . rules of moral behaviour, which I think are more or less common to the human race.

"Answers to Questions on Christianity,"
in *God in the Dock*

Ransom at last understood why mythology was what it was—gleams of celestial strength and beauty falling on a jungle of filth and imbecility.

Perelandra

B Y now we know well enough that Lewis was convinced there is but a single reality in and beyond the universe. But there is more to be said if we are to grasp his thought fully. He realized that not all moral, physical, aesthetic, and metaphysical truth could reach human beings through Christian sources of revelation. After all, if a pagan or atheist who builds a house wants his work to endure, he must make it correspond to the same physical laws and properties of the universe as constrained the architects of Gothic cathedrals; for though there may be Christian architects, there are no Christian principles of physics. A vast amount of truth is necessarily embedded in the cultures of the world, independent of Christianity. Lewis was neither puzzled nor offended by this fact, for God had structured the universe in an orderly fashion, fully intending that it be basically intelligible to human beings in everyday life. There is, he was convinced, a direct correspondence between heavenly or absolute reality and earthly, imperfect existence. The two are vastly different in degree, but not in essence. Reality is the same everywhere.

> Beyond all doubt, His idea of "goodness" differs from ours; but you need have no fear that, as you approach it, you will be asked simply to reverse your moral standards. When the relevant difference between the Divine ethics and your own appears to you, you will not, in fact, be in any doubt that the change demanded of you is in the direction you already call "better." The Divine "goodness" differs from ours, but it is not sheerly different: it differs from ours not as white from black but as a perfect circle from a child's first attempt to draw a wheel. But when the child has learned to draw, it will know that the circle it then makes is what it was trying to make from the very beginning.[1]

The context is that of morality, but Lewis made the same point with regard to many aspects of earthly experience.

The illustration that Lewis used, of a child's attempt to draw a circle, has a Platonic cast—and not coincidentally, for Lewis adduced by way of philosophical argumentation some of the same points that Plato introduced into his dialogues. Like Plato, he held that "a man does not call a line crooked unless he has some idea of a straight line."[2] The idea of straightness is not something that can be directly visualized, nor can anyone ever draw a perfectly straight line; such attempts belong to the realm of imperfect phenomena. Yet the concept of straightness is, in some unfathomable way, present in every person's mind. Furthermore, it is not dependent for its validity upon the mind of the individual person, but is a universal reality. Lewis could strongly agree with Plato that mathematical principles express absolute realities and are as timeless and perfect as the Platonic Forms. Upon occasion he was willing to describe objects in the heavenly realm (such as in the new Narnia that appears at the end of *The Last Battle*) as if they were perfect embodiments of the Platonic Forms of each of them. In such ways he showed an intellectual affinity for what Plato was trying to convey in his doctrine of the Forms, even though he had little interest in the particular way in which Plato formulated that concept.

So much, then, for matters of physical laws and mathematics; what about values? Lewis treated objective value at length in his small volume *The Abolition of Man*.[3] He was prompted to write the book by his discovery of some textbooks designed for boys and girls in the upper forms of English schools in which the authors subtly advocated a theory of the subjectivity of values. Presumably drawing upon the work of logicians and semanticists who had noted pitfalls in the use of the verb "to be," and in particular the use of predicates, the authors had reached the conclusion that all statements that people may make purporting to be assertions about value ("beautiful," "good," "ill," "joyful" and "simpering" would be instances of such predicates) are, in fact, subjective; they say something about how the person making the statement regards things in his or her environment, but they do not say anything necessarily factual about things themselves. Lewis singled out one example in particular from such a textbook. Regarding a tourist's comment upon seeing a waterfall, the authors had declared, "When the man said *That is sublime* . . . he was not making a remark about the waterfall, but a remark about his own feelings. What he was saying was really *I have feelings associated in my mind with the word 'Sublime,'* or shortly, *I have sublime feelings*." [4] Lewis could easily show the absurdity of the notion that "this is sublime" means "I have sublime feelings"; presumably what those authors should have said was that "this is sublime" means "I attribute sublimity to the waterfall"—with the implication that the sublimity was in the viewer's mind, not in the waterfall. But if carried into practice rigorously, Lewis pointed out, such a philosophical stance would invalidate all aesthetic and moral judgments and require the scrapping of most of mankind's imaginative literature. To say that the authors were simply trying to point out to young writers some pitfalls of pathetic and bathetic thought does not, he was convinced, get at the heart of the matter. What is involved is a fundamental philosophical question: Is all value only subjective, or is there some value that is absolute?

We already know, of course, his answer. There is such a thing as objective value in the universe. It is not false, he asserted, to suppose that a waterfall can be sublime, for the waterfall may be of such a nature that it merits the description.

> The reason why Coleridge agreed with the tourist who called the cataract sublime and disagreed with the one who called it pretty was of course that he believed inanimate nature to be such that certain responses could be more "just" or "ordinate" or "appropriate" to it than others. And he believed (correctly) that the tourists thought the same. The man who called the cataract sublime was not intending simply to describe his own emotions about it: he was claiming that the object was one which *merited* those emotions.[5]

Lewis did not attempt to demonstrate the reality of objective value deductively; he did, however, insist, as we have found that he does elsewhere in his writings, that until fairly recent times all philosophers and great religious teachers have assumed that there was objective value in the universe.

> This conception in all its forms, Platonic, Aristotelian, Stoic, Christian, and Oriental alike, I shall henceforth refer to for brevity simply as "the *Tao*." . . . What is common to them all is something we cannot neglect. It is the doctrine of objective value, the belief that certain attitudes are really true, and others really false, to the kind of thing the universe is and the kind of things we are. Those who know the *Tao* can hold that to call children delightful or old men venerable is not simply to record a psychological fact about our own parental or filial emotions at the moment, but to recognize a quality which *demands* a certain response from us whether we make it or not. . . . And because our approvals and disapprovals are thus recognitions of objective value or response to an objective order, therefore emotional states can be in harmony with reason (when we feel liking for what ought to be approved) or out of harmony with reason (when we perceive that liking is due but

cannot feel it). No emotion is, in itself, a judgement: in that sense all emotions and sentiments are alogical. But they can be reasonable or unreasonable as they conform to Reason or fail to conform.[6]

Knowledge of this objective reality may at times be found by a person who looks inside himself, but more often it comes to light through proper education. Lewis wrote at some length, and with no small passion, about the importance of nurturing the young correctly in the traditions of common human morality. "When the age for reflective thought comes," he said, following Aristotle, "the pupil who has been thus trained in 'ordinate affections' or 'just sentiments' will easily find the first principles in Ethics." [7]

These and similar passages show clearly that Lewis assumed that anything on which the vast majority of human beings can agree is very likely to be true. Although this way of thinking has an inductive dimension, since it requires evidence concerning what people do in fact say and do, it is at the same time heavily deductive, inasmuch as it may be said to grow out of the philosophical conviction that higher levels of reality will inevitably manifest themselves on lower levels. Inductive evidence is necessary concerning any specific issue, but the overarching principle is a deductive one. In viewing judgment as valid when it is on a large enough scale, Lewis was expressing a conviction held by Plato; not infrequently one finds in Plato's dialogues the assumption that something is likely to be true when "everybody thinks the same way," or "everyone knows that this is so." When such circumstances existed, Plato was inclined to suppose that people were but recalling, however imperfectly, the heavenly truths that their souls had known before being incarnated on the Earth. In any case, the knowledge was inherent within human beings and therefore valid. Lewis wrote in a similar vein. If, for instance, one takes the view that God's ability to answer petitionary prayer is philosophically improbable, then—he said—the difficulty is that "one has to say that the whole historical tradition of Christian prayer (including the Lord's Prayer itself) has been wrong." [8] It is obvious that Lewis doubted that the whole historical tradition of Christian prayer has, in fact, been wrong. What the mental mechanism might be by which absolute truth could be apprehended, even imperfectly, by human beings, he did not attempt to say.

Lewis illustrated this essentially Platonic idea in numerous other ways. When the unicorn enters Aslan's country at the conclusion of the eschatological cataclysm that ushers in the heavenly Narnia, he cries joyfully: "I have come home at last! This is my real country! I belong here. This is the land I have been looking for all my life, though I never knew it till now." [9] The longing to which the unicorn (i.e., Lewis himself) alludes is not simply a romantic *Sehnsucht,* much less a purely emotional experience; it is a faint glimmer of absolute reality from within the soul of the unicorn; now, in the heavenly realm, that submerged reality, which transcends both the senses and all communicative powers, is perceivable for the first time in its true nature. Circumstances have elicited from the unicorn's self a potential knowledge not unlike that in the *Meno,* where Plato tells how Socrates led an untutored boy to discover that he "knew" geometrical truths.

There is a sense in which the elements of absolute reality lying within the individual person, and capable in varying ways of being utilized by the mind, can be understood as being innate. Although he shied away from the term, [10] Lewis was willing upon occasion to employ it; in *Miracles,* for instance, he speaks of man's "innate sense of the fitness of things." [11] The kind of knowledge, or potential knowledge, to which he alluded as being resident within persons may also in some measure be thought of as intuitive. He preferred to attribute intuitive knowledge of heavenly reality to angels but not to men, as he says in *The Four Loves;* [12] yet he seems to mean not that human beings are devoid of intuition of reality, but that angels have that intuition far more fully. After all, according to the venerable tradition embedded in the Model, angels and mortals share much; they do not have perfect knowledge, but must themselves be instructed in order to know God and his will properly.

We have been considering universal truths in rather broad terms thus far, and have seen that Lewis was prepared to accept a variety of phenomena in human experience as reflecting absolute reality: certain concepts, such as straightness or circularity; mathematical principles; even religious practices such as prayer which are widely regarded by human beings as having objective value. We shall now turn to three particularly important ways, from Lewis's point of view, in which objective truth may be said to be the common property of all, or at least a significant number, of human beings at many different times and places. These are reason, universal moral principles, and mythology. We shall want to give close attention to each of these, commencing with reason.

Among the popular Protestant spokesmen of the twentieth century, Lewis is rather distinctive in his emphasis upon the place of reason in theological thought. More than one reader of his apologetic works has been surprised to find a carefully wrought argument for the existence of God staring him in the face.[13] In order to argue rationally that God exists one must first establish the validity of reason itself, and Lewis was quite prepared to do so. He approached the problem by pointing out that some persons vehemently argue that reason is strictly a biological, mechanistic process, in which brain cells behave deterministically. Of those who make this claim he asked, How is your mind able to decide that its functions are determined by nature, unless your power to reason somehow stands outside the natural process? If reason is not extranatural, rational inferences about nature's irrationality are themselves irrational. Ransom and the evil Weston carry on this sort of debate in Perelandra. Weston speaks first:

> "Reasoning itself . . . has nothing to do with the real universe. Even the ordinary scientists—like what I used to be myself—are beginning to find that out. . . . They don't say in so many words, of course, but what they're getting to, even before they die nowadays, is what all men get to when they're dead—the knowledge that reality is neither rational nor consistent nor anything else. In a sense you might say it isn't there. 'Real' and 'Unreal,' 'true' and 'false'—they're all only on the surface. They give way the moment you press them."
>
> "If all this were true," said Ransom, "what would be the point of saying it?"

"Or of anything else?" replied Weston. "The only point in anything is that there isn't any point." [14]

Weston grasps Ransom's point but obstinately refuses to concede it, so committed is he to a false view of reality. All that he can do is to iterate, "The only point is that there isn't any point"—a logical impossibility. Those who deny the objective validity of reason must use reason in spite of their denial of its validity. The reductio ad absurdum of their claim means that the only alternative, that of supposing that reason is indeed valid, must be correct. All reasoning must assume that inference is valid.

> At least one kind of thought—logical thought—cannot be subjective and irrelevant to the real universe: for unless thought is valid we have no reason to believe in the real universe. We reach our knowledge of the universe only by inference. The very object to which our thought is supposed to be irrelevant depends on the relevance of our thought. A universe whose only claim to be believed in rests on the validity of inference must not start by telling us that inference is invalid. That would really be a bit too nonsensical. I conclude then that logic is a real insight into the way in which real things have to exist. In other words, the laws of thought are also the laws of things: of things in the remotest space and the remotest time. This admission seems to me completely unavoidable and it has very momentous consequences. [15]

Among the consequences of which Lewis spoke are the refutation not only of naturalism, materialism, and determinism—all of which he rather hastily turned into bedfellows—but also of the Calvinistic doctrine of the total depravity of man. [16]

What is the proper way to reason? It is in man's nature to be rational, even when he has never heard of logic or syllogisms. Although there are numerous pitfalls to commonsense reasoning, Lewis tended to believe that the mind has processes, put there by God, which, given sufficient Socratic dialectic or similar activity, enable a person to distinguish correct inferences from spurious ones. He also accepted the validity of formal logic, which began with Aristotle and has been refined subsequently; like mathematics, syllogistic reasoning is absolute and, when properly conducted, is universally valid. As in mathematics, certain concepts used in reasoning cannot themselves to proved, but are axiomatic: a thing cannot, for instance, both be and not be at the same time and in the same place unless one alters the meaning of language.

Lewis made a particular point of rejecting the popular notion that reason is supposed to be at the opposite pole from supernaturalism, and could point to a long history of the use of reason within the supernatural, objectivist, Old Western Culture. Genuinely inimical to supernaturalism, however, was myopic rationalism. Several characters in Lewis's novels exemplify this kind of inadequate reasoning: Mr. Enlightenment in *The Pilgrim's Regress*, MacPhee in *That Hideous Strength*, the Fox in *Till We Have Faces* and, in part, Trumpkin in *Prince Caspian*. All of these personages believe themselves to be engaging in objective reasoning, whereas from Lewis's point of view they represent nineteenth-century rationalism, which is but naturalism in disguise. He was not without a certain amount of sympathy for such persons, whom he frequently represented as sincere but blind to their own restrictive, unimaginative presuppositions. In his autobiography he fondly recalled his own teacher, William T. Kirkpatrick, a positivist who taught him the absoluteness and importance of logic. Lewis had his character Ransom explicitly affirm the utility of the positivist MacPhee to the Company of Logres: "He is our sceptic; a very important office." [17] Ultimately MacPhee's conclusions are erroneous, because he has begun with false premises and has misunderstood the data he uses in reasoning; nevertheless, in matters that are less than cosmic his reasoning is valid and helpful, and his heart is in the right place.

To say that reason is valid when properly carried out is to say that it has validity apart from the individual's own mind. What is reasonable, in a philosophical sense, to one person must be reasonable to others. A syllogism can lead to but one conclusion, regardless of who does the reasoning. It is true that people do not always reach the same conclusions when they reason, but that is because they differ in their presuppositions, employ different data, or make some error in the process. Lewis summed it all up in his statement, "There are a dozen views about everything until you know the answer. Then there's never more than one." [18] Reason is not dependent upon any individual mind; it is a universal reality that can be tapped by anyone at any time, as necessary. Like Plato's Forms—indeed, as one of Plato's Forms—it exists apart from individual reasoners. "It is clear that my Reason has grown up gradually since my birth and is interrupted for several hours each night. I therefore cannot be that eternal self-existent Reason which neither slumbers nor sleeps. Yet if any thought is valid, such a Reason must exist and must be the source of my own imperfect and intermittent rationality." [19] Lewis is particularly attacking certain idealists who had gone so far as to deny to reason any existence at all except within individual human minds.

Lewis goes on to argue that the existence of God can be rationally deduced from the very nature of reason itself. If reason is not to be regarded as a part of natural processes but stands outside natural order, then it must be said to belong to the realm of the supernatural; and since, as he has shown, the reality of reason cannot be said to depend upon individual reasoning minds, but must exist independently of them, then there must be a supreme rational mind that is supernatural. "Human minds, then, are not the only supernatural entities that exist. They do not come from nowhere. Each has come into Nature from Supernature: each has its tap-root in an eternal, self-existent, rational Being, whom we call God." [20] He does not use *God* here in the Christian sense, as a personal deity who is active in history, to whom can be attributed emotions such as love and anger. He is speaking of God philosophically, as the ground or totality of perfect reason. Indeed, he makes no sharp distinction between the universal principles of reasoning and God himself. Thus he makes explicit what is only implicit in Plato's dialogues: God can, metaphorically, be said to be not only the Good, the One and the Beautiful, but also the Rational.

What does it mean to say that God is rational? As Lewis saw

things, it means that God is not capricious, but orderly, consistent, and just. If asked whether God created reason or reason was inherent in reality, he would respond that, since the two cannot be separated, the question is meaningless. Yet he would not cavil at the popular assumption that God created all absolute law; in *The Voyage of the Dawn Treader* he has Aslan say to Lucy, "Do you think I wouldn't obey my own rules?" [21] In any event, God never alters any aspects of reality, for reality is himself. Lewis was thoroughly in accord with the mainstream of Western Christian theology, represented most notably by Thomas Aquinas, which holds that God is not able to be, or do, things that at the same time are inconsistent with one another. He is, in other words, subject to—or at least always in conformity with—the logical principle of noncontradiction. Because this is so, human propositions about God must be formulated accordingly. "We must attack wherever we meet it the nonsensical idea that mutually exclusive propositions about God can both be true," asserted Lewis. [22]

Likewise God cannot act irrationally with the Earth or mankind. Since rationality is an absolute, Lewis argued, the rationality of human beings must bear some resemblance to that of God. [23] The only essential difference is that human beings do not know what God knows, and therefore are seldom able to make momentous decisions that are based upon full information. God knows all; therefore he operates on a higher level of rationality than do his rational creatures. If he at times seems to be behaving capriciously, or even perversely, it is only an apparent violation of the proper divine nature. When MacPhee observes in *That Hideous Strength* that the supernatural happenings at St. Anne's are "clean contrary to the observed laws of Nature," one of the company reproves him: "The laws of the universe are never broken. Your mistake is to think that the little regularities we have observed on one planet for a few hundred years are the real unbreakable laws; whereas they are only the remote results which the true laws bring about more often than not." [24] Lewis had another member of the company proffer a literary illustration of this concept of higher laws: " 'Shakespeare never breaks the real laws of poetry,' put in Dimble. 'But by following them he breaks every now and then the little regularities which critics mistake for the real laws. Then the little critics call it "license." ' " [25] Lewis made essentially the same asseveration in *Miracles*. God can "invade the natural world" and perform acts that appear to human beings as miraculous, when in fact no higher laws of the universe have been broken at all. He was convinced that the nineteenth-century rationalists and their numerous twentieth-century descendants who reject a priori all evidence of miracles of this sort have allowed their assumptions to dominate their thinking.

It should not be thought, as some critics have at times suspected, that Lewis employed reason simply as an apologetic device, subtly and perhaps even unscrupulously chopping logic much as a demagogue uses half-truths to beguile the unsophisticated. No one can read very far in his voluminous writings without realizing that he was utterly committed to the view of reason that he sets forth in so many ways. Unlike some theologians and philosophers, he had no fear whatever of reason. In neither his literary scholarship nor his Christian belief did he ever openly reject it in favor of emotionalism or aestheticism. Christianity, he insisted, should never be contrary to reason. Without claiming infallibility in his own reasoning, he was exceptionally harsh toward writers who, in his judgment, violated the principles of logic or introduced false data into logical processes. [26]

In his attitude toward reason Lewis enjoyed much wider company than simply that of Plato; the Old Western tradition included the Christian Platonists of Alexandria, was continued in Aquinas and in the Renaissance humanists, and lingered in the seventeenth century before rationalism began to be corrupted (in Lewis's judgment) by materialism and naturalism. Thinkers in this tradition broadly agreed that the dictates of reason must be true, wherever found, and that even articles of Christian belief must not be contrary to reason. Lewis was fully aware, of course, of an anti-rational strain in Christian and Western thought, as expressed in Tertullian, Occam, Duns Scotus, the Reformers in part, Pascal, and a host of nineteenth- and twentieth-century theologians such as Kierkegaard and Barth; even Augustine, in spite of his affinities for Neoplatonic thought, tended to sympathize with the view that reason is more the Devil's harlot than the handmaid of God. But it was precisely such thinkers, except in some measure Augustine, whom Lewis found to be misguided and unintelligible.

Broadly speaking, Lewis's position with regard to reason approached that of scholastic thinkers in the tradition of Aquinas, who held that although syllogistic reasoning was always valid, it had circumscribed applicability. Above reason was higher truth, that of God himself, which was partially revealed to mankind through Christ and the church, and was apprehended through faith. By faith the scholasticists meant, largely, assent to Christian doctrine, and Lewis did not reject this aspect of Christianity; he did, however, give a more modern and personal meaning to the concept of faith.[27] Repeatedly he makes a leap from reasoned argumentation to the tenets of Christianity. Reason, he asserts, can lead a person to give intellectual assent to God, but it cannot bring one face to face with the living God himself. "Faith, as we know it, does not flow from philosophical argument alone; nor from experience of the Numinous alone; nor from moral experience alone; nor from history alone; but from historical events which at once fulfil and transcend the moral category, which link themselves with the most numinous elements in Paganism and which . . . demand as their presupposition the existence of a Being who is more, but not less, than the God whom many reputable philosophers think they can establish." [28] More than once, when he has carried a rational argument as far as he can take it, Lewis declares something like, "But God himself has taught us in the Scriptures what is right," and proceeds to explicate some tenet of Christianity. Nevertheless, he cannot accept Tertullian's dictum, "I believe because it is absurd." With Aquinas, he holds that revealed truth and man's response in faith are never contrary to reason; they are but loftier planes in the almost infinite levels of reason that emanate from God himself.[29]

There is a second important way in which things in the phenomenal world will, when practiced properly, constitute a true, if limited, mirror of reality. Lewis asserted as a concomitant of his Christian objectivism that concepts of right human conduct are rooted in reality. In advancing this idea he knew full well that he might find much more skepticism here than he faced with regard to reasoning. After all, do not peoples' ideas of right and wrong differ widely around the world? By way of reply he granted, to begin with, that in any culture there will be moral notions which arise from local circumstances and prejudices; yet he could dismiss these as being peripheral to the central moral traditions of mankind. He emphasized not what was different among the many moralities of the world but what was common to them. This commonality he variously called the law of human nature, moral law, or the rule of decent behavior. Although this moral law manifests itself in human thought, it is a cosmic reality that exists quite apart from individual human minds, just as mathematical truths exist even when there are no human minds to apprehend them.[30] "We must believe that the conscience of man is not a product of Nature. It can be valid only if it is an offshoot of some absolute moral wisdom, a moral wisdom which exists absolutely 'on its own' and is not a product of non-moral, non-rational Nature." In Christian terms, this absolute moral law is bound up with the very nature of God himself.[31]

This concept was central to Lewis's understanding of morality, and appears frequently in his writings, fiction as well as nonfiction. Typical is the comment of the sage Professor Dimble in *That Hideous Strength*: "Of course there are universal rules to which all goodness must conform." [32] Lewis knew well enough, however, that it was not enough simply to declare his conviction, for there were many thinkers who would deny that any such innate awareness of moral law, or indeed any absolute moral law at all, exists. He was prepared to rebut their arguments.

> Some people say the idea of a Law of Nature or decent
> behaviour known to all men is unsound, because
> different civilisations and different ages have had quite
> different moralities. But this is not true. There have been
> differences between their moralities, but these have
> never amounted to anything like a total difference. If
> anyone will take the trouble to compare the moral
> teaching of, say, the ancient Egyptians, Babylonians,
> Hindus, Chinese, Greeks and Romans, what will really
> strike him will be how very like they are to each other

and to our own. . . . I need only ask the reader to think what a totally different morality would mean. Think of a country where people were admired for running away in battle, or where a man felt proud of doublecrossing all the people who had been kindest to him. You might just as well try to imagine a country where two and two made five. Men have differed as regards what people you ought to be unselfish to—whether it was only your own family, or your fellow countrymen, or everyone. But they have always agreed that you ought not to put yourself first. Selfishness has never been admired. Men have differed as to whether you should have one wife or four. But they have always agreed that you must not simply have any woman you liked.[33]

In saying this Lewis did not actually prove that there is a universal moral law, but only that people tend to act in broadly similar ways in similar circumstances. Some critics would doubtless also point out that the common denominator among the world's value systems is so low as to have little value; after all, to Christians it is not at all a bagatelle for a moral system to permit four wives, but a most serious breach of divine law. Still, Lewis's basic line of argumentation will not be dismissed lightly by many of his readers.

What is particularly important about absolute moral law at this juncture is the way in which it enters human experience. It is related to reason, insofar as its demands can be said to be in harmony with the greater cosmic order, which Lewis has already found to be reasonable. Men should be good, even as reality itself is good. Like the laws of mathematics, human beings in various parts of the world may independently learn of the same moral law and put it into practice, as, indeed, they have done in ways that Lewis noted. Yet, again like mathematics, moral law can efficiently be taught from teacher to pupil, from father to son, and from a declining culture to a rising one. Moral law is not intuitive in the biological sense; yet all normal, mature persons have the capacity for knowing what the universal moral law expects of them, even when they are not consciously aware of that knowledge.[34] Much like Plato, Lewis supposed that people must have within their minds some mechanism by which all moral options that occur to their conscious minds may be judged against an absolute standard. He argued: "The moment you say that one set of moral ideas can be better than another, you are, in fact, measuring them both by a standard, saying that one of them conforms to that standard more nearly than the other. But the standard that measures two things is something different from either. You are, in fact, comparing them both with some Real Morality, admitting that there is such a thing as a real Right, independent of what people think, and that some people's ideas get nearer to that real Right than others." [35] The innate standard of moral law cannot itself be brought to the conscious mind in all its fullness any more than God can be described; it is, we might say, preverbal, or even nonverbal. That fact, however, does not prevent a person from sensing accurately what the universal law demands of him. It goes without saying that each person is free to heed or reject the demands of this moral law most of the time. Lewis did not speculate about the nature of this mechanism; Plato offered the mythological explanation of the soul's recollection of heavenly realities that it had known before descending to the Earth and growing forgetful of the wonders it had previously known. As a Christian Lewis had little interest in the Platonic myth of recollection as such, or in its sister theory of the reincarnation of souls.[36] He was content to state what to him was the obvious fact that people do have an innate ability to distinguish broadly between right and wrong.

Lewis argued that it is a false dichotomy to set reason against such things as childhood training and the moral standards of a person's social group, as if one must choose only one or the other. It is possible, he emphasized, that a position on a moral question can be taken both according to reason and according to one's training, or the beliefs of one's society or peers. There is no reason to suppose, he pointed out, that just because a person has learned something from parents and teachers or found it supported by customary practice within his culture, it necessarily be only a human invention. As he so often did, he illustrated his point with an analogy: "We all learned the multiplication table at school. A child who grew up alone on a desert island would not know it. But surely it does not follow that the multiplication table is simply a human convention, something human beings have made up for themselves and might have made different if they had liked? I fully agree that we learn the Rule of Decent Behaviour from parents and teachers, and friends and books, as we learn everything else. But some of the things we learn are mere conventions which might have been different—we learn to keep to the left of the road, but it might just as well have been the rule to keep to the right—and others of them, like mathematics, are real truths." [37] He added that the moral law that reason mediates to man belongs to the same class as mathematics.

Lewis explicitly called upon the ancients to attest to the correctness of this understanding of morality. "The belief that to recognise a duty was to perceive a truth—not because you had a good heart but because you were an intellectual being—had roots in antiquity. Plato preserved the Socratic idea that morality was an affair of knowledge; bad men were bad because they did not know what was good. Aristotle, while attacking this view and giving an important place to upbringing and habituation, still made 'right reason' . . . essential to good conduct. Stoics believed in a Natural Law which all rational men, in virtue of their rationality, saw to be binding on them." [38] He went on to note that even the apostle Paul shows essentially this kind of understanding of the roots of morality; there is a law "written in the hearts" even of Gentiles, whether or not they are familiar with the divinely revealed Scriptures of the Hebrew people.

Now, what are the basic principles of morality that man can derive from his innate awareness of right and wrong? To answer this Lewis did not work deductively from the nature of absolute good, but inductively from an examination of what the moral codes of religions and cultures around the world and through the centuries have actually asserted. In *The Abolition of Man* he assembled his evidence under eight rubrics. Drawing upon dozens of literary works, representing assorted cultures and individual opinions around the world for nearly four millennia (much of which information he had gleaned by poring over the *Encyclopedia of Religion and Ethics*),[39] he found that the common moral law prohibits murder and encourages concern for humanity; promulgates social cohesion, including regard for ancestors, protection of the weak, and care for the young; disparages marital infidelity; promotes honesty and disparages all forms of deception and exploitation; extols mercifulness; recommends magnanimity; praises temperance in all things; inculcates nobility of demeanor; and finds value in the sacrifice of oneself for a larger cause.[40]

From these considerations Lewis drew the obvious conclusion: It is impossible that there could ever be any really worthwhile new morality. There can be only one morality, that which is in accord with reality, and that morality has already become generally known to mankind through the centuries—just as the laws of mathematics, physics, and chemistry have come to be known and cannot be expected to be overthrown by any new theories. Even as far back as the first century A.D. Christianity brought no new ethical code into the world; for what Jesus and the apostles did was to demand sincere adherence to a divine moral law which was already known quite well in its essential outlines, but which had been violated by mankind.

> Let us very clearly understand that, in a certain sense, it is no more possible to invent a new ethics than to place a new sun in the sky. Some precept from traditional morality always has to be assumed. We never start from a *tabula rasa*: if we did, we should end, ethically speaking, with a *tabula rasa*. New moralities can only be contractions or expansions of something already given. . . .
>
> I deny that we have any choice to make between clearly differentiated ethical systems. I deny that we have any power to make a new ethical system. I assert that wherever and whenever ethical discussion begins we find already before us an ethical code whose validity has to be assumed before we can even criticize it. For no ethical attack on any of the traditional precepts can be made except on the ground of some other traditional precept. . . .
>
> Men say "How are we to act, what are we to teach our

children, now that we are no longer Christians?" You see, gentlemen, how I would answer that question. You are deceived in thinking that the morality of your father was based on Christianity. On the contrary, Christianity presupposed it. That morality stands exactly where it did; its basis has not been withdrawn for, in a sense, it never had a basis. The ultimate ethical injunctions have always been premises, never conclusions. Kant was perfectly right on that point at least: the imperative is categorical. Unless the ethical is assumed from the outset, no argument will bring you to it.[41]

Hence "the real job of every moral teacher is to keep on bringing us back, time after time, to the old simple principles." [42] Lewis never tired of insisting that we recognize an objective standard of good underlying the diverse moralities of the world. He found his view to be in the mainstream of the Old Western tradition.

> Until modern times no thinker of the first rank ever doubted that our judgements of value were rational judgements or that what they discovered was objective. It was taken for granted that in temptation passion was opposed, not to some sentiment, but to reason. Thus Plato thought, thus Aristotle, thus Hooker, Butler and Doctor Johnson. The modern view is very different. It does not believe that value judgements are really judgements at all. They are sentiments, or complexes, or attitudes, produced in a community by the pressure of its environment and its traditions, and differing from one community to another. To say that a good thing is good is merely to express our feeling about it; and our feeling about it is the feeling we have been socially conditioned to have.[43]

At this point he touches on a topic that was the chief motivation for his writing of The Abolition of Man, the present-day school of subjectivism that denies all objective reality.

To be sure, in the heavenly realm where God dwells there is no need for any moral principles or duties at all; in that country, said Lewis, everyone "is filled full with what we should call goodness as a mirror is filled with light." [44] Absolute morality is not abrogated, but is present without verbalization, compulsion or the possibility of deviation. Indeed, many of the earthly embodiments of divine moral law, such as prohibitions against incest and adultery, cannot be relevant in the heavenly realm at all, for in heaven there is no physical sexuality or marriage. Neither can the universal deprecation of self-indulgence be expected to be directly applicable; Lewis indicates as much when the saved Narnians enter the heavenly Narnia:

> Everyone raised his hand to pick the fruit he best liked the look of, and then everyone paused for a second. This fruit was so beautiful that each felt, "It can't be meant for me . . . surely we're not allowed to pluck it."
> "It's all right," said Peter. "I know what we're all thinking. But I'm sure, quite sure, we needn't. I've a feeling we've got to the country where everything is allowed." [45]

This passage is in sharp contrast with that in which Ransom, newly arrived on luxuriant Perelandra and still very much within the sphere of mortal existence, feels a proper urge not to be gluttonous. Having eaten an indescribably delicious fruit, he is about to feast on the same plant a second time when he suddenly realizes he is no longer hungry or thirsty. "His reason, or what we commonly take to be reason in our own world, was all in favour of tasting this miracle again; the childlike innocence of fruit, the labors he had undergone, the uncertainty of the future, all seemed to commend the action. Yet something seemed opposed to this 'reason.' It is difficult to suppose that this opposition came from desire, for what desire would turn from so much deliciousness? But for whatever cause, it appeared to him better not to taste again. Perhaps the experience had been so complete that repetition would be a vulgarity—like asking to hear the same symphony twice in a day." [46] The next day Ransom enjoys a tactile delight that likewise tempts him to repetition, and he again finds himself refusing a second experience. The thought occurs to him: "This itch to have things over again, as if life were a film that could be unrolled twice or even made to work backwards . . . was it possibly the root of all evil? No: of course the love of money was called that. But money itself—perhaps one valued it chiefly as a defence against chance, a security for being able to have things over again, a means of arresting the unrolling of the film." [47] In the heavenly realm, the divine moral law makes irrelevant all such necessary restraints upon earthbound people.

But let us return to the world we live in. We have already seen Lewis's emphasis upon reason as a divine gift that all persons, Christians and non-Christians alike, can utilize. Such is the case also with universal morality. Pagan morality can be finely honed. Since there is only one God and one natural moral law that all persons can at least partly sense, Lewis readily reached the conclusion that every act or thought that is itself good is pleasing to God, whether done by a Christian or a pagan. For this he had, in addition to philosophical arguments, biblical support, for Jesus' parable of the good Samaritan assumes that such is the case. In the last of the Narnian stories, Aslan, in the role of Christ, admits into the forecourt of his heavenly kingdom a young Calormene, a member of a cruel race who venerate the demonic Tash. The Calormene has worshipped a false god, but he has done so in good faith, and that sincerity saves him. "Child," says Aslan to him, "all the service thou hast done to Tash, I account as service done to me." [48]

There is yet a third major way in which reality is manifested widely in human experience. The nobler forms of paganism, Lewis asserted, contain many insights into reality. He reasoned that if there is indeed but a single reality in the universe from which all meaning is derived, then paganism must contain many reflections of reality that are at least partially correct. To the extent that non-Christians use mathematical principles, engage in reasoning, perceive moral principles, and so forth, they are dealing with the true nature of the universe. Under no circumstances can Christians justifiably claim that all truth is to be found within Christianity and nowhere else. This stance is entirely consistent with Lewis's objectivism.

Although all religions and cultures necessarily have some consonance with reality, not all ways to God are equally valid. Although more attracted than he sometimes cared to admit to those dark recesses of man's religious quest which he depicted in *Till We Have Faces*, Lewis was eager to give intellectual assent to that which was clear and bright in religion.[49] He read enough about the religions of the world that he could speak with some confidence about them, although he can never be said to have developed expert knowledge in any of them. In view of his predilection for clarity in religion, we are not surprised to find that he was especially interested in those religions that have a well-developed body of theological tradition. Chief among these, in ascending order, were Buddhism, Islam, Hinduism, Judaism, and Christianity. He also perceived orderliness in Confucianism, but not much that suggested to him an actual religion. To these religions he was quite prepared to add Platonism, which he regarded as being among the most religious of the philosophical systems.[50]

Lewis found certain important reflections of reality to be contained within the pagan mythologies that tell of a slain, risen god who is able, through his sacrifice, to transform nature or humanity. He rejected all facile psychological or anthropological interpretations of these numerous myths, and did not find their impetus primarily in the environmental needs of those who used them. He also emphatically rejected the explanation given by some Christian thinkers that such stories are but the sly, deceptive work of the Devil. He found a ready explanation for these myths in his Christian objectivism.

> Christians who think, as I do, that in mythology divine and diabolical and human elements (the desire for a good story), all play a part, would say: "It is not accidental. In the sequence of night and day, in the annual death and rebirth of the crops, in the myths which these processes gave rise to, in the strong, if half-articulate, feeling (embodied in many Pagan "Mysteries") that man himself must undergo some sort of death if he would truly live, there is already a likeness permitted by God to that truth on which all depends.

The resemblance between these myths and the Christian truth is no more accidental than the resemblance between the sun and the sun's reflection in a pond, or that between a historical fact and the somewhat garbled version of it which lives in popular report, or between the trees and hills of the real world and the trees and hills in our dreams." [51]

He concluded, "There is a real connection between what Plato and the myth-makers most deeply were and meant and what I believe to be the truth. I know that connection and they [since they lived before the time of Christ] do not. But it is really there. It is not an arbitrary fancy of my own thrust upon old words. One can, without any absurdity, imagine Plato or the myth-makers if they learned the truth, saying, 'I see . . . so that was what I was really talking about. Of course. That is what my words really meant, and I never knew it.' "[52]

Then, like a latter-day Dante, Lewis added that he should perhaps not talk about what Plato or Virgil or the myth-makers would have said, but of what they said when they in fact observed the Christ-event. "For we can pray with good hope that they now know and have long since welcomed the truth; 'many shall come from the east and the west and sit down in the kingdom.' "[53]

It is this sense of the affinity between Christianity and what Lewis regarded as the best of ancient thought that makes the good-hearted, searching pagan superior, in Lewis's thinking, to the modern person who has cut himself off from that understanding of reality, begun in paganism and brought to completion in Christianity, which is his religious heritage. "A Pagan," he wrote, "as history shows, is a man eminently convertible to Christianity. He is essentially the pre-Christian, or sub-Christian, religious man. . . . The Christian and the Pagan have much more in common with one another than either has with the writers of the *New Statesman*." [54]

Lewis was prepared to go so far as to assert that paganism can provide for the Christian mythological images that say something more relevant about reality than abstract theological language does, or that is at least supplementary to it. Thus it was possible for him to write at length of Venus in his chapter on Eros in *The Four Loves*. He dealt with the symbol and myth of Venus in detail in two of his planetary romances. In *Perelandra* he imaginatively adapted the tradition of the birth of Venus from the foamy sea. When Ransom first sees her, the Green Lady appears, as it were, rising from the sea, and she subsequently inhabits the floating islands that glide over the swelling sea as one who is in her proper element. The constant changes of shapes of the waves and of the islands is a motif also related to the pagan goddess. Lewis elsewhere quoted his colleague Edgar Wind by way of clarification of this concept: "Only from the 'chaotic realm of change,' only from 'that formless nature of which every creature is composed,' can Venus arise in her beauty." [55] The very planet itself has a sensuous warmth evocative of the emotion of love, and to no small extent its intellectual aspects as well.

To speak of Venus leads to an aspect of paganized Christianity that Lewis found particularly fascinating: the idea, present in the writings of Spenser and others, that there were two Venuses, a heavenly and an earthly one. [56] This doubling had arisen out of the need to reconcile two disparate concepts—the assumption that Venus, as a perfect celestial being, could not be enmeshed in anything sordidly earthly, and the fact that pagan mythology was replete with stories of her activities in the sublunary region. *Venus vulgaris* was far lower than *Venus coelestis*, yet was like her in qualities, even as in the Epistle to the Hebrews the earthly tabernacle of God was like the heavenly, but imperfect. The same earthly mirroring of heavenly realities could be found in all the planetary deities. [57] Upon occasion Lewis found this contrivance useful in his fiction. Toward the end of *Perelandra* he introduced the celestial Venus: like human beings a creature of God, yet so rarified a substance as to be barely visible to a mortal such as Ransom. When with some difficulty she and her companion, the celestial Mars, have manifested themselves in a form that to some extent approximates earthly phenomena, Ransom is at once awed and curious.

He asked them how they were known to the old poets of

129

Tellus. When and from whom had the children of Adam learned that Ares was a man of war and that Aphrodite rose from the sea foam? . . . It comes, they told him, a long way round and through many stages. There is an environment of minds as well as of space. The universe is one—a spider's web wherein each mind lives along every line, a vast whispering gallery where (save for the direct action of Maleldil) though no news travels unchanged yet no secret can be rigorously kept. . . . In the very matter of our world, traces of the celestial commonwealth are not quite lost. Memory passes through the womb and hovers in the air. The Muse is a real thing. A faint breath, as Virgil says, reaches even the late generations. Our mythology is based on a solider reality than we dream: but it is also at an almost infinite distance from that base. And when they told him this, Ransom at last understood why mythology was what it was—gleams of celestial strength and beauty falling on a jungle of filth and imbecility. His cheeks burned on behalf of our race when he looked on the true Mars and Venus and remembered the follies that have been talked of them on earth.[58]

In *That Hideous Strength* Lewis returned to the same theme and had the earthly Venus appear, in all her rich sensuousness, to the love-deficient Jane Studdock. For purposes of the novel, though in defiance of the Model, he later allowed the heavenly archetype of Venus to descend to the Earth briefly, manifesting love on a plane that far surpassed that of the Venus of Earth.[59]

When writing as though specific myths were true, Lewis did not expect his readers to take him literally. He was trying to suggest that, even in its imperfect and fallen state, the human mind is capable of flashes of valid insight pertaining to the structure of reality. The idea is quite at home in Platonic thought. More specifically, it can be related to the theology of the Christian Platonists of the early centuries of the church, who sought admubrations of truth in pagan mythology. The fathers diligently noted aspects of pagan tradition that seemed to accord with

Christian concepts of God, of man, and of virtue; these they concluded were valid insights, so far as they went. Indeed, they had been God's divine preparation for the Christian gospel that was to come. What had been an imperfect apprehension of truth in pagan philosophy and religion was now a full and perfect revelation through Jesus Christ.

> I believe that in the huge mass of mythology which has come down to us a good many different sources are mixed—true history, allegory, ritual, the human delight in story telling, etc. But among these sources I include the supernatural, both diabolical and divine. We need here concern ourselves only with the latter. If my religion is erroneous then occurrences of similar motifs in pagan stories are, of course, instances of the same, or a similar error. But if my religion is true, then these stories may well be a *preparatio evangelica*, a divine hinting in poetic and ritual form at the same central truth which was later focussed and (so to speak) historicised in the Incarnation. To me, who first approached Christianity from a delighted interest in, and reverence for, the best pagan imagination, who loved Balder before Christ and Plato before St Augustine, the anthropological argument against Christianity has never been formidable. On the contrary, I could not believe Christianity if I were forced to say that there were a thousand religions in the world of which 999 were pure nonsense and the thousandth (fortunately) true. My conversion, very largely, depended on recognizing Christianity as the completion, the actualization, the entelechy, of something that had never been wholly absent from the mind of man. [60]

What was least perfectly understood in paganism was, of course, that aspect of Christianity represented by the person of Jesus Christ. Yet even in this regard paganism had ample adumbrations. Plato pictured a perfectly just man who would be persecuted by his ignorant, jealous fellow men. The mystery religions told of gods who died and rose. Such ideas were, so to speak, good dreams sent to the human race by God.[61] The early fathers of the church were more inclined to attribute such insights to the wiles of the Devil than to God's beneficence, but for Lewis such anticipations were only good. Their fault lay in their incompleteness, but the insight itself, pointing toward a heavenly reality, had to be from and about God. Whatever is true is good, even though the Devil may intercept the message and twist it in an attempt to use it for his own purposes.

Behind the willingness of some church fathers to find values in pagan mythology may have been, in part, the desire to find a common ground with paganism so that Christianity might be the more appealing to Gentiles. Their willingness may also have stemmed from their conviction that so vast and rich a system as paganism, like nature itself, could not be dismissed as being totally unrelated to the order of the universe. The fathers may also have had personal affection for classical learning that they could not easily dismiss. Certainly Lewis could have agreed with all of these concerns. He, too, wanted to find a place in the cosmic scheme for that which he had learned to know and love so deeply, and to use that wisdom for yet higher purposes. He did not understand this to be syncretism; for syncretism, as such, implies only the interweaving of disparate religious concepts, and says nothing about the intrinsic coherence of the synthesis, whereas Lewis's preoccupation was with the plausibility of any philosophical theology. Furthermore, his loyalty to Christian doctrine restrained him from openly finding values in paganism except those that could be subsumed under Christianity. The church, he once said, is "the only concrete organization which has preserved down to this present time the core of all the messages, pagan and perhaps pre-pagan, that have ever come from beyond the world." [62] When pagan religion is compared directly with Christianity, it generally comes out second-best. "The Sky-Father himself," he wrote of Zeus, "is only a Pagan dream of One far greater than Zeus and far more masculine than the male." He elsewhere declared, "Paganism does not merely survive but first becomes really itself in the very heart of Christianity." [63] Christianity was the unit by which he measured all other philosophical and religious viewpoints—or at least by which he intended to do so; he can hardly be blamed if, in matters where there were no doctrinal strictures, he chose as valid those elements in paganism that accorded most closely with his own philosophical frame of reference.

Thus far we have spoken of the place of paganism at that level of Lewis's thought where philosophical argumentation and conceptualization are paramount. We should note, however, that Lewis freely and joyfully embraced paganism for imaginative purposes—not, in such instances, so much because there was no other way to say what he wished, but simply because it delighted him to fabricate new settings for old concepts and discarded materials of other cultures. One such fabrication is Merlin, the magician, in *That Hideous Strength*, and in the Narnian tales there is, as we have seen, a seemingly endless variety of *longaevi* trooping through the adventures. Another highly useful function of paganism in Lewis's fiction is that it affords a signal device for communicating holy joy. Lewis was convinced that God and goodness are endless sources of joy; yet, apart from some Christian mysticism, he found little in Christian history or theology that depicted earthy, hearty pleasure, such as the spontaneous leap into dance, the sudden burst of song, laughter at a good joke, and the riotiousness of ecstasy. Paganism offered an enrichment to the relatively staid Christian tradition, and Lewis embraced it eagerly. He did not rely upon paganism for all such expressions, but his occasional utilization of it for this purpose is memorable. In *Prince Caspian*, the second of the Narnian stories, at one point we find Aslan at the center of a dance of *longaevi* that includes Bacchus and Silenus. [64] The episode shows clearly both the values and the limitations of paganism for Lewis. The bacchic romp is a worthy counterbalance to sobersided Christian practices, yet it is a sanitized paganism. There is no exploitation of others or blackness of deeds, only wholesome joy that echoes cosmic ecstasy. The joy centers around a legitimately good figure, Aslan, and, for all its utter exuberance, is never excessive; when it is finished, there is not the emptiness of exhaustion, but intellectual alertness and readiness to hear the wisdom of Aslan. Lewis's depiction would have been considerably more convincing if pagan practices had, in fact, generally been so elevated.

In all of these ways Lewis found the absolute to impinge upon the phenomenal world—in the validity of reason, the universal perception of the existence of God and laws of human behavior, and the nobler insights in pagan myth. It is obvious that he had a relatively high estimate of the capability of the human mind to perceive, however imperfectly, heavenly truths. In holding the potentialities of the human mind in high esteem, he inevitably stood in opposition to the Calvinistic doctrine of the total depravity of man. Lewis never abandoned his optimism about the possibilities that lay within the individual person. In that respect he remained to the last a true Platonist and Renaissance man.

6

Imagination and the Mystical Ascent

I think that all things, in their way, reflect heavenly truth,
the imagination not least.

Surprised by Joy

One has a glimpse of a country where . . . every one . . . is
filled full with what we should call goodness as a mirror is
filled with light. But they do not call it goodness. They do
not call it anything. They are not thinking of it. They are too
busy looking at the source from which it comes. But this is
near the stage where the road passes over the rim of our
world. No one's eyes can see very far beyond that.

Mere Christianity

T would be difficult to overestimate the importance of the
imagination in the Christian objectivism that Lewis cham-
pioned. *Ratio*, for all its importance, was, as we have seen, a
lesser stage of rational thought. *Intellectus* represented a loftier
form of reason, which included human imagination and was
capable of lifting the spiritual adept ever closer to absolute reality.
Although the imagination might entertain, its noblest and most
essential function was that of guiding the mind toward the higher
truths that gave meaning to existence. Lewis insisted that those
who suppose imagination to be only a psychological or physiological activity of the mind are wrong. When functioning as it should,
in secular as well as religious contexts, imagination is the most
important means by which higher truths can be communicated.

135

Holding such strong and hardly commonplace convictions, Lewis was concerned at a number of places in his writings to elucidate his understanding of imagination. He wrote, "I am a rationalist. For me, reason is the natural organ of truth; but imagination is the organ of meaning. Imagination, producing new metaphors or revivifying old, is not the cause of truth, but its condition. It is, I confess, undeniable that such a view indirectly implies a kind of truth or rightness in the imagination itself." [1] He was concerned to dispel the popular notion that whatever is imaginative is, by its very nature, false or nonexistent. What the ordinary person fails to perceive is that there are some aspects of reality that can be conveyed in no other way than imaginatively. Inasmuch as reality itself transcends the most abstract language, the imagination can offer, when properly focused, higher integrative levels, helping to lead the receptive mind toward a supraverbal apprehension of reality that draws upon the mind's innate capabilities of recognizing truth when presented with it. Thus by imagination Lewis meant something far more important than the aesthetic experience of the fabrication of fantasies.

The extent of his commitment to imagination, both intellectually and emotionally, is revealed in a letter that Lewis wrote to the Milton Society of America: "The imaginative man in me is older, more continuously operative, and in that sense more basic than either the religious writer or the critic. It was he who made me first attempt (with little success) to be a poet. It was he who, in response to the poetry of others, made me a critic, and in defence of that response, sometimes a critical controversialist. It was he who after my conversion led me to embody my religious belief in symbolical or mythopoeic forms, ranging from *Screwtape* to a kind of theologised science-fiction. And it was of course he who has brought me, in the last few years, to write the series of Narnian stories for children." [2] Such a statement warns the reader that he claimed for his fiction not simply that it was a valid vehicle for philosophical and religious truth, but that it might in some instances be the superlative one. [3]

Lewis was thus giving assent to the venerable, though by no means universally held assumption that poetic language "is by

no means merely an expression, nor a stimulant, of emotion, but
a real medium of information," whether (he carefully added)
that information be false or true.[4] Certain kinds of imaginative
statements do indeed, he argued, say something truthful, however flamboyantly garbed, about reality. In this category he
placed the world view represented by the Model, of which, as
we have seen, his fiction is but a latter-day expression. Inasmuch as there is only one reality, even those persons and cultures that stand outside the Old Western Culture in which the
Model took shape must willy-nilly reflect some measure of that
reality in their more serious imaginative works. Though
immensely subtler, the human imagination is, in its own distinctive way, just as absolute as are universal moral laws or syllogisms. All are part and parcel of the same underlying reality
that is itself inaccessible to the mind through any direct means.[5]

One of the specific values of the imaginative approach to
reality is that it allows for the expression of those dark, sensuous, awesome aspects that the prose of rationalism and abstraction seldom provides. In his poem "Reason" Lewis set the
murky side of reality in sharp contrast to the clear brightness of
ratio.

> Set on the soul's acropolis the reason stands
> A virgin, arm'd, commercing with celestial light,
> And he who sins against her has defiled his own
> Virginity: no cleaning makes his garment white;
> So clear is reason. But how dark, imagining,
> Warm, dark, obscure and infinite, daughter of Night:
> Dark is her brow, the beauty of her eyes with sleep
> Is loaded, and her pains are long, and her delight.[6]

One ignores each at great peril. Speaking from his conviction
that reality is one, Lewis longed for the ultimate harmonization
of the two faces of reality, the cool Athene and the warm Deme-
ter:

> Oh who will reconcile in me both maid and mother,
> Who make in me a concord of the depth and height?

Who make imagination's dim exploring touch
Ever report the same as intellectual sight? [7]

He may have been thinking of Goethe's Faust, in whom two
similar spirits are struggling, and in whose wide experiences no
earthly reconciliation can ever be found. In his own *Till We Have
Faces* he personified the contrasting aspects of reality in two of
the characters. The Fox is the epitome of rationalism, Ungit that
of the dark mysteries of the supernatural. Still, neither figure
encompasses the full range of the two dimensions, for in the Fox
reason has degenerated into sterile skepticism and in Ungit the
rich sensuousness of cosmic mystery has become selfish cruelty.
Broadly speaking, Lewis did himself some injustice when, in the
poem just quoted, he implicitly identified imagination with the
warm, obscure, and sensuous dimension of experience; for in
his fiction he frequently emphasized the imagination as leading
not to obscurity but to clarity. Indeed, he suggested that the
divergent yet parallel paths of *ratio* and imagination come together at the borders of Aslan's country.

Lewis was emphatic in his insistence that imaginativeness not
be confused with creativeness. The static structure of reality and
the absoluteness of God permit no genuine creativeness on the
part of human beings. The most that a person can hope to do is
to devise things that reflect the existing order and beauty of the
universe. The proper function of all human endeavor is to imitate reality as closely as possible.

> Applying this principle to literature, in its greatest
> generality, we should get as the basis of all critical
> theory the maxim that an author should never conceive
> himself as bringing into existence beauty or wisdom
> which did not exist before, but simply and solely as
> trying to embody in terms of his own art some
> reflection of eternal Beauty and Wisdom. Our criticism
> would therefore from the beginning group itself with
> some existing theories of poetry against others. It
> would have affinities with the primitive or Homeric
> theory in which the poet is the mere pensioner of the

Muse. It would have affinities with the Platonic
doctrine of a transcendent Form partly imitable on
earth; and remoter affinities with the Aristotelian
doctrine of mimesis and the Augustan doctrine about
the imitation of Nature and the Ancients.[8]

The alternative to the imitation of reality is not the creation of a
new reality but the assembling of a meaningless jumble of elements that philosophically approximates nothingness.

Although he derived his theory of imitation from what he
regarded as the mainstream of Western philosophical tradition,
Lewis most frequently spoke of it in the context of the Christian
faith. Here his argument was essentially based on Scripture.
Jewish and Christian tradition asserts that God created all that
is, including mankind; nowhere does the Bible say that human
beings ever create anything. The proper function of human
beings is to mirror God's truth. "We—even our poets and musi-
cians and inventors—never, in the ultimate sense, *make*. We only
build. We always have materials to build from. All that we can
know about the act of creation must be derived from what we
can gather about the relation of the creatures to their Creator."[9]
Or, as he says elsewhere, " 'Creation' as applied to human
authorship seems to me to be an entirely misleading term. We
re-arrange elements He has provided. There is not a vestige of
real creativity *de novo* in us. Try to imagine a new primary colour,
a third sex, a fourth dimension, or even a monster which does
not consist of bits of existing animals stuck together."[10] Lewis
takes the New Testament as a guide on the question of creativeness. He argues:

In the New Testament the art of life itself is an art of
imitation: can we, believing this, believe that literature,
which must derive from real life, is to aim at being
"creative," "original," and "spontaneous"? "Origi-
nality" in the New Testament is quite plainly the pre-
rogative of God alone; even within the triune being
of God it seems to be confined to the Father. The duty
and happiness of every other being is placed in being

139

derivative, in reflecting like a mirror. Nothing could be more foreign to the tone of scripture than the language of those who describe a saint as a "moral genius" or a "spiritual genius," thus insinuating that his virtue or spirituality is "creative" or "original." If I have read the New Testament aright, it leaves no room for "creativeness" even in a modified or metaphorical sense. Our whole destiny seems to lie in the opposite direction, in being as little as possible ourselves, in acquiring a fragrance that is not our own but borrowed, in becoming clean mirrors filled with the image of a face that is not ours.[11]

Appropriately, he cited Augustine of Hippo in support of his stance.

Lewis carried his conviction of the essential erroneousness of all attempts at the creation of new ideas into all of his thought. In matters of theology he had nothing but scorn for all talk of "new" theology for present-day Christians. A new theology is a contradiction in terms. The most that is possible is for a theologian to devise new ways of setting forth the one absolute truth. Here one discerns the conceptual basis for Lewis's own firm traditionalism as a Christian. Although his orthodoxy could conceivably be explained on personal grounds, Lewis himself rooted it squarely in his philosophy of religion. He could not bring himself to suppose that millions of Christians in the course of nearly twenty centuries had misapprehended truth so badly that the credal affirmations of the church and the scripture should be in need of revision. The universe, as he saw it, simply did not function in that manner.

Lewis's theory of the imitation of reality strikes a hard blow at the egocentrism of the artist and inventor. It is fashioned of the same stuff as his criticism of subjectivism. Lewis strongly denounced those who would set up their own experiences and productions as valid absolutes.

The unbeliever may take his own temperament and experience, just as they happen to stand, and consider them worth communicating simply because they are facts or, worse still, because they are his. To the Christian his own temperament and experience, as mere fact, and as merely his, are of no value or importance whatsoever; he will deal with them, if at all, only because they are the medium through which, or the position from which, something universally profitable appeared to him. . . . Thus St Augustine and Rousseau both write *Confessions*; but to the one his own temperament is a kind of absolute (*au moins je suis autre*), to the other it is "a narrow house, too narrow for Thee to enter—oh make it wide. It is in ruins—oh rebuild it." . . . In this sense, then, the Christian writer may be self-taught or original.[12]

In alluding to the self-taught person he is referring to his belief in something akin to innate ideas. This is not atypical; as we have seen, he used one concept to undergird or illuminate another, thereby weaving the fabric of his thought the firmer.

Dismissing, then, the notion of human creativeness, Lewis proceeded to deal with imitation. He was quite prepared to speak of human imitativeness; indeed, as if seeking to compensate for his rejection of creativeness he encouraged a high degree of imaginativeness. His distinction spared him any embarrassment at borrowing from earlier genres and literary devices, including the Model. By the very act of denying the possibility of true creativeness to himself, he seems to have set himself free psychologically to become highly inventive. It cannot be denied, of course, that much that Lewis would call imaginativeness others would call creativeness, although Lewis would insist that the distinction is not merely a semantic one.

Essentially imagination was for Lewis just what the common use of the term would suggest: an exceptionally inventive way of seeing things. As such it had affinities with romanticism, but it was by no means so narrowly limited. In Lewis it was far more than feeling, and certainly not vague sentiments; it was, first and foremost, images. Several times Lewis explained how his works of fiction began. Regarding *The Lion, the Witch, and the*

Wardrobe he stated: "The *Lion* all began with a [mental] picture of a Faun carrying an umbrella and parcels in a snowy wood. . . . At first I had very little idea how the story would go. But then Aslan came bounding into it. I think I had been having a good many dreams of lions about that time. Apart from that, I don't know where the Lion came from or why He came. But once He was there he pulled the whole story together, and soon He pulled the other six Narnian stories in after Him." [13] The fact that he capitalized the pronoun here when referring to Aslan and alluded to the lion as if he were actual is consistent with his Christian objectivism. He did believe that what Aslan represented, though not the image itself, was real and objective. "All scriptural imagery," he once ventured, is "a merely symbolical attempt to express the inexpressible." [14] He came close to implying that his inspiration for the lion had no discernable human genesis at all, but came directly from God, or Christ, himself, whether in the dreams to which he alluded or in some subtler way. In any case, his fictional use of Aslan could do no more than mirror the one absolute good story in the world, that which received its definitive earthly expression in the story of Christ found in the New Testament. [15]

Lewis did not intend one to suppose that mental pictures are the sole, or necessarily even the central element in his fiction. Once the picture of a faun hurrying along in the woods had been set down on paper, there came the laborious task of devising plausible and interesting things to happen in the faun's world. "If you are very lucky (I have never been as lucky as all that) a whole set [of pictures] might join themselves so consistently that there you had a complete story: without doing anything yourself. But more often than not (in my experience always) there are gaps. Then at last you have to do some deliberate inventing, have to contrive reasons why these characters should be in these various places doing these various things." [16] In *Perelandra* the sole picture seems to have been that of the floating islands. Of that work he declared: "The starting point of the second novel, *Perelandra*, was my mental picture of the floating islands. The whole of the rest of my labours in a sense consisted of building up a world in which floating islands could exist. And then of

course the story about an averted fall developed. This is because, as you know, having gotten your people to this exciting
country, something must happen." [17] Except for the few instances in which Lewis described how his stories grew, we have
no way of knowing which parts represent mental pictures and
which constitute calculated elaborations that give order and
richness to the material.

It is not to be thought that Lewis was so enamored of the
mental pictures he saw that he rigorously included all of them in
his fiction. "A very large part," he said, "of what comes up from
the unconscious and which, for that very reason, seems so
attractive and important in the early stages of planning a book,
is weeded out and jettisoned long before the job is done." [18] Nor
should it be thought, as apparently many readers have, that he
began his fictional works with a conscious moral purpose. The
mental pictures seem to have been entirely amoral in nature. On
this matter he was explicit: "Some people seem to think that I
began by asking myself how I could say something about Christianity to children; then fixed on the fairy tale as an instrument;
then collected information about child-psychology and decided
what age group I'd write for; then drew up a list of basic
Christian truths and hammered out 'allegories' to embody them.
This is all pure moonshine. I couldn't write in that way at all.
Everything began with images. . . . At first there wasn't even
anything Christian about them; that element pushed itself in of
its own accord." [19] "I've never started from a message or a
moral," he once asserted. "The story itself should force its moral
upon you. You find out what the moral is by writing the story."
He did not mean to suggest that he wrote randomly, as a com-
puter today can be programmed to "write" poetry; he meant
rather that metaphysical truth will tend to manifest itself by a
mental process that he nowhere attempts to analyze. This process was far different from the origin of "those dreary sociologi-
cal dramas that appear from time to time, started with a didactic
purpose—to a make a preconceived point—and they've got no
further." [20]

Lewis was not belittling religious content in fiction, but only
insisting that any religious element be on a firmer basis than

143

pedestrian moralizing. "Everything in the story should arise from the whole cast of the author's mind," he said. "The matter of our story should be a part of the habitual furniture of our minds." [21] In a letter to a former student he declared: "Art and Literature . . . can only be healthy when they are either (a) admittedly aiming at nothing but innocent recreation or (b) definitely handmaids of religious or at least moral truth. . . . But the great *serious irreligious* art—art for art's sake—is all balderdash; and incidentally never exists at all when art is really flourishing." [22] Behind this statement lies Christian objectivism. Lewis was suggesting that since all that art can do is to copy the existing sole reality, any art that sets itself up as autonomous—perhaps expressionism or surrealism in the twentieth century, though he gave no examples—is, in fact, cut off from the living stream that nourishes all art. He was typically directing his barbs at subjectivism and nihilism, at what happens when the imagination is not subjected to the clear light of the accumulated wisdom of the Old Western Culture in which the Model so long held sway.

Lewis found considerable support for his interest in imaginativeness in the writings of Plato, who, although placing the arts under certain strictures, was himself imaginative and inclined to regard fiction as a highly useful tool in the education of the masses. Plato had permitted the rulers of his ideal state to press upon the populace whatever fiction was lofty and ennobling, and permitted them to assert that the fiction was literally true. Lewis had no desire to palm off fiction as fact, but he recognized some of the same values that Plato found in noble fiction—in what we may call mythology or elevated metaphor. He ill concealed his distaste for those thinkers who lacked this intellectual dimension. "Those who have prided themselves on being literal, and who have endeavoured to speak plainly, with no mystical tomfoolery, about the highest abstractions, will be found to be among the least significant of writers: I doubt if we shall find more than a beggarly five per cent of meaning in the pages of some celebrated 'tough-minded' thinkers, and how the account of Kant or Spinoza stands, none knows but heaven. But open your Plato, and you will find yourself among the great creators of metaphor, and therefore among the masters of meaning." [23] This same distaste would also apply to those Platonic scholars who have been so unimaginative as to think that all meaning in Plato is limited to those statements that can be treated as logical propositions.

Early in his career Lewis had turned to allegory as a means of conveying his philosophical and religious concerns; the major result was *The Pilgrim's Regress*. He soon abandoned allegory as a prime vehicle for communication, although some of his later fiction is tinged with allegorical elements. In the final analysis, allegory could not pass muster because it was too artificial, too procrustean and too restrictive. Analogy suited his purposes much better, and he made extensive use of it in his everything he wrote, including his scholarly studies. Sometimes his analogies were simple ones, as when he likened moral law and human instincts to the tune of a piano and to the keys.[24] At other times they are elaborate, as when he delineated the person of the Green Lady of Perelandra in ways that show her to be modeled after Eve. Lewis had little fear of making false analogies, though he doubtless tried to use ones that he believed were valid. If challenged in any specific instance he would probably have insisted that his analogies were never intended to prove his case, but only to illustrate it. Yet he was enough of a Platonist to harbor a persistent suspicion that his analogies were something more than expendible marginalia. Believing that reality manifested itself through transposition from higher planes to lower ones, he tended to share with Plato the assumption that there is a correspondence of pattern among things great and small. The original itself can never be directly perceived, but one can circle around it by means of "hints, similes, metaphors"—all of which involve analogy. This form of understanding is, Lewis said, "the very essence of our life as conscious beings." [25]

Of particular significance is myth. In countless ways Lewis revealed his commitment to this means of communication. Myth is, he acknowledged, imagination in its most metaphysically significant, aesthetically satisfying and potentially ennobling form. It is not a primitive, outdated means by which human beings long ago tried to describe something that can today be more accurately explained by science or abstraction. It is the faded, and sometimes not so faded, recollection of supernatural realities. When Wisdom (i.e., philosophy) tries to convince John in *The Pilgrim's Regress* that all of the episodes in his spiritual pilgrimage are nothing but mythology, God speaks directly to John in rebuttal: "Child, if you will, it *is* mythology. It is but truth, not fact: an image, not the very real. But then it is My mythology. The words of Wisdom are also myth and metaphor: but since they do not know themselves for what they are, in them the hidden myth is master, where it should be servant: and it is but of man's inventing. But this is My inventing, this is the veil under which I have chosen to appear even from the first until now. For this end I made your senses and for this end your imagination, that you might see My face and live." [26] His other writings often echo this belief in the higher truths of mythology.

The mythology that Lewis found most reflective of reality was, not surprisingly, the Bible's. Thus broadly viewed, myth can include history. In the planetary romances Ransom momentarily speculates that "the distinction between history and mythology might itself be meaningless outside the Earth." [27] In general, however, Lewis held that myth may reflect metaphysical reality without being literally true or factual. Upon occasion he distinguished between myth and history, above all with regard to Christianity. "Here is the very thing you like in poetry and the romances," he wrote, "but this time it's true." [28] Although elsewhere myth may have metaphysical truth without necessarily being factual, in the Christ-event myth and history become one. The life, death, and resurrection of Christ constitute a unique event, charged with potentiality. "The heart of Christianity is a myth which is also a fact. The old myth of the Dying God, *without ceasing to be myth*, comes down from the heaven of legend and imagination to the earth of history." Without the mythological dimension, the sheer historical fact of Christ would have less meaning. "Even assuming (which I most constantly deny) that the doctrines of historic Christianity are merely mythical, it is the myth which is the vital and nourishing element in the whole concern. . . . [It is] the myth, that abides. . . . It is the myth that gives life." [29] Judged by the

unique standard of the Christ-myth, all other myths are imperfect. In a long letter that he wrote to his friend Arthur Greeves
just after becoming a Christian, he declared:

> In Pagan stories I was prepared to feel the myth as
> profound and suggestive of meanings beyond my
> grasp even tho' I could not say in cold prose "what it
> meant." Now the story of Christ is simply a true myth:
> a myth working on us in the same way as the others,
> but with this tremendous difference that *it really
> happened*: and one must be content to accept it in the
> same way, remembering that it is God's myth where
> the other are men's myths: i.e. the Pagan stories are
> God expressing Himself through the minds of poets,
> using such images as he found there, while Christianity
> is God expressing Himself through what we call "real
> things." Therefore it is *true*, not in the sense of being a
> "description" of God (that no finite mind would take
> in) but in the sense of being the way in which God
> chooses to (or can) appear to our faculties. The
> "doctrines" we get *out of* the true myth are of course *less*
> true: they are translations into our *concepts* and *ideas* of
> that which God has already expressed in a language
> more adequate, namely, the actual incarnation,
> crucifixion, and resurrection.[30]

He did not depart from this basic conviction throughout the
remainder of his life.

Myth need not be cast in prose; indeed, no small amount of it
is found in the form of poetry.[31] Good poetry is, indeed, by its
very nature allusive and metaphorical in its representation of
reality, though not all poetry can be called mythological.[32] Lewis
was in thorough agreement with Dante that myth and poetry,
along with allegory and other forms of symbolism, are God's
primal ways of communicating with mankind. Consistent with
his philosophical objectivism, he insisted that the greatest
poets—above all Christian ones, but to a lesser extent pagan
ones as well—are but channels through which truth is me-

147

diated.[33] The poet creates nothing new, but only imitates; the greater the poet, the clearer and more beautiful is his representation of the objective reality of the universe.

> I think Dante's poetry, on the whole, the greatest of all the poetry I have read: yet when it is at its highest pitch of excellence, I hardly feel that Dante has very much to do. There is a curious feeling that the great poem is writing itself, or at most, that the tiny figure of the poet is merely giving the gentlest guiding touch, here and there, to energies which, for the most part, spontaneously group themselves and perform the delicate evolutions which make up the *Comedy*. When the ascent from one sphere to the next is compared to progress in virtue, the last thing I am inclined to do is to exclaim "How did he think of that?"; given the metaphysics (which are not his own) and the physics (which are Ptolemy's) and the scheme of an ascent to heaven (which is from Cicero, Martianus Capella, and Alanus), it seems almost as if this simile must occur, and that the inexhaustible potency of such a passage demanded nothing more from the poet than that he should not meddle nor spoil it, that he should let it take its course and then write down what had happened as well as he could. The very nature of his universe seems to fill his key words—words such as *love, light, up, down, high, low, sun, star* and *earth*—with such a wealth of significance that their mere mention, at those points where the literal narrative requires them, becomes solid poetry "more gold than gold" without more ado. . . . I draw the conclusion that the highest reach of the whole poetic art turns out to be a kind of abdication, and is attained when the whole image of the world the poet sees has entered so deeply into his mind that henceforth he has only to get himself out of the way, to let the seas roll and the mountains shake their leaves or the light shine and the spheres revolve, and all this will *be* poetry, not things you write poetry about.[34]

The only way that greater precision than Dante's in the description of reality could be achieved, Lewis was convinced, would be by the writing of still greater poetry, not by the abandoning of poetry for abstract prose.

It follows that Lewis scorned all attempts to strip myth to its bare, conceptual bones, and more specifically attempts to de-mythologize Christianity.[35] Take away myth, he insists, and beneath will lie either new myth or nothing at all.

> The critic may still ask us why the imagery—which we admit to be untrue—should be used at all. But he has not noticed that any language we attempt to substitute for it would involve imagery that is open to the same objections. To say that God "enters" the natural order involves just as much spatial imagery as to say that He "comes down"; one has simply substituted horizontal (or undefined) for vertical movement. To say that He is "re-absorbed" into the Noumenal is better than to say He "ascended" into Heaven, only if the picture of something dissolving in warm fluid, or being sucked into a throat, is less misleading than the picture of a bird, or a balloon, going up. All language, except about objects of sense, is metaphorical through and through. To call God a "Force" (that is, something like a wind or a dynamo) is as metaphorical as to call Him a Father or a King. On such matters we can make our language more polysyllabic and duller: we cannot make it more literal.[36]

Still, he was not prepared to grant that all mythological statements are of equal validity, and we have already noted his affirmation that the best insights of pagan mythology are but gleams of celestial strength and beauty by comparison with the truths conveyed by the great Christian myth.

It was in myth that Lewis found some justification for the relative lack of character-development that we have noted in his fiction. Aware that some critics had complained that his novels lacked plausible, interesting characters, he pointed out (working on the assumption that his novels were of the same genre as myth) that myth does not demand psychological character-study; on the contrary, he argued, attention to characterization in the modern psychological sense of that term might well distract the reader from the myth itself. Indeed, in the telling of myth the customary literary criteria do not apply at all.

> The critical problem with which we are confronted is whether this art—the art of myth-making—is a species of literary art. The objection to so classifying it is that the Myth does not essentially exist in *words* at all. We all agree that the story of Balder is a great myth, a thing of inexhaustible value. But of whose version—whose *words*—are we thinking when we say this? For my own part, the answer is that I am not thinking of any one's words. No poet, so far as I know or can remember, has told this story supremely well. I am not thinking of any particular version of it. If the story is anywhere embodied in words, that is almost an accident. What really delights and nourishes me is a particular pattern of events, which would equally delight and nourish if it had reached me by some medium which involved no words at all—say by a mime, or a film. . . . Any means of communication whatever which succeeds in lodging those events in our imagination has, as we say, "done the trick." After that you can throw the means of communication away.[37]

In his essay "On Science Fiction" he carried this same principle over to science fiction as well, presumably on the grounds that that literary genre is basically related to mythology. Such writing, he declared, ought not to contain "any deep or sensitive characterization," and that if it does do so it is, in fact, at fault. From his point of view, the characters in science fiction need to be those to whom things happen rather than the focal points of the story. If the characters become the central concern as such, then the distinctive science-fictional environment will be lost. "He who is to see strange sights must not himself be strange," he asserted. "He ought to be as nearly as possible Everyman or Anyman." [38]

Finally there is the matter of children's fiction as a theological vehicle. Few writers of fiction, and much less children's fiction, have ever given so elaborate and consistent a rationale for their work as Lewis did. He once described the child's response to fantasy: "Fairy land arouses a longing for what he knows not what. It stirs and troubles him (to his life-long enrichment) with a dim sense of something beyond his reach and, far from dulling or emptying the actual world, it gives a new dimension of depth." He wrote his stories about Narnia, he said, because sometimes "a children's story is the best art-form for something you have to say." [39] In *That Hideous Strength* he found occasion to imply much the same thing. While waiting in a small country hotel, his character Mark Studdock discovers a sitting-room containing old bound volumes of *The Strand* magazine. "In one of these he found a serial children's story which he had begun to read as a child but abandoned because his tenth birthday came when he was half way through it and he was ashamed to read it after that. Now, he chased it from volume to volume till he had finished it. It was good. The grown-up stories to which, after his tenth birthday, he had turned instead of it, now seemed to him, except for *Sherlock Holmes*, to be rubbish." [40] Lewis would not, of course, limit the validity of his observations to children's stories; indeed, he was trying to suggest that the common distinction between children's and adults' stories is only partially warranted. He could not expect that children comprehend adult literature, but he was prepared to argue that adults can continue to find value in substantial children's literature. His planetary romances were in no small measure children's fiction written for adults, a fact that he made amply clear when he subtitled *That Hideous Strength* "A Modern Fairy-Tale for Grown-ups." Yet the converse is also just as true: the Narnian tales are in a significant way grown-ups' fiction written for children; and perhaps that fact explains why some adults continue to find those stories worth the reading.[41]

All of Lewis's imaginative devices revolve essentially around the apprehension of reality. We are not surprised, therefore, to find that Lewis invested some of his richest imaginative thought in the description of the progress of the self toward God. Thus we find ourselves turning again, as Lewis's thought has so often required us to do, to ultimate matters. Lewis called this experience of enlightenment by a variety of names as occasion seemed to him to warrant, and described it in many places in his writings. Particularly illuminating is his statement in his autobiography about his discovery while still a young man of the existence of a mystical path to the transcendental. "I thus understood that in deepest solitude," he confided, "there is a road right out of the self, a commerce with something which, by refusing to identify itself with any object of the senses, or anything whereof we have biological or social needs, or anything imagined, or any state of our own minds, proclaims itself sheerly objective. Far more objective than bodies, for it is not, like them, clothed in our senses—the naked Other, imageless (though our imagination salutes it with a hundred images), unknown, undefined, desired." [42] The very wording of this passage has echoes of both Plato's description of the Good in the *Symposium* and the apostle Paul's several near-credal encomiums to God and Christ. Although brief and deceptively simple in wording, this statement is profoundly reflective of the core of Lewis's religious and philosophical thought. It not only sums up the Christian objectivism that we have been explicating but proclaims the belief that a person can enter the presence of this transcendent reality. This is the language of mysticism.

It may seem strange to think of Lewis as a mystic, for most scholarly studies of his thought have said little, indeed nothing at all, about this aspect of his religious views. Perhaps the oversight is understandable; after all, one does not usually expect that an avowed rationalist will at the same time have mystical tendencies. Lewis himself seemed to deny any mystical concerns when, in *Letters to Malcolm*, he declared, "You may wonder that my intense desire to peep behind the scenes has not led me to attempt the mystic way." [43] But in denying that he had taken the mystic way, Lewis had in mind the kind of mysticism in which subjectivism predominated, to the neglect of the objective reality that gave validity to the experience. Such easy mysticism could lead to the assumption that the central factor in religion was not content but mode or style. He refused to allow mysticism to blur the distinctions among religions or to become a sufficient religion in itself.

> One thing common to all mysticisms is the temporary shattering of our ordinary spatial and temporal consciousness and of our discursive intellect. The value of this negative experience must depend on the nature of that positive, whatever it is, for which it makes room. . . .
> I do not at all regard mystical experience as an illusion. I think that it shows that there is a way to go, before death, out of what may be called "this world"—out of the stage set. Out of this; but into what? That's like asking an Englishman "Where does the sea lead to? " He will reply, "To everywhere on earth, including Davy Jones's locker, except England." The lawfulness, safety, and utility of the mystical voyage depends not at all on its being mystical—that is, on its being a departure—but on the motives, skill, and constancy of the voyager, and on the grace of God.[44]

It is the port that counts, not the voyage. There is, of course, only one port; all other alleged harbors are but rocky crags upon which a badly navigated ship will founder. He continued: "I shouldn't be at all disturbed if it could be shown that a diabolical mysticism, or drugs, produced experiences indistinguishable (by introspection) from those of the great Christian mystics. Departures are all alike; it is the landfall that crowns the voyage." He also stated the point less metaphorically: "The true religion gives value to its own mysticism; mysticism does not validate the religion in which it happens to occur." [45] Even with these caveats he still had ample room for mysticism in his approach to religion. So long as the pilgrim keeps his focus upon the objective goal of his journey, mysticism can be a viable path for him to follow.[46]

Lewis knew, as we do, that mysticism could not be disentangled from the Platonic-Christian tradition of the West. We have earlier noted that he held Plato to be a religious philosopher, a veritable mystagogue into realities that those less sensitive failed to perceive. The form of Platonism enunciated by Plotinus must be regarded, by any standard, as a mystical one. Indeed, as soon as one postulates a ground of being that lies beyond all human grasp and yet is that which is most to be desired, one is already involved in mysticism. The expressions of the Model in the Middle Ages, and above all in the Renaissance, were often suffused with mystical elements. Unlike many of the mystics who stood outside the Platonic tradition, these thinkers did not turn their backs on the material world but saw phenomena as lower levels in a vast hierarchy of being that could be ascended like a ladder. A less formal variant of this latter view saw reality as something glimmering faintly but persistently through the profusion of earthly phenomena.

Steeped in the history of Old Western Culture, Lewis had every occasion to develop an interest in mysticism. Yet in many ways he was temperamentally and intellectually an unlikely candidate for that approach to religion. He came from a most unmystical Protestant background, and the lifelong love of reasoned argumentation that he learned from his teacher Kirkpatrick militated against anything other than a matter-of-fact, unimaginative approach to religion. If he had thought like many other nominal Christians of his time, he would have been a supernaturalist in name only, and otherwise a materialist, empiricist, and relativist—with perhaps a dash of Protestant pietism thrown in to sweeten the dour rationalism. Yet once he became a supernaturalist—first a theist, then a Christian—in his early manhood, he took the implications of that position seriously. His friends, particularly Barfield, Tolkien, and Williams, gave strong reinforcement to his views.

In finding a place for mysticism in this thought, Lewis never slipped into the Gnostic heresy of rejecting the phenomenal world as being either nonexistent or utterly evil. His stance was more extraversive than that of the Gnostic or the flagellant; he cherished the world for the glimpses it provided of greater reality. Neither did he advocate a mysticism that denigrated human individuality. To him the notion of the dissolution of the self into the Godhead was abhorrent. He longed for an ecstatic experience of God, but one of intensified sensations and increased mental processes, not the loss of the discrete self. His mysticism was, from first to last, the activity of a sensitive, malleable, and yet fully controlled mind. Imagination suggested, but reason directed him in his religious and philosophical peregrinations. He wanted not to lose himself, but to find himself in God.[47] In insisting upon his individuality, he set himself apart from many mystics, Christian and otherwise. He was willing to grant, however, that there was more than one path toward the beatific vision. "Didn't people dispute once," he asked in one of his later works, "whether the final vision of God was more an act of intelligence or of love?" He answered his own query: "That is probably another of the nonsense questions."[48]

For the most part, each viable path to God is vibrant and invigorating, not the austere void of the Neoplatonic *via negativa*.[49] The ascent is made not out of one's disinterested, intellectual inclinations but because God pulls man like a magnet. Man, as creature, needs to turn to the source of his being. In *The Four Loves* Lewis observed that a few exalted souls may reach beyond sheer need-love for God, but that if such persons should attempt to transcend need-love entirely the mystical heights would become illusory. "It would be a bold and silly creature," he wrote, "that came before its Creator with the boast, 'I'm no beggar. I love you disinterestedly.'"[50] It is to such extremes, he believed, that the Neoplatonic ascent can lead. The major difference between the Platonic and Christian paths to the absolute was in precisely this matter. The Platonist basically has no divine help in the ascent, whereas the Christian affirms that he has the support of the absolute itself: Father, Son, and Holy Spirit.

Always a teacher, Lewis delighted in serving as mentor to his reader and occasionally came close to being a hierophant in cosmic mysteries. The most imaginative and dramatic representations of the spiritual ascent appear in his fiction. In *The Pilgrim's Regress* he uses the device of a pilgrimage around the world, which in all essentials is comparable to an upward spiritual journey. This pilgrimage, like those in some of his other novels, is, in effect, a provocative trip through the highways and byways of the mind, and in particular of competing philosophies. The theme of religious pilgrimage is also prominent in the Narnian tales. It appears in the first story of the series, where the children, who have only recently arrived in Narnia, respond to the talking beaver's whispered invitation, "Come further in," and thereafter begin their education in Narnian history, cosmology, soteriology and eschatology.[51] Although Narnia is not itself a perfect world by any means, it is a dimension in which sensations are sharper, the central issues of life are seen more clearly, the mind of the deity can be read more directly than in our world, and the possibility for living an unambiguously moral life is greater.

By far the lengthiest presentation of the ascent toward ultimate reality appears in the third Narnian story, *The Voyage of the Dawn Treader*, which in its series of fantastic episodes is remarkably similar to a psychedelic experience. As is often the case with reported psychedelic experiences, the episodes are strung together loosely; each is—quite literally in this book—an island unto itself. The voyagers travel by stages from the Lone Islands, which are closest to the everyday Narnian world (and to ours) to islands which are increasingly remote from ordinary experience. On the Island of Ramandu their adventure involves the dawn, a theme which presages a growing qualitative difference in the nature of their surroundings, and even in the nature of their quest. "Every night they saw that there rose in the east new constellations which no one had ever seen in Narnia and perhaps, as Lucy thought with a mixture of joy and fear, no living eye had seen at all. Those new stars were big and bright and the nights were warm." [52] The island has a gentle, hospitable terrain; on it they find the ruins of a great palace, in the midst of which is a magical table set with a supernatural feast—Aslan's Table, heavy with the "promise of all happiness." The food is renewed daily as a part of a great cosmic renewal, typified by the rising of the sun. The voyagers witness the rite in which the priestly Ramandu greets the dawn. "Once or twice before, the

Narnians had wondered whether the sun at its rising did not look bigger in these seas than it had looked at home. This time they were certain. There was no mistaking it. And the brightness of its ray on the dew and on the table was far beyond any morning brightness they had ever seen. And as Edmund said afterwards, 'Though lots of things happened on that trip which *sound* more exciting, that moment was really the most exciting.' " [53] This first stage in the mystical initiation is followed by some elucidation provided by Ramandu, who functions both as a priest and as the voyagers' mystagogue.

The Narnians set forth from Ramandu's Island on the final phrase of their journey. At once they begin to feel that they have gone beyond their ordinary world. Lewis utilized a variety of symbols to convey the otherness of this growing participation in another dimension of existence. "All was different. For one thing they all found that they were needing less sleep. One did not want to go to bed nor to eat much, nor even to talk except in low voices. Another thing was the light. There was too much of it. The sun when it came up each morning looked twice, if not three times, its usual size." [54] The water becomes transparent, and, when sampled, proves no longer to be salty but sweet. The drinking of it gives one an unearthly vigor; it is perceived as being like "drinkable light" in its nature. [55] All those on board imbibe, and notice a strange result: "As I have said before, there had been too much light ever since they left the island of Ramandu—the sun too large (though not too hot), the sea too bright, the air too shining. Now, the light grew no less—if anything, it increased—but they could bear it. They could look straight up at the sun without blinking. They could see more light than they had ever seen before." [56] And so the journey continues. As the Narnians drink more of the water of the supernatural ocean, some of the sailors who had been elderly begin to appear younger. Everyone on board is filled with an excitement. The ship passes through a vast field of blooming white lilies, from which arises a sweet but not narcotic odor—"a fresh, wild, lonely smell that seemed to get into your brain and make you feel that you could go up mountains at a run or wrestle with an elephant." [57]

Finally, when their boat can navigate the shallows no longer, the Narnians turn back, leaving Edmund, Lucy, Eustace, and the mouse Reepicheep to forge ahead toward their goal, which they have long realized is Aslan's country. Gliding with a gentle current they move eastward, needing neither to sleep nor to eat. "When the third day dawned—with a brightness you or I could not bear even if we had dark glasses on—they saw a wonder ahead . . . a long, tall wave—a wave endlessly fixed in one place as you may often see at the edge of a waterfall." [58] This wave is the barrier between the world of Narnia and the realm of the supernatural, the domain of the deity. Because the time is not yet right, the children are not permitted to enter Aslan's country, but, like Moses viewing the promised land, they glimpse that other realm.

> For now they saw something not only behind the wave but behind the sun. They could not have seen even the sun if their eyes had not been strengthened by the water of the Last Sea. But now they could look at the rising sun and see it clearly and see things beyond it. What they saw—eastward, beyond the sun—was a range of mountains. It was so high that either they never saw the top of it or they forgot it. None of them remembers seeing any sky in that direction. And the mountains must really have been ouside the world. For any mountains even a quarter of a twentieth of that height ought to have had ice and snow on them. But these were warm and green and full of forests and waterfalls however high you looked. And suddenly there came a breeze from the east, tossing the top of the wave into foamy shapes and ruffling the smooth water all round them. It lasted only a second or so but what it brought them in that second none of those three children will ever forget. It brought both a smell and a sound, a musical sound. [59]

Only little Reepicheep, whom Aslan has called to himself, is permitted to reach the goal of his spiritual journey. Setting out in a tiny craft he disappears over the huge wave and is seen no more. Later, in *The Last Battle*, the reader learns that he has remained from that time onward in Aslan's country—as indeed he must, since he is one of the privileged few who have been translated bodily to paradise—living joyfully in the presence of his Lord. Thus Lewis discreetly drew a veil over Aslan's country. He had brought his reader to the very gateway of the Empyrean, but there he preferred to stop, at least for purposes of this story. As he said about the Christian Heaven in another context, "No one's eyes can see very far beyond that." [60] In the final Narnian story he was to be bolder.

It is especially important to observe that Lewis's descriptions of mystical ascent to the absolute have a strongly integrative function within the stories. They are not, like the adventures of Alice in Wonderland, a series of nearly unrelated episodes that suggest psychosis. They are always set within the framework of Christian objectivism, and as such have more, not less, meaning than typical literary fantasies. We see illustrated Lewis's concern that the imagination be controlled and ordered by the conscious mind and by the cumulative wisdom of the Old Western Culture. Lewis revealed his role as teacher and apologist for Christianity in an exchange between the children and Aslan at the end of *The Voyage of the Dawn Treader*:

> "Please, Aslan," said Lucy. "Before we go, will you tell us when we can come back to Narnia again? Please. And oh, do, do, do make it soon."
>
> "Dearest," said Aslan very gently, "you and your brother will never come back to Narnia."
>
> "Oh, *Aslan!*" said Edmund and Lucy both together in despairing voices.
>
> "You are too old, children," said Aslan, "and you must begin to come close to your own world now."
>
> "It isn't Narnia, you know," sobbed Lucy. "It's *you*. We shan't meet *you* there. And how can we live, never meeting you?"
>
> "But you shall meet me, dear one," said Aslan.
>
> "Are—are you there too, Sir?" said Edmund.

"I am," said Aslan. "But there I have another name. You must learn to know me by that name. This was the very reason why you were brought to Narnia, that by knowing me here for a little, you may know me better there." [61]

That other name is, of course, Christ. Lewis is saying, in good Platonic fashion, that in describing truth by myth and related imagery he intends that the reader be led to perceive a likeness to the Christian gospel.

Less extensive but fully as sustained in intensity is the ascent toward the ultimate that Lewis introduced at the end of *The Last Battle*. There Lewis constructed, around the theme "Further up and further in," the ascent from the mutable Narnia into the heavenly Narnia through various unfolding vistas, each of which provides an appropriate advance in metaphysical understanding and joy for the blessed. [62] Whereas in *The Voyage of the Dawn Treader* he had left the curtain lowered between the Narnians and Aslan's kingdom, here he lifted it and allowed the reader to enter the paradisal scene.

Occasionally there are shorter passages in the Narnian stories that describe mystical exieriences. One of the most dramatic and imaginative appears in *Prince Caspian*, where Lucy encounters her beloved lord and friend Aslan. [63] The lion comes to Lucy in the privacy of the night, while Peter, Susan, and Edmund are sleeping. The latter three children have doubted Lucy's insistent statement that she has gotten glimpses of Aslan during the previous day (these being typical of Lucy's ability to receive intuitions of an unseen higher reality), and they continue to sleep (that being symbolical of their relative spiritual insensitivity) during Lucy's encounter. One is reminded not only of the story of Jesus' encounters with his Father while his three disciples slept but also of Plato's analogy of the cave. In any case, the account depicts Lucy as first hearing a voice that calls her name once, and then a little later a second time, when she is wide awake. She sits up, trembling with anticipation, and sees a glade of trees commence to move in response to a strange music.

She rises and enters into her supernatural experience with an aplomb worthy of a medieval mystic.

> She went fearlessly in among them, dancing herself as she leaped this way and that to avoid being run into by these huge partners. But she was only half interested in them. She wanted to get beyond them to something else; it was from beyond them that the dear voice had called. . . .
>
> A circle of grass, smooth as a lawn, met her eyes, with dark trees dancing all round it. And then—oh joy! For *He* was there: the huge Lion, shining white in the moonlight, with his huge black shadow underneath him. . . .
>
> She rushed to him. She felt her heart would burst if she lost a moment. And the next thing she knew was that she was kissing him and putting her arms as far around his neck as she could and burying her face in the beautiful rich silkiness of his mane.
>
> "Aslan, Aslan. Dear Aslan," sobbed Lucy. "At last."
>
> The great beast rolled over on his side so that Lucy fell, half sitting and half lying between his front paws. He bent forward and just touched her nose with his tongue. His warm breath came all round her. She gazed up into the large wise face.
>
> "Welcome, child," he said.
>
> "Aslan," said Lucy, "you're bigger."
>
> "That is because you are older, little one," answered he.
>
> "Not because you are?"
>
> "I am not. But every year you grow, you will find me bigger."
>
> For a time she was so happy that she did not want to speak. But Aslan spoke.
>
> "Lucy," he said, "we must not lie here for long. You have work in hand." [64]

Here is Christ-mysticism in its full medieval splendor. Lucy, whom we have found to typify the ideal Christian novice, approaches Aslan with the passion of a bride, and lies in ecstasy in his large, comforting arms. Side by side, bodies enwined, they kiss in a subtly erotic way. Lucy takes the lion into her body through the symbol of his quickening breath. When he has consummated the spiritual marrige, the lion promptly sets her to do his will and his work.

Mysticism is also present in the planetary romances, sometimes in the form of episodes of ecstatic experience and occasionally as full-fledged representations of an ascent toward the ultimate. Among the former is the description of the arrival of Ransom on Venus, which includes an experience of bodily levitation; [65] the latter finds expression in the mystical flight of Ransom in the concluding episode of the book. As we have noted earlier, the planetary romances trace, among other things, the intellectual and spiritual development of the protagonist. Ransom is engaged in his own mystical ascent. When the reader first meets him in *Out of the Silent Planet* he is a retiring philologist. During his adventures on Malacandra he advances rapidly in his knowledge of the spiritual realm, but remains largely a spectator. In the several years that follow this initiation, he becomes an expert in medieval metaphysics as well as taking on a more cosmic role in the affairs of the planet Perelandra. By the time of *That Hideous Strength* he has become the Pendragon, the chief earthly hierophant of divine mysteries; he is accustomed to receiving supernatural visitations, is said to be ageless, has special robes that befit his station, and even lounges on a dias that resembles a throne. As a final evidence of his successful passage through these increasingly elevated plateaus of spiritual achievement, he is transported to the Third Heaven of Perelandra, where he will never die but live in endless peace. [66] The extravagance of this character-development is extreme; Ransom's bodily translation to the Third Heaven is nothing less than an apotheosis. What motivated Lewis to take such uncharacteristic liberties with the person of Ransom is difficult to say, apart from the obvious consideration of Lewis's high opinion of the potentialities of man.

There are other, sometimes less neatly schematic, instances of spiritual pilgrimage in Lewis's fiction. Orual, in *Till We Have Faces*, undergoes a long and tortuous growth in grace, from initial ignorance and vanity to a modicum of self-understanding and self-forgetfulness that helps her to accept her human lot. Yet there are few spiritual exhilarations in her life, and even by the end of her anguished existence she has grasped only a few insights into the nature of reality. Those who respond favorably to the neat certainties of the quintessential C. S. Lewis are likely to feel dissatisfaction with the results of Orual's pilgrimage. If there is any development to be discerned at all within Lewis's thought over the decades, it is in his increasing tendency to tolerate ambiguity and irony in the human experience.

The concepts of the imagination and of the nature of the self's journey toward the absolute are fundamental to Lewis's thought; about that there can be no doubt. There nevertheless remains another frame of mind that cannot be ignored. In his theological treatises Lewis was willing, upon occasion, to forego all philosophical nuances and cautions and to speak directly about the vision of God and the final state of the soul in the presence of God. Here was Lewis the believer speaking. As a Christian pietist he could assert, with the simple faith of the biblical writers, "In the twinkling of an eye, in a time too small to be measured, and in any place, all that seems to divide us from God can flee away, vanish leaving us naked before Him." [67] Gone is the mystical ascent to God, the ladder that leads, rung by rung, from this world into the clouds. Gone is philosophical inquiry, with its rational bent. Gone is romanticism, with its rich sensuousness and imaginativeness. In the place of these there is a simple meeting of God and man. Writing in this mood Lewis can, without anxiety over the loss of individuality, speak of one's "surely and swiftly approaching his final union with God, vision of God, and enjoyment of God." [68] This is the traditional language of Christian theology, slightly adapted to Lewis's own style. Although naive and simplistic, this conviction was as much a part of him as the loftiest of philosophical statements.

In all his imagery Lewis showed himself to be God-intoxicated. He had known the stab of longing for that which lies forever out of sight, yet which is constantly leaving evidences of its existence and signals of its utmost importance to mortals. He lived in the conviction that ultimate reality alone could provide hope, beauty, joy, and, in the final reckoning, meaning to life. He had been privileged to have the curtain that conceals the infinite lifted slightly for brief moments, and he had glimpsed the inexpressible—or at least the forecourts of reality. From his vantage point a short distance up the vast ladder of being he could turn back to view the phenomenal world and there perceive patches of Godlight, largely unnoticed by the majority of persons, that fitfully but magnificently illuminate the dark wood of life.

7

The Self

How did other people . . . find it so easy to saunter through the world with all their muscles relaxed and a careless eye roving the horizon, bubbling over with fancy and humour, sensitive to beauty, not continually on their guard and not needing to be? What was the secret of that fine, easy laughter which he could not by any efforts imitate? Everything about them was different. They could not even fling themselves into chairs without suggesting by the very posture of their limbs a certain lordliness, a leonine indolence. There was elbow-room in their lives.

That Hideous Strength

*C*HARACTERISTICALLY, C. S. Lewis developed his concept of human nature as carefully as the rest of his philosophy of religion. Bringing together elements of Platonic anthropology, Christian doctrine, Renaissance humanism, modern psychology, and personal predilections, he produced a picture that gave human beings a remarkably high position in the order of reality. Rejecting the relatively low estimate of the place of humankind in the scheme of creation that is generally found within the medieval versions of the Model, he went back to the text of the Bible and found there justification for the conviction that human beings are made in the image of God. This belief doubtless accorded with his own deepest wishes, and was at the same time reinforced by the Renaissance thought that he knew so well. It was also highly compatible with Platonism, for although Plato did not suppose that the Good had any unadulterated physical manifestation, he adhered to no concept of essential human depravity. With so much support in traditional thought, Lewis was fully prepared to assert that "when we come to man, the highest of the animals, we get the completest resemblance to God which we know of." [1]

The similarity to which he alludes may in some measure be literal. Lewis thought of God as profoundly male, and often betrayed his presupposition that the male is the dominant sex. [2] It is, however, primarily a spiritual similarity that he had in mind: a likeness between the divine and human processes of rationality that give God and man an affinity for one another. He never abandoned a viewpoint to which he came shortly before his conversion to personal theism:

> We mortals, seen as the sciences see us and as we
> commonly see one another, are mere "appearances."
> But appearances of the Absolute. In so far as we really
> are at all (which isn't saying much) we have, so to
> speak, a root in the Absolute, which is the utter reality.
> And that is why we experience Joy: we yearn, rightly,
> for that unity which we can never reach except by
> ceasing to be the separate phenomenal beings called
> "we." Joy was not a deception. Its visitations were
> rather the moments of clearest consciousness we had,
> when we became aware of our fragmentary and
> phantasmal nature and ached for that impossible
> reunion which would annihilate us or that self-
> contradictory waking which would reveal, not that
> we had had, but that we *were*, a dream. [3]

The depreciation indicated by the words "which isn't saying much" and "our fragmentary and phantasmal nature" is frequent in Lewis's writings. Always concerned to check what he regarded as dangerous human tendencies toward undue self-vaunting, Lewis often (and with some Platonic and Christian justification) reminded his readers of the gap between the divine and man. Yet in less guarded moments, particularly in his fiction, he largely forewent the denigration of human beings and exalted them as those to whom God gave the Earth for their use. In the Narnian stories he quite deliberately gave dominion to human beings over a region that is, in all essentials, an animal-land.[4] Quite explicit also was his giving of dominion over the planet Perelandra to the humanoids Tor and Tinidril.[5] In *Perelandra* he placed emphasis upon the fact that dominion over the planet has been transferred, by the express command of Maleldil, from the awesome planetary intelligence that had ruled for preceding aeons to the relatively frail, naive humans. It would be hard to find amid the literature of the Renaissance or the Enlightenment a more dramatic representation of the transfer of authority from the gods to human beings.

How is it possible for a frail, weak reed like man to occupy so exalted a role? Certainly human beings are very near the bottom of the scale of reality, dwelling on Earth like benighted captives in a prison. Doubtless the difficulty lay partly in the structure of the Model, which gave man so humble a state. Seen from another perspective, human beings are wondrously high in the scale of being. Is not man vastly superior to God's other creatures in his powers of reasoning and invention? Does not the Old Testament say that God created men only a little lower than the angels, and gave them dominion over the earth? Lewis could no more than Plato bear to concede that humanity is but the excrescence of primal muck. In his poem "On Being Human" he meditates on this matter.

> Angelic minds, they say, by simple intelligence
> Behold the Forms of nature. They discern
> Unerringly the Archtypes, all the verities
> Which mortals lack or indirectly learn.
> . . . .
> But never an angel knows the knife-edged severance
> Of sun from shadow where the trees begin,
> The blessed cool at every pore caressing us
>   —An angel has no skin.
>
> They see the Form of Air; but mortals breathing it
> Drink the whole summer down into the breast.
> The lavish pinks, the field new-mown, the ravishing

Sea-smells, the wood-fire smoke that whispers *Rest*.
. . . .

Far richer they! I know the senses' witchery
Guards us, like air, from heavens too big to see;
Imminent death to man that barb'd sublimity
And dazzling edge of beauty unsheathed would be.
Yet here, within this tiny, charm'd interior,
This parlour of the brain, their Maker shares
With living men some secrets in a privacy
Forever ours, not theirs.[6]

Reveling, as he does, in this earthiness, vibrancy, and sensuality, Lewis not only agrees that God has made man only a little lower than the angels, but speculates that in some ways human beings have more in common with God than do those ethereal beings. His bold assertion of the cosmic importance of man may involve a non sequitur, but it is understandable.

Inhabiting, as they do, the sublunary region, human beings are imperfect and live in an imperfect environment, where occasion for thinking wrongly and doing evil abounds. For all their imperfections, however, they retain the possibility of ascending to higher levels of reality and ultimately of leaving this realm entirely and being with God.[7] Plato had spoken of this process metaphorically or analogically: the human soul has bits of divine reality resident within it, but these scraps are often submerged by ignorance, error, and dullness; hence the ascent is long and arduous, and at any time the soul may falter and descend to lower levels. He proposed the idea that the soul could ascend to reality only through a series of repeated incarnations in physical bodies, either noble or ignoble depending upon one's conduct in the previous incarnation. Interestingly enough, some versions of the Model regarded the soul as pre-existent, and a few toyed with the Platonic idea of reincarnation. Aside from some infrequent, casual, and hesitant speculation, Lewis had no interest in either of these two ideas on a theological level.[8] With many other aspects of Plato's anthropology, however, he is in considerable agreement.

Plato had found within the self three aspects: the intelligent or rational element, typified by the mind; the willful or spiritual element, represented by the chest; and the sensate or appetitive element, exemplified by the stomach and reproductive organs. The proper state of the self is one of harmony, in which the rational element uses the spirited to control the appetitive. The self that functions smoothly is happy and able to carry out an appropriate role in society; it is also capable of fixing its gaze upon higher realities that will ultimately bring it into the presence of very reality itself. Conversely, the self that is in disorder—Plato used, among other things, the image of a chariot out of control—is unhappy and unable to achieve its highest potentialities.

The Model took over most of the Platonic psychology intact, but enriched it with assorted materials. Lewis described its mature form in *The Discarded Image*. [9] Although actually but a single entity with three parts, the soul was often described as if it were three separate souls. The rational soul was that which separated human beings from animals and made them akin to angels, who were likewise rational. It was man's most distinctive element. "Rational" meant more than simply "syllogistic" or "logical." It included, appropriately enough, both *ratio*, essentially logical reasoning, and *intellectus*, understanding in its widest range of meaning, including the ability to apprehend innate truths that transcended syllogisms. The latter was the seat of knowledge of right human conduct and that part of the person which made the ascent toward the ultimate. Second in esteem came the "sensitive" soul, corresponding to Plato's spirited element. In the Model the term designated the five senses—the outward senses, they were called—as well as memory, estimation, imagination, fantasy, and common sense, which were collectively called the five "wits." Here an elaboration of the Platonic self is evident, for Plato had not given this "middle term" between the intellect and the appetites such specific psychological or physiological functions. Last came the "vegetable" soul, which corresponded closely to Plato's lowest element. Lewis looked upon this anthropology of the Model and its Platonic component with fascination, and he adapted it broadly to his interests. "To be a complete man," he wrote, "means to have the passions obedient to the will and the will offered to God." [10]

Lewis gave careful consideration to the disorder that results when the rational part of the self is unable to control the appetitive by means of the will and habituation. In *The Abolition of Man* he deals with the problem at considerable length:

> Without the aid of trained emotions the intellect is powerless against the animal organism. . . . We were told it all long ago by Plato. As the king governs by his executive, so Reason in man must rule the mere appetites by means of the "spiritual element." The head rules the belly through the chest—the seat, as Alanus tells us, of Magnanimity, of emotions organized by trained habit into stable sentiments. The Chest—Magnanimity—Sentiment—these are the indispensible liaison officers between cerebral man and visceral man. It may even be said that it is by this middle element that man is man: for by his intellect he is mere spirit and by his appetite mere animal. [11]

This understanding of the human situation was largely compatible with Christian doctrine, which held that human beings were created by God with the elements of their souls in proper order. These creatures violated the divine order and allowed their appetites to gain control. By eating the forbidden fruit, Adam and Eve threw themselves into disorder—in Christian terms, into sin. Human beings thus alienated themselves from God, even as in Platonic thought a person ruled by the appetites is alienated from what is real and good. To be sure, Plato assumed that the disordered person was largely ignorant of what was best, whereas the Christian position, while recognizing that some spiritual illness might be the outgrowth of ignorance, was that such a condition should be understood as willful disobedience of God, either by the person or by his or her remote ancestors. Christianity presupposed that there was a dark, evil power in the world, actively seeking to corrupt the divine orderliness in persons; Platonic thought included no such demonic power.[12]

Lewis was most concerned to explicate the nature of the rational part of the soul. Rational creatures, he stated, are those with the ability not only to think abstractly and logically but to apprehend values—that is, to be sensitive to the higher forms of reason with which we have by now become acquainted. One who is governed by reason in this sense means "by 'good' something more than 'good for me' or even 'good for my species.' " Inasmuch as they belong to the animal kingdom, human beings exercising this sort of reason may be called spiritual animals.[13] In seeking the highest good possible, the spiritual animal is reflecting, in a limited way, the rationality and goodness that are in the Godhead itself. God, who is spirit, "created the soul. Its values may be expected, therefore, to contain some reflection or antepast of the spiritual values."[14] Thus by the process that Lewis called transposition, higher reality manifests itself in ways that, although increasingly imperfect as one goes down the scale of reality, nevertheless mirror in some degree the heavenly archetype, or "antepast" as Lewis experimentally dubbed it in this passage. *Ratio* can give conscious direction to the promptings of *intellectus*, while *intellectus* can afford glimpses of reality that *ratio* alone could never have provided. Lewis noted that these glimpses constitute a kind of holiness that came to him even in his pre-Christian days, "before I really knew what it was."[15] Later his conscious reason gave coherence to these experiences and all the other facets of life.

Lewis concretely illustrated his conception of the tripartite soul in his fiction. In the Narnian stories he did so in the most convenient manner possible: the English children who appear in the novels represent the parts of the soul. The four Pevensie children—Peter, the eldest; next, Susan; then Edmund; and, youngest of all, Lucy—serve this purpose exceptionally well. Lucy, who is clearly the author's favorite, exemplifies the rational soul. Lewis chose, however, to have Lucy embody not so much *ratio* as *intellectus*. She has keener spiritual eyes than any of the others, and is therefore quicker to perceive divine realities. It is she who first has the experience of Narnia; and, like Plato's philosopher who comes back into the cave where the chained prisoners think that the shadows they see represent the sum of reality, she finds that the other children only scoff at her description of the other world. She is especially attuned to Aslan; she not only sees him physically on occasions when the other children do not, but also is sensitive to Aslan's wishes as they are not. It is her nature always to be "drinking in everything more deeply than the others"[16] and interpreting the mind of Aslan to the others on various occasions. There is more than a touch of romanticism in Lewis's characterization of Lucy, the innocent child who sees truth better than her sophisticated elders and who, if heeded, can guide her party into right paths; yet that image doubtless also owes something to Jesus's statements about the insights and innocence of children. Even the name Lucy, though the same as that of Owen Barfield's daughter, to whom the first of the Narnian stories is dedicated, is suggestive of the function of Lucy in the stories. She is a type of the person who, though not yet all-knowing and certainly not perfect, is in the process of being initiated into higher truths, of becoming, and already partly being, a light-bearer. In the Platonic sense, she is one in whom the mind is functioning properly, directing the will so that her entire self is wholesome. She is never prey to her appetitive self, for her orientation toward Aslan (even before she hears of him) acts as a rudder to her craft. Lucy's strength and charm serve as a corrective to any facile judgment that Lewis was subtly hostile to women in his writings. Appropriately enough Lewis provides, as Lucy's symbol, a vial containing a cordial that restores the sick to health.[17] Thus Lucy serves as an aide to Aslan himself in his task of bringing wholeness of self—salvation—to the Narnian world.

Peter, as the eldest of the group, assumes the role of ostensible leader of the four, and ultimately becomes the High King of Narnia. Although his mannerisms and language are particularly medieval—or perhaps because they are so—he is a reasonably close approximation of Plato's guardian class, who correspond in turn to the spirited, habituated element in the individual soul. Although he is not lacking in common sense, he acts most often on the basis of an ingrained code or morality, much as Plato expected that his warrior class would do. He is relatively solemn, matter-of-fact in facing problems, and of unhesitating moral rectitude. He is the defender of Aslan's laws, which he perceives in a rather straightforward manner. His insights are sensible but seldom imaginative, and the quality of mercy seldom motivates him. His special magical device is a sword, accompanied by a shield. The sword is suggestive of his namesake, the apostle Peter, who also became the manifest leader of the believers in Christ and then the spiritual ruler of Christendom; otherwise, however, the boy has none of the traditional characteristics of the apostle. He is far better understood in Platonic terms, as the middle element between the intellect and the appetites. With the help of Lucy's spiritual insight, he is able to rule his subjects in an enlightened manner, like a true Platonic guardian.

Edmund, the third eldest Pevensie child, is a case-study in Platonic psychology. Lewis initially conceived Edmund as one in whom the appetites held sway. As the first Narnian story begins, he is a greedy, shortsighted, and disloyal boy whose hedonism and selfishness are characterized by his love of the confection called Turkish delight—the highest good that he can imagine. He is, in Platonic terms, a person whose self is in disorder because the appetites have subdued reason and demoralized the spirited element. The other children intuitively perceive Edmund's disorder, even though they are helpless to alleviate it. Edmund is obviously seeking his own good, as he erroneously understands it to be. Because his vision is limited he is moving in the wrong direction morally and metaphysically; his need, therefore, is to be able to perceive what his best interests really are.

It was important to Lewis that Edmund be shown as undergoing a reform of personality, even though to do so meant to lose his prime example of a platonically disordered self. As the story progresses, Edmund gains more information about the White Witch, who has led him into error, and his own rational processes cause him to discern the ephemeral, self-destructive nature of his former loves. Growing ashamed of the results of his foolishness and greed, he becomes receptive to the instruction that Aslan imparts word and deed. To this extent he represents the ideal student of philosophy, who responds positively to his teacher's nudges and comes to a more realistic understanding of the nature of the Good. He is very much like one of the prisoners in Plato's analogy of the cave: His ascent into the real world is by degrees, and not without a certain amount of initial resistance on his part. But he does eventually complete the spiritual journey.

There is, however, another major aspect to the growth of Edmund's self: the Christian. Lewis did not simply have Edmund develop a more appropriate view of what was in his best interest; he had him be saved. Edmund does nothing that earns him merit in Aslan's eyes, nor does he save himself. His redemption is ultimately Aslan's free gift to him as a sinner. As according to Christian doctrine Christ died for the sins of mankind, so Aslan dies a sacrificial death on the stone table to atone for Edmund's sins.[18] Thus Lewis fuses, in much the same manner as some theologians had done in centuries before him, the Platonic and Christian concepts of how one enters into a proper relationship with the absolute and the Good. After his salvation Edmund lives a life of exemplary rectitude from both the Platonic and the Christian point of view.[19] He is no longer controlled by his lower elements and is no longer in disorder. Lewis thus transforms him into Edmund the Just, meaning by the title not simply that he is fair-minded, but that the elements of his soul function harmoniously, with higher reason in control and his mind directed toward the absolute.

In an even broader sense Lewis accepted the Christian belief that, properly speaking, there is no possibility for a person to have a truly ordered self apart from the redemptive work of Christ. Christ becomes the model for the balanced self. "God himself, as Son, from all eternity, renders back to God as Father by filial obedience the being which the Father by paternal love eternally generates in the Son. This is the pattern which man was made to imitate—which Paradisal man did imitate—and wherever the will conferred by the Creator is thus perfectly offered back in delighted and delighting obedience by the crea-

174

ture, there, most undoubtedly, is Heaven, and there the Holy Ghost proceeds." [20] It is not that by becoming a Christian a person takes on perfect harmony of self; Lewis knew well enough that Christians are still vulnerable to sin, and do sin. What one does is to rely upon Christ to impute righteousness, and to await the putting on of an incorruptible body in Heaven.

We have yet to consider the fourth of the Pevensie children, Susan. Since he has already matched three of the children to the three elements of the soul, Lewis had nothing new with which to identify the elder girl. [21] His solution was to allow Susan to represent a particularly modern form of personality disorder that he deplored. Plato had assumed that if a person had a disordered self, it was because the spirited element or the appetites had come to dominate the reason. He did not clearly envision a situation in which something might go wrong within the reasoning part of the mind; yet Lewis perceived that disorder could indeed occur within the rational self, producing twisted metaphysics and mores of the sort found in materialism, naturalism, and relativism. It is this kind of disorder that he allowed Susan to embody. From the outset, yet more notably as the Narnian stories unfold, Susan plays the role of the pragmatist, the scoffer, the positivist, the unimaginative child of the nineteenth and twentieth centuries. She is the victim, not of her appetites, but of her limited rationality. In her, reason can achieve no more than shortsighted practicality and common sense; all higher reason is lacking. In spite of her actual experiences in Narnia, she has made up her mind that events can happen only in a mechanistic way; therefore she gradually shuts Narnia and Aslan from her mind as nonexistent. Her plight is far worse than Edmund's, for she is moving not only toward spiritual disorder but toward disintegration of the self. Lewis handles her brusquely enough: In *The Last Battle* she is missing from the band of friends of Narnia. When someone inquires about her absence, the other children matter-of-factly explain:

"My sister Susan," answered Peter shortly and gravely, "is no longer a friend of Narnia."
"Yes," said Eustace, "and whenever you've tried to

175

get her to come and talk about Narnia or do anything about Narnia, she says 'What wonderful memories you have! Fancy your still thinking about all those funny games we used to play when we were children!' "

"Oh Susan! " said Jill, "she's interested in nothing now-a-days except nylons and lipstick and invitations. She always was a jolly sight too keen on being grown-up." [22]

For Susan, being grown-up means regarding God, beauty, and imagination as worthless fantasies. It is not surprising that Lewis did not permit her to enter the heavenly Narnia, for she has alienated herself from Heaven forever, like the ghosts of Hell in *The Great Divorce*. [23]

Some other persons in the Narnian tales also embody aspects of the tripartite soul in noticeable fashion. Although he had achieved a satisfactory reorientation of Edmund's personality in the first of the Narnian stories, Lewis felt the continuing need for a figure with disordered personality, if for no other reason than to heighten the action and provide better character differentiation. In *The Voyage of the Dawn Treader* he introduced a new boy, Eustace Scrubb, who has much the same spiritual malady that had beset Edmund. Eustace's punishment for his selfishness, greed, and quarrelsomeness is to be turned into a dragon. [24] Lewis had utilized the fairy-tale figure of a dragon much earlier in *The Pilgrim's Regress;* there the Northern Dragon represents tension, hardness, possessiveness, coldness, and anemia, and was cannibalistic and hoarded gold, just as he does in the Narnian story. [25] Lewis could not bring himself to leave Eustace unredeemed, and soon had him undergo a metamorphosis in which Aslan strips away his dragon's body with his sharp, divine claws. [26] Having tasted a bit of Hell, Eustace is henceforth a much more integrated, ordered self. One might also mention the talking mouse, Reepicheep, who is an almost pure type of Plato's spirited element or guardian. [27] There are, of course, many characters in the stories whose personalities do not reflect Platonic psychology in any striking way, but it cannot be expected that Lewis could develop all personages equally in terms of his philosophical orientation; a considerable amount of his space is devoted to telling interesting, fast-paced stories.

The situation is somewhat similar in the planetary romances. There Lewis permitted some of his protagonists to exemplify states of the tripartite soul.[28] Ransom, who is the most elaborately drawn character in Lewis's fiction except for Orual in *Till We Have Faces*, is a type of human soul in healthy condition. Indeed, he approximates more than any other of Lewis's characters the ideal Platonic person.[29] Although not so broadly educated as Plato's philosopher-ruler should be, he is one in whom the intellect is functioning properly. He reasons not only by *ratio*, as can his enemy Weston, but also by *intellectus*; he can therefore grow in wisdom, as Weston cannot. Lewis did not attempt to explain why Ransom has an affinity for eternal verities while Weston does not, and perhaps no explanation is possible; Ransom is what he is and Weston is what he is. Each character develops until the full implications of his personality become apparent: Ransom ascends into the ethereal, while Weston sinks into nonentity. Even while just commencing his initiation into cosmic truths on Perelandra, Ransom is guided by his *intellectus* in passing tests that most other persons would fail, such as his wise refusal to gorge himself on delicious fruit that a greedier person would not have resisted. He thus fulfills, on an adult level, much the same role that Lucy fulfills on a child's level.[30]

As for Weston himself, we have already seen that he is the personification of all that is potentially destructive and wrongheaded in modern science and materialism. In this regard he corresponds to Susan in the Narnian stories. But here the spiritual, and ultimately physical, malaise is far worse. Weston is profoundly evil. He is at heart bestial, for he has surrendered to the baser elements of his soul, including jealousy and cruelty.[31] When the reader first encounters him in *Out of the Silent Planet* his failing is identified almost entirely as his dedication to scientism (as Lewis called it), although hints of his destructive lower self are present. By the time that Satan has possessed him in *Perelandra* he has forgotten most of his scientism, for Satan has no interest in that per se, and he is a base creature of appetites—a cosmic horror that resembles, though in much more acute form, the dragon that the boy Eustace became when he surrendered to his appetites.[32]

A more straightforward embodiment of the appetitive element of the soul is Devine, whose sole motivation in *Out of the Silent Planet* is greed. He is lacking in even the pretense of moral concern, and when the opportunity arises he displays a low sensuality. He reappears in *That Hideous Strength* under the alias of Lord Feverstone; there he is suave and calculating but as immoral and self-centered as ever. Like all human beings, he can employ logic up to a point, but he often resorts to false data or subtly twisted syllogisms, with the result that his conclusions are erroneous and even dangerous. Thus he exemplifies what Edmund or Eustace might have been as adults if they had not responded to the intervention of divine redemptive power.

Is there, then, no turning back of the soul once it has commenced a downward drift? To be sure there is; otherwise the sacrificial death of Christ would mean nothing. Nevertheless, the way to spiritual health is not an easy one. Lewis presented a fictional world that is relatively static: The good tend to remain good and the evil remain evil, with relatively few exceptions. His novels resemble, in this regard, Greek tragedies, in which the interest consists not in how the protagonists can alter their fate (for they cannot) but in how their personalities unfold as they respond to the inevitable. Lewis was not, however, a determinist. Neither was he able to accept the Calvinistic doctrine of predestination. As he said through the person of George MacDonald in *The Great Divorce*, the doctrine of predestination "shows (truly enough) that eternal reality is not waiting for a future in which to be real; but at the price of removing Freedom which is the deeper truth of the two." [33] People are what they are because they have made crucial choices throughout their lives. Although these choices necessarily appear within a temporal framework, they are essentially timeless manifestations of the true desires of those persons. Hence Lewis regarded each person as responsible for his or her ultimate state of beatitude or damnation.

Among the most interesting and provocative instances of one

of Lewis's fictional personages regaining his divinely intended spiritual health is that of a ghost from Hell in *The Great Divorce* who bears on his shoulder a red lizard "twitching its tail like a whip and whispering things in his ear" (p. 99). The animal is symbolic of the appetitive element of the soul; it has left its rightful place and has assumed control of the whole self. When an angel offers to kill the lizard—an act of divine grace—the ghost shrinks back, for he does not really wish the monster's influence to be broken. Several times the angel asks, "May I kill it? " Each time the ghost answers evasively.

> "Please, I never meant to be such a nuisance.
> Please—really—don't bother. Look! It's gone to sleep of
> its own accord. I'm sure it'll be all right now. Thanks
> ever so much."
> "May I kill it? "
> "Honestly, I don't think there's the slightest
> necessity for that. I'm sure I shall be able to keep it in
> order now. I think the gradual process would be far
> better than killing it." (Pp. 100–101)

The angel persists, calmly rejecting all excuses until at last the ghost tells him, in an instant of decision, "Do what you like." The angel strangles the reptile and flings it away as the ghost screams in agony. Then Lewis, as narrator, records: "For a moment I could make out nothing distinctly. Then I saw, between me and the nearest bush, unmistakably solid but growing every moment solider, the upper arm and the shoulder of a man. Then, brighter still and stronger, the legs and hands. The neck and golden head materialised while I watched, and if my attention had not wavered I should have seen the actual completing of a man—an immense man, naked, not much smaller than the Angel" (p. 103). The former inhabitant of Hell, the ghost in bondage to himself, has now assumed his true nature and is like the angels in Heaven. He will not return to Hell with the others, but will remain in the realm of reality. As for the lizard, Lewis writes:

> At the same moment something seemed to be

happening to the Lizard. At first I thought the operation had failed. So far from dying, the creature was still struggling and even growing bigger as it struggled. And as it grew it changed. Its hinder parts grew rounder. The tail, still flickering, became a tail of hair that flickered between huge and glossy buttocks. Suddenly I started back, rubbing my eyes. What stood before me was the greatest stallion I have ever seen, silvery white but with mane and tail of gold. It was smooth and shining, rippled with swells of flesh and muscle, whinneying and stamping with its hoofs. At each stamp the land shook and the trees dindled.

The new-made man turned and clapped the new horse's neck. It nosed his bright body. Horse and master breathed each into the other's nostrils. . . . In joyous haste the young man leaped upon the horse's back. Turning in his seat he waved a farewell, then nudged the stallion with his heels. They were off before I well knew what was happening. There was riding if you like! (Pp. 103–4)

Lewis's imagery here of the spiritually healthy person controlling his passions as a strong rider manages his horse was probably influenced directly by Plato's description of reason as a charioteer keeping the appetites under close rein. The man rides off, like Apollo in his glory, into a landscape similar to that of Aslan's country in *The Last Battle,* and disappears into the rose-brightness of Heaven's everlasting morning while the earth, woods, and waters—in other words, nature—sing with joy. "The Nature or Arch-nature of that land rejoiced to have been once more ridden, and therefore consummated, in the person of the horse. It sang, *'The master says to our master, Come up. Share my rest and splendour till all natures that were your enemies become slaves to dance before you and backs for you to ride. . . . Overcome us that, so overcome, we may be ourselves'* " (p. 105). Thus, says Lewis, does appetite, which threatened to destroy man when it dominated him, become a magnificent, ennobling servant when it is subjected to him.

The appetitive element of the soul is not itself evil. Lewis did not, like the Gnostics regard all that is material or earthy as inimical to the good. Like Plato he recognizes that the phenomenal world has its part in the grand cosmic design. For this stance he had ample biblical warrant as well. Nevertheless, the New Testament contains many passages that encourage the Christian to live a moderate, self-controlled life, and stronger tendencies towards asceticism arose subsequently within Christianity. Lewis had a discernably high regard for the disciplined Christian life, which at times veered toward asceticism.[34] He wanted to control his appetites so that his body would serve his mind the better, but he did not pummel his flesh for the salvation of his soul. Indeed, he preferred to regard the appetites as a potential boon; after all, if they served no proper function, God would not have placed them in the human body. Hence he could write, "Every *natural* thing which is not itself sinful can become the servant of the spiritual life, but none is automatically so." [35]

Lewis was not inclined to dissect the appetites after the fashion of a psychologist, but he did once suggest that "sensuality really arises more from the imagination than from the appetites; which, if left merely to their own animal strength, and not elaborated by our imagination, would be fairly easily managed." [36] Among his ephemeral writings there is a short, whimsical paragraph dealing with this matter.

> "You are always dragging me down," said I to my Body. "Dragging *you* down! " replied my Body. "Well I like that! Who taught me to like tobacco and alcohol? You, of course, with your idiotic adolescent idea of being 'grown-up.' My palate loathed both at first: but you would have your way. Who put an end to all those angry and revengeful thoughts last night? Me, of course, by insisting on going to sleep. Who does his best to keep you from talking too much and eating too much by giving you dry throats and headaches and indigestion? Eh? "And what about sex? " said I. "Yes, what about it? " retorted the Body. "If you and your wretched imagination would leave me alone I'd give

you no trouble. That's Soul all over; you give me orders and then blame me for carrying them out." [37]

Thus he recognized, to an extent that Plato perhaps never fully did, that the mind is the seat not only of reason but of the appetites as well.

Like many another thinker, Lewis was inclined to suppose that the best way to keep unwanted passions out of the mind was to be preoccupied with such strong positive thoughts that troublesome notions could find no entry.[38] In reporting to his brother Warren a conversation he had had with their father, he wrote: "I was talking I think about not letting one's mind brood on fears or grievances. He replied, 'What on earth do you mean by controlling the imagination? One controls one's appetites.' That is the whole psychology of his generation in a nutshell, isn't it? A man sits thinking of whiskey and making 'iron rules' not to drink any, with much contortion of the face and 'Oh Lords' until the inevitable moment when he finds some excellent reason for breaking the iron rule. The idea of a simpler method—that of applying his mind to something else and using a little concentration—would never occur." [39] Plato, convinced that no person knowingly acts against his own genuine best interests, would have approached the problem differently: He would have tried, through argumentation and illustration, to lead the unfortunate man to realize that drinking was not in his best interest, that the momentary pleasure to be gotten from drinking was far less than the long-term pleasure to be had from not drinking. And, one may venture to add, he would probably not have succeeded in persuading him. How effective Lewis's solution would be is a debatable matter.

Lewis nowhere presented a systematic description of the conduct of the well-ordered self. Doubtless he would have suspected that no formulations of right conduct could be more than approximate—not because he believed that proper behavior was relative (he did not) but because of the inherent limitations of all language. Still, his writings contain numerous discussions of right conduct in which he delineated the various important elements of the ordered life. The universal code of right conduct he set forth, as we have noted, in *The Abolition of Man*. The more specific code of Christian life he enunciated in his small book *Christian Behavior,* which became Part 3 of *Mere Christianity.*[40] In his discussion of Christian conduct in that work he stayed closely within traditional Christianity, even to the point of elucidating the meaning contained in the venerable cardinal virtues and the great triad of faith, hope, and love. Inasmuch as his explication of Christian morality is so readily available there, that information need not be repeated. A few special matters pertaining to the good life do, however, warrant some attention.

Traditional and broadly pietistic though it is, Lewis's understanding of right conduct is not effete. Hatred is a case in point. Although he inculcated love and generally denounced hating, Lewis was quite prepared to commend hate under certain circumstances. His logic was simple and Aristotelian. That hate is a human emotion cannot be denied, and one must suppose that God would not have implanted in persons any emotion for which there was not some legitimate purpose. Hence there must be legitimate objects of hatred; the only need is to determine what these may be. Irrational or self-serving hatred, or the hatred of persons, must routinely be excluded,[41] but it is quite appropriate for one to hate what is inimical to God or to the Good. Thus the Christian can and should hate Satan and all that is evil. In his protracted struggle with Weston in *Perelandra*, Ransom experiences justifiable hate:

> An experience that perhaps no good man can ever have
> in our world came over him—a torrent of perfectly
> unmixed and lawful hatred. The energy of hating,
> never before felt without some guilt, without some dim
> knowledge that he was failing fully to distinguish the
> sinner from the sin, rose into his arms and legs till he
> felt that they were pillars of burning blood. What was
> before him appeared no longer a creature of corrupted
> will. It was corruption itself to which will was attained
> only as an instrument. Ages ago it had been a Person:
> but the ruins of personality now survived in it only as
> weapons at the disposal of a furious self-exiled

183

negation. It is perhaps difficult to understand why this filled Ransom not with horror but with a kind of joy. The joy came from finding at last what hatred was made for. (Pp. 155–56)

Subsequently Ransom kills the Satan-possessed Weston and saves Perelandra from falling into the thrall of evil.

It follows that Lewis was not opposed to violence and killing if such were required for the maintenance of world order.[42] In order to save the world from the onslaught of evil, says Ransom in *That Hideous Strength*, "we must be ready both to kill and die."[43] This stance was contrary neither to Plato, who had assumed that the ideal state would need to have soldiers to defend the right, nor to traditional Christians, who had long been familiar with the concept of a just war. The Narnian tales are amply supplied with episodes of battle between the forces of Aslan and those of evil; these are, however, relatively mild compared with the bloody slaughter of the enemies of Maleldil that climaxes *That Hideous Strength*. Some of Lewis's defense of the concept of the just war may be attributable to the threat that the Axis powers posed for Britain during World War II, a time when extremely few voices were heard in support of pacifism anywhere among the Allied Nations; still, his convictions went deeper than that crisis.

It should not be thought that Lewis was giving tacit approval to the notion that the end justifies the means. War is not an unjust means used for some ultimate good purpose; battle with evil is inherent in the full meaning of being a Christian. He strongly insisted that the means one employs lie within the bounds of morality. In *That Hideous Strength* Ransom tells his Company of Logres that they cannot be like their enemies, "breaking all the rules whenever we imagine that it might possibly do some vague good to humanity in the remote future."[44] Indeed, the very means by which one does things are ends, in the sense that means are all the things that one does in life; and God judges a person by the way he has gone about living. Generally those who claim that the end justifies the means have no nobler ends than means.

The Self

The life of the self in which all of the parts are in harmony is far more than one of intellectual concepts or routine responsibilities; it is one that is intensely satisfying. What gives such a life its value is the fact that it imitates the nature of the divine insofar as possible. "Since God is blessed, omnipotent, sovereign and creative, there is obviously a sense in which happiness, strength, freedom and fertility (whether of mind or body), whenever they appear in human life, constitute likenesses, and in that way proximities, to God." [45] Happiness includes joyousness, jocundity, and a mature sense of humor; fertility consists of seminality, sensuousness (but not license), and energy. These vigorous elements Lewis found, inter alia, in the Christian Platonism of his Renaissance mentor Spenser, as a perusal of *Spencer's Images of Life* readily evinces. [46] The ordered self has an individuality and spontaneity that spring from the very nature of the universal processes, and it is not reluctant to express itself, as we have seen, in dancing, singing, and a kind of orderly ecstasy that was quite different from a romantic or nihilistic loosing of all restraints.

The self that is in harmony is one that turns toward God in prayer and worship and toward fellow creatures in love and service. [47] Unlike Plato, Lewis had little interest in the structure of society, and indeed was suspicious of all attempts to reform the social order through human endeavor. His social program was simple and pietistic: If enough persons live Christian lives, society will function well. Toward religious institutions and their rites Lewis had ambivalent feelings. On the one hand, his respect for doing things in established ways and his general respect for authority within society prompted him to attend Anglican services dutifully, and even to dislike departures from the customary order of worship; on the other, his love of freedom and his dislike of all regimentation tended to lead him away from almost all kinds of cultus. Public worship was to him, one of his friends has noted, a duty rather than a delight. "I have," he confessed, "a sort of spiritual *gaucherie* which makes me unapt to participate in any rite." [48] The relative absence of religious institutions in Lewis's writings, and particularly in his fiction, suggests the ambivalence of his thought on cultus. One does find, however, considerable interest in private religious practices in Lewis's apologetic works and occasionally in his fiction.[49]

Lewis was greatly concerned about the proper education of the self. Not only in *The Abolition of Man* but at several places in the Narnian stories he fired oblique salvos at subjectively oriented education.[50] How, then, does one apprehend reality? Plato had been convinced that learning was essentially an interior process rather than something done by the teacher to the pupil. The soul had within it the potentiality for perceiving reality; the task of the teacher was largely that of facilitating the process of self-discovery. To account for the innate affinity of the soul for absolute truth, Plato was led to postulate the eternal existence of the individual soul, and to suppose that it ultimately had a divine origin. There was a measure of commonality between this view and Christian doctrine, to the extent that both held the soul to be something other than material and to continue to exist after the death of the body. Christians did not, however, believe in the existence of the soul prior to conception, nor did they believe that the individual soul undergoes repeated rebirths.

Where Plato and Christianity diverge, Lewis predictably sided with Christianity in his theological treatises. Yet in his fiction he sometimes fell back upon Platonic and Neoplatonic thought, perhaps in part because it afforded him a dramatic and philosophical dimension that Christian doctrine lacked. Thus we find, for instance, Ransom's descent into the atmosphere of Malacandra described in ways that suggest the Neoplatonic descent of the soul from the celestial realm into the sublunary region. When later Ransom goes to the capital of the planet, the oyarsa says to him, "Creatures of your kind must drop out of heaven into a world." [51] By "creatures of your kind" the planetary governor seems to mean "souls" of the sort that exist in all human beings.

It follows from this conception of the soul's descent into the earthly miasma that the soul will grow forgetful of its heavenly origin during its earthy incarnation. Alsan says to Jill Pole in *The Silver Chair*, "Here on the mountain I have spoken to you clearly:

I will not often do so down in Narnia. Here on the mountain, the air is clear and your mind is clear; as you drop down into Narnia, the air will thicken. Take great care that it does not confuse your mind." [52] Jill's mind does indeed grow forgetful and confused, as it must in spite of Aslan's caution. But, clouded though the soul's vision of the good is on Earth, there remains in each person a flickering, sputtering flame of divine truth that can be fanned into a clearer, more illuminating light under suitable circumstances. This concept is, of course, Plato's famous theory of recollection, and Lewis accepted the insight unhesitatingly. Like Plato, he was impressed by the fact that people have a particular ability to compare experiential data with some kind of standard deep within their minds—a standard that cannot, in most instances, be brought to light and examined methodically, yet one that seems to him to be as absolute in its judgments as a mathematical principle. He gave, among others, this homey example: "A young man meets a girl. The whole world looks different when he sees her. Her voice reminds him of something he has been trying to remember all his life, and ten minutes casual chat with her is more precious than all the favours that all other women in the world could grant. He is, as they say, 'in love.' " [53] What the young man is doing, Lewis assumed, is unconsciously comparing the girl in his presence with a standard of womanliness resident in his mind, and finding that the girl measures up exceptionally well to that standard. Lewis's reasoning here is essentially the same as that pertaining to the universal validity of basic moral judgments, and is consistent with both Platonism and his own objectivism. The standard of beauty in the young man's mind, he opined, is not simply a subjective preference but a reflection of absolute beauty. He did not bother to consider why, if the standard of beauty is absolute and universal, all other young men ought not also to fall in love with this same girl; if pressed, however, he would doubtless answer that there is indeed such a thing as fundamental agreement among men of normal intelligence as to what constitutes feminine beauty, all cultural vagaries aside.

Lewis illustrated this concept of recollection at numerous

places in his works. When the English children who enter Narnia are first told by the Beaver about Aslan their response is immediate and unlearned.

> None of the children knew who Aslan was any more than you do; but the moment the Beaver had spoken these words everyone felt quite different. Perhaps it has sometimes happened to you in a dream that someone says something which you don't understand but in the dream it feels as if it had some enormous meaning—either a terrifying one which turns the whole dream into a nightmare or else a lovely meaning too lovely to put into words, which makes the dream so beautiful that you remember it all your life and are always wishing you could get into that dream again. It was like that now. At the name of Aslan each one of the children felt something jump in his inside. Edmund felt a sensation of mysterious horror. Peter felt suddenly brave and adventurous. Susan felt as if some delicious smell or some delightful strain of music had just floated by her. And Lucy got the feeling you have when you wake up in the morning and realise that it is the beginning of the holidays or the beginning of summer. [54]

The children are recollecting something that has always been inside them, but that previously had not come to consciousness for lack of the right stimulus. With proper reminders, conceivably from within but more often from outside, they can kindle the smoldering divine flame and live their lives in greater accord with the reality of God. They still have need, of course, for much instruction about and experience of Aslan himself if they are to ascend higher on the spiritual path. [55] The same concept of recollection appears in *The Last Battle,* where the unicorn exclaims as he enters Aslan's country that he has "come home at last." This, he says, "is the land I have been looking for all my life, though I never knew it until now," and then he adds, "The reason why we loved the old Narnia is that it sometimes looked a little like this" (p. 171). The same idea also appears in the planetary romances. In a moment of reflection upon the delights of Perelandra that he has learned to know, Ransom senses a correspondence between the external impressions of the planet and his unconscious knowledge of something akin to those impressions. "The cord of longing which drew him to the invisible isle seemed to him at that moment to have been fastened long, long before his coming to Perelandra, long before the earliest times that memory could recover in his childhood, before birth, before the birth of man himself, before the origins of time. It was sharp, sweet, wild, and holy, all in one." These recollections are not so much Jungian archetypes as buried memories of reality itself, of which the archetypes are but universal manifestations in the mind of man.[56] And they have nothing whatever to do with the Freudian model of the mind.

It will be noticed that in the preceding instances the earthly stimulus for recollection of the absolute is much less intense than the thing recalled. This is as it should be in Lewis's Christian objectivism. The copy cannot be more real than reality itself. The object of one's spiritual longing must always be purer, brighter, more beautiful, and more satisfying than any earthly adumbrations of it. Thus the water on Malacandra "was not merely blue in certain lights like terrestrial water but 'really' blue." [57] As the unfallen planet Malacandra is to Earth in intensity, so infinitely more must reality itself be than all phenomenal manifestations of it. The degrees of the hierarchy of reality are so many that, as elsewhere in his metaphysics, Lewis tended to drift off into an intellectual version of cosmic mysticism.

This essentially Platonic psychology of recollection had already been acclimatized to Christianity centuries earlier. In the thought of Augustine there is a fairly close approximation to the Platonic concept. Within each person there is a self-instructor which guides the soul toward the true light; this instructor is identified as none other than Christ himself, whose spirit is actively teaching within each believer and, to some extent, within the nonbeliever as well. This inner revelation is powerfully supplemented by external instruction of the kind that comes through Christ's earthly incarnation, as remembered in the New Testament and the church.

The person whose soul is engaged in religious edification is one who at first has only the dimmest of inklings about reality. It is not surprising that Lewis prefaced Book 1 of *The Pilgrim's Regress* with three quotations that deal with precisely this matter of recollections: first Plato, then Boethius, then Hooker, all of whom Lewis knew stood within the venerable line of philosophic tradition that he identified as Old Western Culture and the Model. The emphasis in that work is upon the length, difficulty, and number of by-ways of the road that leads to knowledge. Thus for Lewis the doctrine of the recollection of the soul is intimately linked with the spiritual ascent of the soul toward reality, and has eschatological overtones.

The goal of the soul is, of course, to be with God. At times Lewis wrote as if the soul's deepest longing is for the extinction of individuation, for the merging of itself with its divine source. "The state in which a man is 'nearest' to God are those in which he is most surely and swiftly approaching his final union with God, vision of God and enjoyment of God." [58] The individual soul is to be "taken into the dance," [59] to become an inseparable part of the absolute. To the extent that selfhood implies selfishness it must be abandoned. "The golden apple of selfhood, thrown among the false gods, became an apple of discord because they scrambled for it. They did not know the first rule of the holy game, which is that every player must by all means touch the ball and then immediately pass it on. To be found with it in your hands is a fault: to cling to it, death. But when it flies to and fro among the players too swift for eye to follow, and the great master Himself leads the revelry, giving Himself eternally to His creatures in the generation, and back to Himself in the sacrifice, of the Word, then indeed the eternal dance 'makes heaven drowsy with the harmony.' " [60] Still, Lewis loved his individuality, and above all his own, discrete mind; and there runs clearly throughout his works an unquenchable desire for self-fulfillment rather than self-annihilation. He was able to hold the two contrary concepts together by postulating, as supernaturalists before him had often done, that in the denial of the self there is fulfillment of the self. Ultimately he was unable to go very far beyond this paradox.

When considering the ultimate fate of the soul, Lewis took his departure directly from Christian teaching, where the concepts of Heaven and an afterlife for the individual person were highly developed. The only goal toward which the well-ordered self may and should look is Heaven. After all, the serious business of Heaven is joy for its participants.[61] To be sure, getting into Heaven will undoubtedly involve pain for the self, just as Eustace had to undergo the cleansing claws of Aslan. But the result will be the same sort of shining, vigorous spiritual being that rode off into Heaven in *The Great Divorce*. Likening human beings to rabbits, Lewis once declared, "We shall bleed and squeal as the handfuls of fur come out; and then, surprisingly, we shall find underneath it all a thing we have never yet imagined: a real Man, an ageless god, a son of God, strong, radiant, wise, beautiful and drenched in joy." [62] Elsewhere he described the heavenly state of the soul in terms of glory—glory as brightness, splendour, and luminosity: "We are to shine as the sun, we are to be given the Morning Star. . . . The poets and the mythologies know all about it. We do not want merely to *see* beauty, though, God knows, even that is bounty enough. We want something else which can hardly be put into words—to be united with the beauty we see, to pass into, to receive it into ourselves, to bathe in it, to become part of it." [63] He was not contradicting what he had said elsewhere. The self is not being swallowed up in the godhead to the point that no individuality is left. He was using the hyperbolic language of the mystic and the preacher, not the cool language of the theologian. He continued:

> Some day, God willing, we shall get *in*. When human souls have become as perfect in voluntary obedience as the inanimate creation is in its lifeless obedience, then they will put on its glory, or rather that greater glory of which Nature is only the first sketch. For you must not think that I am putting forward any heathen fancy of

being absorbed into Nature. Nature is mortal; we shall outlive her. When all the suns and nebulae have passed away, each of you will still be alive. . . . And in there, in beyond Nature, we shall eat of the tree of life. At present, if we are reborn in Christ, the spirit in us lives directly on God; but the mind, and still more the body, receives life from Him at a thousand removes. . . . What would it be to taste at the fountain-head that stream of which even these lower reaches prove so intoxicating? Yet that, I believe, is what lies before us. The whole man is to drink joy from the fountain of joy. As St. Augustine said, the rapture of the saved soul will "flow over" into the glorified body. In the light of our present specialized and depraved appetites we cannot imagine this *torrens voluptatis,* and I warn everyone most seriously not to try. But it must be mentioned, to drive out thoughts even more misleading—thoughts that what is saved is a mere ghost, or that the risen body lives in numb insensibility. The body was made for the Lord, and these dismal fancies are wide of the mark.[64]

This heavenly joy is not, he cautioned, to be confused with the mere prolongation of earthly happiness.[65] Even though he had no choice in his fiction except to liken heavenly joys to earthly delights, he tried to suggest that the heavenly joys are more than quantitative; they are qualitative as well, and the most wondrous of them lie beyond all present mortal anticipations.[66] Such was his confidence in the outcome of the present earthly existence for the soul that has turned toward God.

Evil and Eschatology

Bad cannot succeed even in being bad as truly as good is good. If all Hell's miseries together entered the consciousness of yon wee yellow bird on the bough there, they would be swallowed up without trace.

The Great Divorce

N his understanding of evil Lewis was influenced by both Christianity and Platonism. He had relatively little to say about natural evil—the sort of thing that happens when, say, someone breaks a leg or a steamship sinks—but he presupposed that in a world in which there was genuine freedom there must be the possibility that evil could occur. A world without evil would be not only deterministic but boring. He also accepted in considerable measure the traditional argument that the presence of evil makes the good all the more apparent and desirable.[1] The only naturally evil creature on Malacandra—there are no morally evil ones, save for the newly arrived human beings—is the *hnakra*, a dragon-like creature that has been placed there by Maleldil. When Ransom objects to the existence of such an animal, his Malacandran companion declares that "the *hnakra* is our enemy, but he is also our beloved," and goes on with a paean to the creature that is reminiscent of the encomiums to certain fearsome creatures in the Book of Job. "I do not think," he concludes, "the forest would be so bright, nor the water so warm, nor love so sweet, if there were no danger in the lakes. . . . I drank life because death was in the pool."[2] The beast does not behave maliciously; it is his divinely appointed nature to kill. Lewis's willingness to concede that evil may serve some larger good purpose was probably heavily influenced by his monism, as well as the fact that in the Old Testament God is said to be the creator of even loathsome, dangerous creatures. Underlying this viewpoint one may also detect the familiar concept of Aristotelian-Christian theology that God has put nothing in the world that is not in some integral way related to the whole and that does not serve some ultimate—and therefore ultimately good—purpose. It is in such a way that Lewis justified, in part, the existence of pain in human experience.[3]

Moral evil—that is, the wrongness human beings do, such as stealing and murdering—constituted a more difficult problem. For his solution to that problem Lewis borrowed from Plato a central philosophical insight that was only inchoate in Christian thought, the conviction that evil is not an entity in its own right but the corruption of goodness. He was aware of the belief of certain medieval thinkers that God had no opposite. "Every sin," he wrote, "is the distortion of an energy breathed into us."[4] In one of his letters he declared, "I don't think evil, in the strict sense, can *create*. It can spoil something that Another has created."[5] He emphasized this conviction in *The Great Divorce*, where he asserted that "bad cannot succeed even in being bad as truly as good is good."[6] Evil feeds upon the good, manipulates it, conceals it, and otherwise attempts to destroy it. It is nothing more than a parasite; it has no roots of its own.

The most explicit discussion of the nonentity of evil in Lewis's writings appears in *Mere Christianity*, where Lewis is in the process of denying validity to the claims of metaphysical dualism—the view that there are two independent, competing and very nearly matched opposing forces in the universe that are constantly engaged in a contest for superiority, winner take all. He had no small fascination with dualism, and confessed that "next to Christianity Dualism is the manliest and most sensible creed on the market."[7] Nevertheless, the idea of two competing realities was absurd from the Platonic point of view. Although dualism took evil seriously, it required the supposition that there can be an evil that is virtually as real and powerful as the good. Such a view, Lewis argued, involves a basic metaphysical error.

> If Dualism is true, then the bad Power must be a being who likes badness for its own sake. But in reality we have no experience of anyone liking badness just because it is bad. The nearest we can get to it is in cruelty. But in real life people are cruel for one of two reasons—either because they are sadists . . . or else for the sake of something they are going to get out of it—money, or power, or safety. But pleasure, money, power, and safety are all, as far as they go, good things. The badness consists in pursuing them by the wrong method, or in the wrong way, or too much. . . . You can be good for the mere sake of goodness: you cannot be bad for the mere sake of badness. . . . Goodness is, so to speak, itself; badness is only spoiled goodness. And there must be something good first before it can be spoiled. . . . It follows that this Bad Power, who is supposed to be on an equal footing with the Good Power, and to love badness in the same way as the Good Power loves goodness, is a mere bogy. In order to be bad he must have good things to want and then to pursue in the wrong way: he must have impulses which were originally good in order to be able to pervert them. But if he is bad he cannot supply himself either with good things to desire or with good impulses to pervert. He must be getting both from the Good Power. And if so, then he is not independent. He is part of the Good Power's world: he was made either by the Good Power or by some power above them both. . . . Do you now begin to see why Christianity has always said that the devil is a fallen angel? That is not a mere story for the children. It is a real recognition of the fact that evil is a parasite, not an original thing. The powers which enable evil to carry on are powers given it by goodness. All the things which enable a bad

man to be effectively bad are in themselves good things—resolution, cleverness, good looks, existence itself. That is why Dualism, in a strict sense, will not work.[8]

In *Perelandra* Lewis had the Green Lady, who, for all her lack of knowledge about the universe, is filled with fundamental insight into Maleldil and the reality that he constitutes, say: "How can I step out of His will save into something that cannot be wished? Shall I start trying not to love Him—or the King—or the beasts? It would be like trying to walk on water or swim through islands. Shall I try not to sleep or to drink or to laugh? . . . To walk out of His will is to walk into nowhere" (p. 116). That is what evil is: not a walk to another, competing reality, but a walk to nowhere. The sentiment is far more Platonic than biblical, though it is doubtful that Lewis realized that he was stressing one view much more than the other. At times he almost outdid Plato in his monism. In one of his letters he went so far as to accuse Plato—somewhat wrongly—of holding a metaphysical dualism. "I fear," he wrote, "Plato thought the concrete flesh and grass bad, and have no doubt he was wrong."[9] In his concern to find a place even for flesh and grass within his system, he was doubtless reflecting his commitment to mainstream Christian thought, which had always held that God's created world was good.

Although he accepted as mythologically truthful, if not necessarily factual, the biblical account of how Satan got a foothold on Earth and subsequently introduced evil to all parts of the globe, Lewis was more concerned with the present reality of evil than its origin. He was strongly influenced by the cosmology of the Model, which saw the Earth as miasmic battleground of good and evil and the planets as free of corruption. His fictional Mars is free from sin (though once long ago it had been victimized by Satan), as is his fictional Venus. The plot of *Perelandra* is built upon Satan's attempt to break free of his present earthly quarantine and establish a foothold on the unsullied Perelandra. Lewis was so intent upon contrasting Earth with Perelandra and

Malacandra that he described the Earth almost as if Christ had never come to it; in this regard the unconscious influence of Platonism dominated his Christian frame of reference. Earth is represented as a dark planet, sealed off from the rest of the universe to prevent its contamination from escaping. The Oyarsa of Malacandra describes it in gloomy language: "I have been down into the air of Thulcandra . . . which the small ones called Tellus. A thickened air as full of the Darkened as Deep Heaven is of the Light Ones. I have heard the prisoners there talking in their divided tongues." [10] This passage draws upon both Plato's analogy of prisoners in a cave and the story of the tower of Babel in the Book of Genesis. The deplorable state of Earth is the direct result of Satan's having entered its sphere long ago. [11] Lewis had the Oyarsa of Malacandra summarize, in his own distinctive manner, those remote cosmic happenings:

> Once we knew the Oyarsa of your world—he was brighter and greater than I—and then we did not call it Thulcandra. It is the longest of all stories and the bitterest. He became bent. That was before any life came on your world. Those were the Bent Years of which we still speak in the heavens, when he was not yet bound to Thulcandra but free like us. It was in his mind to spoil other worlds besides his own. He smote your moon with his left hand and with his right he brought the cold death on my *harandra* before its time; if by my arm Maleldil had not opened the *handramits* and let out the hot springs, my world would have been unpeopled. We did not leave him so at large for long. There was great war, and we drove him back out of the heavens and bound him in the air of his own world as Maleldil taught us. There doubtless he lies to this hour. [12]

In this passage Lewis came closer than anywhere else to picturing Earth in a Gnostic way, as wholly depraved and inimical to what is good. Elsewhere he assumed a more traditional Christian

197

stance and conceived of the Earth as a meeting-ground of good
and evil, where there is light as well as darkness, particularly
since the Incarnation.

Lewis's predominantly monistic view of reality underlies a
dramatic assertion to be found in his writings: Evil is a stance of
mind. After all, if evil is not real, what else can it be but that?
Lewis asserted: "Hell is a state of mind. . . . And every state of
mind, left to itself, every shutting up of the creature within the
dungeon of its own mind—is, in the end, Hell. But Heaven is
not a state of mind. Heaven is reality itself. All that is fully real is
Heavenly." [13] The words are put into the mouth of George
MacDonald, Lewis's ostensible guide, but they are in fact the
sentiments of Lewis himself. The belief that evil is ultimately
nothingness or negation appears prominently in *The Last Battle*,
where we find Narnia in the grip of idolatrous worship. A false
Aslan has been set up, and all Narnians have been directed to
worship the beast. Fierce Calormenes from the land south of
Narnia have joined in the wickedness; together they and the
evildoers in Narnia syncretize the worship of Aslan and the vile
Calormene deity Tash under the composite name "Tashlan."
Lewis depicted Tash as the embodiment of evil, and described
the god's advent vividly. Several of the loyal Narnians are in the
forest as Tash passes through.

> "Faugh! What foul smell is this?"
> "Phew!" gasped Eustace. "It's like something dead.
> Is there a dead bird somewhere bout? And why didn't
> we notice it before?
> With a great upheaval Jewel scrambled to his feet and
> pointed with his horn.
> "Look!" he cried. "Look at it! Look, look!"
> Then all six of them saw; and over all their faces there
> came an expression of uttermost dismay.
> In the shadow of the trees on the far side of the
> clearing something was moving. It was gliding very
> slowly Northward. At first glance you might have
> mistaken it for smoke, for it was grey and you could see
> things through it. But the deathly smell was not the

smell of smoke. Also, this thing kept its shape instead of billowing and curling as smoke would have done. It was roughly the shape of a man but it had the head of a bird; some bird of prey, with a cruel, curved beak. It had four arms which it held high above its head, stretching them out Northward as if it wanted to snatch all Narnia in its grip; and its fingers—all twenty of them—were curved like its beak and had long, pointed, bird-like claws instead of nails. It floated on the grass instead of walking, and the grass seemed to wither beneath it. [14]

By this vile apparition Lewis attempted to show Tash's evil nature. As events later show, Tash is base, appetitive, cruel, and subrational. Most characteristically for Lewis he is insubstantial, like the ghosts from Hell in *The Great Divorce*. This quality prevents him from bending the grass as he moves over it, although Lewis could not resist saying that the grass withered. This insubstantiality superficially resembles that of the eldils of the planetary romances, but in fact is quite different: Tash is less substantial than matter, the eldils more substantial. [15]

Lewis argued that all those in Hell, like Satan and his demons themselves, have locked the door from the inside, making their own prison. Such a viewpoint suggests that salvation rests with the individual person, and that is precisely what Lewis asserted a number of times in his fiction. The persons in Lewis's novels all make their own beds and then must lie in them. "All find what they truly seek," says Aslan in *The Last Battle*. [16] To be sure, his evil characters do not seem to be aware of the consequences of what they most desire. The selfish dwarfs, whose motto is "The dwarfs are for the dwarfs" receive their just reward: isolation from all that is real and beautiful. The wicked witch Jadis in *The Magician's Nephew* cannot escape the same inexorable law, which transcends even Aslan's powers. After she eats one of the forbidden apples in Aslan's garden she flees from goodness. The children report this fact to Aslan.

"Child," he replied . . . "that is what happens to

those who pluck and eat fruits at the wrong time and in the wrong way. The fruit is good, but they loathe it ever after."

"Oh I see," said Polly. "And I suppose because she took it in the wrong way it won't work with her. I mean it won't make her always young and all that?"

"Alas," said Aslan, shaking his head. "It will. Things always work according to their nature. She has won her heart's desire; she has unwearying strength and endless days like a goddess. But length of days with an evil heart is only length of misery and already she begins to know it. All get what they want: they do not always like it." [17]

Selfishness lies, then, at the center of the spiritual malaise of all of Lewis's sinful characters.[18] In *The Great Divorce* such persons live in houses that are forever moving farther apart from one another, like stars in an expanding universe. It is not God who is punishing them, but they themselves, by their own willful actions. Thus Lewis was enunciating his strong disbelief in the doctrine of divine predestination. Each person chooses what he or she will be, and even God in all his omnipotence cannot, or will not, infringe upon that self-determination. When Lucy, ever kindly, begs Aslan through her tears to save the selfish dwarfs from their own blindness, Aslan replies, "Dearest, I will show you both what I can, and what I cannot, do." [19] He comes near the dwarfs and gives a long growl that sets the air shaking, but the dwarfs do not recognize the sound; he shakes his mane and a glorious feast appears before the dwarfs, but to them it tastes like garbage. " 'You see,' said Aslan. 'They will not let us help them. They have chosen cunning instead of belief. Their prison is only in their own minds, yet they are in that prison; and so afraid of being taken in that they cannot be taken out.' " [20] The law that each person gets what he most desires is as immutable as the law of noncontradiction or a mathematical principle, and cannot be separated from the very nature of reality, of God himself.

The most graphic and extended description of the insidious

process by which a person charts his own doom is that of the physicist Weston in the planetary romances. Learned, ambitious, unprincipled, and unrelenting in pursuing his evil cause, Weston first appears in *Out of the Silent Planet* as he is leaving for Malacandra on a mission that he regards as both scientific and humanistic: the establishment of a colony of Earth on the planet to insure the survival of the human species even if mankind disappears from Earth. His cause has the superficial ring of humanitarianism, but Weston soon shows that although he loves mankind in principle he cannot endure individual persons.[21] He eventually denies any purposiveness to life, and he scorns the idea that there is any supernatural dimension to the universe. For him, everything is a matter of scientific analysis and control. He is, as Lewis describes him,

> a man obsessed with the idea which is at this moment circulating all over our planet in obscure works of "scientifiction," in little Interplanetary Societies and Rocketry Cubs, and between the covers of monstrous magazines, ignored or mocked by the intellectuals, but ready, if ever the power is put into its hands, to open a new chapter of misery for the universe. It is the idea that humanity, having now sufficiently corrupted the planet where it arose, must at all costs contrive to seed itself over a larger area: that the vast astronomical distances which are God's quarantine regulations, must somehow be overcome. This for a start. But beyond this lies the sweet poison of the false infinite—the wild dream that planet after planet, system after system, in the end galaxy after galaxy, can be forced to sustain, everywhere and for ever, the sort of life which is contained in the loins of our own species—a dream begotten by the hatred of death upon the fear of true immortality, fondled in secret by thousands of ignorant men and hundreds who are not ignorant. The destruction or enslavement of other species in the universe, if such there are, is to these minds a welcome corollary.[22]

One detects here, along with the invective, a note of near paranoia. Lewis intended that Weston embody scientism at its worst extreme, and with it the assorted evils of social scientism, materialism, evolutionism, and progressivism.[23] He made clear that Weston was no innocuous test-tube manipulator but a dangerous maniac. In order to achieve his lofty-sounding but ill-conceived goals, Weston was willing to kidnap, shoot, and otherwise manhandle his fellow creatures. Animals were things to be used as he saw fit, no matter how painful to them the experimentations might be.

Weston thus represents the ultimate in the dehumanization of man. He is what he is not because he has embraced science (for Lewis was not hostile to science as such, but to scientism, which he believed to be a perversion of what science should be) but because in embracing science he has denied the possibility of the supernatural. He is, then, in Lewis's eyes, modern man writ large: man looking down into the muck to see where he came from, rather than looking to God, where he would see his divinely intended heavenly destination. It is this blindness that prevents him from understanding higher realities when he encounters them. In a humorous episode near the end of *Out of the Silent Planet* Weston meets the Oyarsa of Malacandra but utterly fails to comprehend his situation. He cannot perceive the Oyarsa, but mistakenly thinks that one of the drowsing lower creatures of the planet is the celestial intelligence.

In *Perelandra* Ransom goes to Venus with the specific mission commissioned by the Oyarsa of Malacandra of saving the virginal planet from the evil intentions of Weston, who has been sent there, as he earlier had been sent to Malacandra, by the Bent One (Satan) for the purpose of introducing evil under the guise of progressivism. Weston is his customary self when he first meets Ransom on Perelandra, although already "his face had something about it which seemed subtly unfamiliar."[24] Ransom has an initial debate with him, which begins as a reasoned argumentation but ends with Weston's showing evidences that he is on the verge of possession by Satan. What had appeared as ambition, vanity, and depersonalization in the thought of Weston now begins to unfold in its full horror: It is actually the arrogance of Satan in setting himself against the true lordship of God. Weston howls at Ransom: "Can you understand nothing? Will you always try to press everything back into the miserable framework of your old jargon about self and self-sacrifice? That is the old accursed dualism in another form. There is no possible distinction in concrete thought between me and the universe. In so far as I am the conductor of the central forward pressure of the universe, I am it. Do you see, you timid, scruple-mongering fool? I *am* the Universe. I, Weston, am your God and your Devil. I call that Force into me completely." [25] Now, as one of the characters in another of Lewis's novels ominously declares, "People shouldn't call for demons unless they really mean what they say." [26] Having committed himself to the Devil, Weston thereupon gets just what he has asked for. Satan, or one of his demons, does take possession of him, and in an instant of terror he realizes the full extent of what he has asked for. "Then horrible things began happening. A spasm like that preceding a deadly vomit twisted Weston's face out of recognition. As it passed, for one second something like the old Weston reappeared—the old Weston, staring with eyes of horror and howling, 'Ransom, Ransom! For Christ's sake don't let them—' and instantly his whole body spun round as if he had been hit by a revolver-bullet and he fell to the earth, and was there rolling at Ransom's feet, slavering and chattering and tearing up the moss by handfuls." [27] It is curious that Lewis resorted here to a premodern notion of Devil-possession as insanity. Still, the displacement activity of tearing up moss is suggestive of Satan as one who is both raging and irrational. From this time on Weston is almost totally possessed by the Devil. Sometimes he is calm and reasoning, as when he attempts to seduce the innocent Green Lady into disobeying Maleldil, and at other times—particularly later in the story, as he grows desperate—he is animalistic and physically combative. Weston is virtually dead, but Satan keeps his physical body animate with his magical powers; Ransom calls this monstrosity the Un-man. Before *Perelandra* ends, Ransom, as a surrogate

Christ for the planet, destroys Weston, thereby preventing evil from gaining its desired foothold. The Garden of Eden will continue forever on Perelandra.

In introducing Devil-possession Lewis departed drastically from Platonism. Still, his picture of Satan is a remarkable synthesis. From Plato he took the concept of evil as nothingness; from Chrisianity he borrowed the anthropomorphism and vivid imagery of mythic language; to these he added details of the representation of Satan found in some versions of the Model, as a vile, animalistic creature that is the very antithesis of order and beauty. Not only in the planetary romances but in *The Screwtape Letters* and elsewhere he delineated Satan as having the façade of a calm, suave roué, as superficially the epitome of the gentleman. Satan generally gives the impression that he is a most rational and reasonable fellow, but logic, gentlemanliness, and urbanity are only devices by which he hopes to deceive the unwary and gain his ends. Lewis sums up the picture neatly in *Perelandra*:

> Ransom . . . had full opportunity to learn the falsity of
> the maxim that the Prince of Darkness is a gentleman.
> Again and again he felt that a suave and subtle
> Mephistopheles with red cloak and rapier and a feather
> in his cap, or even a sombre tragic Satan out of *Paradise
> Lost*, would have been a welcome release from the
> thing he was actually doomed to watch. It was not like
> dealing with a wicked politician at all: it was much
> more like being set to guard an imbecile or a monkey or
> a very nasty child. . . . It showed plenty of subtlety and
> intelligence when talking to the Lady; but Ransom soon
> perceived that it regarded intelligence simply and
> solely as a weapon, which it had no more wish to
> employ in its off-duty hours than a soldier has to do
> bayonet practice when he is on leave. Thought was for
> it a device necessary to certain ends, but thought in
> itself did not interest it. It assumed reason as externally
> and inorganically as it had assumed Weston's body.[28]

Aside from some general matters, such as depicting Satan anthropomorphically and presupposing his hatred of goodness, this picture is heavily Platonic. In it Lewis once again stressed the fact that evil cannot be truly rational or intelligent, for that quality is by its very nature good; there is no such thing, properly speaking, as wicked intelligence.[29] True, the Devil can argue logically, for logic is but a tool and, like mathematics, can be employed by the wicked and the good alike. But he is incapable of reasoning in the higher sense, of thinking intelligently beyond syllogisms. He can only mimic goodness, employing politeness (when it suits his purposes) in the place of genuine kindly regard, and displaying an exterior calmness to mask his inner turmoil and violence. In his innermost self he is disorderly, unintelligent, cruel, sensual, and selfish. His mimicry of God is but a perversion of that which is truly good. He is an inveterate liar.[30] Worst of all, he arrogates to himself prerogatives that are God's. It is not without reason, then, that Lewis chose to call Satan the "Bent One" in the planetary romances. Evil is not to be dignified with an independent existence. There can be no true realm of evil set opposite the realm of good; Satan's kingdom exists as a parasite on the one real kingdom. All his power is divine power misused, all his morality is the absolute demand of God twisted. Through and through he is a formless travesty of what is real.

This picture of Satan is an engaging one. In its own way it may be said to stem from the same concern that gave rise to the Calvinistic doctrine of predestination, that of preserving the absoluteness, power, and glory of God. Yet there are attendant conceptual difficulties. The great advantage of the Christian concept of the Devil is that it enables one not to have to attribute moral evil to God. Yet the more that one insists that evil is nothingness the less one can place the responsibility for moral evil upon the Devil. Furthermore, the notion of a Devil that can seduce people into thinking and acting wrongly runs the serious risk of denying the individual accountability of persons—a concept that Lewis was eager to preserve.

Lewis's solution to the problem of accountability was to suppose that Satan could never enter a person unless invited there in some unguarded moment of disharmony among the elements of the soul, when the appetites had gained the upper hand. Weston is not simply the unfortunate victim of arbitrary seizure by Satan, as popular demonology would often have it. In his youth he had, as Lewis made clear, cracked the door open and invited Satan in. So vast was his ego and so ready was he to do anything that might further his ambition that he did not fully perceive his danger. Once given a foothold, Satan continued to take control of more and more aspects of his being, enmeshing him until the bonds were too tight for escape. Lewis never doubted for a moment how little one realizes his mortal danger when he commits some small wrongness, some deed of hubris, some act of dominance over his fellow human beings. He had Weston, in a raging fever, mention in rapid succession several such instances in his past: "They won't let me see my press cuttings. So then I went and told him that if they didn't want me in the first Fifteen they could jolly well do without me, see. We'll tell that young whelp it's an insult to the examiners to show up this kind of work. What I want to know is why I should pay for a first-class ticket and then be crowded out like this." Even in his present state Weston does not comprehend that it is his own many little decisions in life that have led him deeper and deeper into Satan's domain. This is Satan's greatest deception of all, to prevent a person from being able to see the inevitable outcome of his thoughts and deeds, to deceive him into thinking, when he gets what he wanted, that "it's not fair." [31]

Lewis found in Satan the prototype of all sinners, all those who have willed themselves to follow a path away from God. Satan was also the first to misuse the freedom that God gave him when he made him a self.

> The moment you have a self at all, there is a possibility of putting yourself first—wanting to be the centre—wanting to be God, in fact. That was the sin of Satan: and that was the sin he taught the human race. . . . What Satan put into the heads of our remote ancestors was the idea that they could "be like gods"—could set up on their own as if they had created themselves—be their own masters—invent some sort

of happiness for themselves outside God, apart from God. And out of that hopeless attempt has come nearly all that we call human history—money, poverty, ambition, war, prostitution, classes, empires, slavery—the long terrible story of man trying to find something other than God which will make him happy.[32]

Precisely where the point of no return lay for Satan, or for mortals lured by him, Lewis did not attempt to say, and doubtless would have asserted that the point differs from person to person. But about the fact itself he had no doubt. In *The Great Divorce* he had George MacDonald explain that "it begins with a grumbling mood, and yourself still distinct from it: perhaps criticising it. And yourself, in a dark hour, may will that mood, embrace it. Ye can repent and come out of it again. But there may come a day when you can do that no longer. Then there will be no *you* left to criticise the mood, nor even to enjoy it, but just the grumble itself going on forever like a machine." [33] Still, the point of no return lies far down the road for every person; as a Christian Lewis was convinced that the possibility of salvation is open to every person throughout life,[34] and perhaps even in some purgatory in the afterlife; for such is the mercy of God. But God cannot compel souls to turn upward; it is the wayward themselves who, unwittingly, set up their own point of no return.

This loss of selfhood—of freedom, of perceptive powers, of rationality—is the real death of the soul. In the early stages of Satan's onslaught, the person has some residual freedom to resist, but the time comes when it is too late. At one point Weston's old self emerges momentarily and describes is predicament: "You be very careful, Ransom. I'm down in the bottom of a big black hole. No I'm not, though. I'm on Perelandra. I can't think very well now, but that doesn't matter, he does all my thinking for me. It'll get quite easy presently. That boy keeps on shutting the windows. That's all right, they've taken off my head and put someone else's on me." [35] He is, of course, raving, but amid the rambling comments one glimpses the depth of his ensnarement by Satan. It is evident that Lewis's fictional descriptions of Hell do not all employ the same imagery—and there is no reason that they should do so, since Lewis made clear that such depictions are at best imaginative. In the case of Weston, Hell is the gradual, tortured annihilation of the self; in *The Great Divorce* it is the continuation of a dreary, earthlike existence in which one increasingly isolates oneself from all other life, both from other souls and from God himself. Hell does not always involve suffering, at least on a conscious level, but those in Hell are unable to comprehend what heavenly joys they are missing. In all cases the final state of the soul in Hell is nothingness—the same condition that characterizes both evil and Satan.

In view of what we have seen, we are not surprised that Lewis was attracted by the idea of Hell as infinitely small. Although to those inside it Hell appears to be vast, with enough space for the dwellings of the inhabitants to move apart from one another to remote distances, to those in Heaven it appears as the minutest of specks. Lewis used this imagery effectively in *The Great Divorce*. As narrator he mentions to George MacDonald the huge cliff past which the levitating bus rises as it ascends from Hell to the lower regions of Heaven. MacDonald's response is a curious smile.

> "Look," he said, and with the word he went down on his hands and knees. I did the same (how it hurt my knees!) and presently saw that he had plucked a blade of grass. Using its thin end as a pointer, he made me see, after I had looked very closely, a crack in the soil so small that I could not have identified it without this aid.
>
> "I cannot be certain," he said, "that this *is* the crack ye came up through. But through a crack no bigger than that ye certainly came." . . .
>
> "Do you mean then that Hell—all that infinite empty town—is down in some little crack like this?"
>
> "Yes. All Hell is smaller than one pebble of your earthly world: but it is smaller than one atom of *this* world, the Real World. . . . All loneliness, angers,

> hatreds, envies and itchings that it contains, if rolled
> into one single experience and put into the scale against
> the least moment of the joy that is felt by the least in
> Heaven, would have no weight that could be registered
> at all. . . . A damned soul is nearly nothing: it is
> shrunk, shut up in itself." [36]

Thus Hell is just the opposite of the stable in *The Last Battle*, which from the outside appeared to be quite small but inside proved to grow infinitely large until it contained the whole of the heavenly Narnia.[37] Once again Lewis has delighted in inverting our usual assumptions about reality.

It should not be supposed from such considerations that Lewis believed that evil, Satan, and Hell were trivial, and that eventually God would redeem even these, or would reveal that they were nothing but pedagogical devices for wayward humans. He insisted that evil was a power that had to be reckoned with. The damned soul would most assuredly perish forever, as also Satan ultimately would. In this matter he took sharp issue with his respected teacher MacDonald, who believed that all creation, including the very Devil himself, would in due course be saved. The entire logic of Lewis's Christian objectivism led him to believe that evil had to perish. The very sacrifice of Christ on the cross could not alter that situation, for God could not redeem that which would not allow itself to be saved. "In the long run the answer to all those who object to the doctrine of hell is itself a question: 'What are you asking God to do?' To wipe out their past sins and, at all costs, to give them a fresh start, smoothing every difficulty and offering every miraculous help? But He has done so, on Calvary. To forgive them? They will not be forgiven. To leave them alone? Alas, I am afraid that is what He does." Lewis preferred to speculate about Hell relatively little, for reasons that accord with his objectivism. "We know much more about heaven than hell, for heaven is the home of humanity . . . but hell was not made for men. It is in no sense *parallel* to heaven: it is 'the darkness outside,' the outer rim where being fades away into nonentity." [38] It was Heaven that captured his very being, and just as he was sure that the only persons in Hell are those who choose to be there, so he was convinced that "no soul that seriously and constantly desires joy will ever miss it." [39]

Many other passages besides those we have examined illustrate Lewis's understanding of evil. Uncle Andrew, the bumbling and sometimes unintentionally humorous dabbler in black magic in *The Magician's Nephew*, is the Narnian tales' equivalent of Weston. He represents misguided science. [40] The way in which he consorts with magic in his investigations is not unlike the far more massive undertaking of the N.I.C.E. in *That Hideous Strength*, but whereas Lewis rained down doom upon the latter he was charitable toward the old uncle, asserting at the end of the story simply that the man never tried any magic again as long as he lived. [41] The most obvious personifications of evil in the Narnian tales are the witches who, though differing in some details, are essentially the same demonic figure, possessed of great magical powers and forever intruding into the peaceful realm of Narnia their attempts to gain and keep control over the inhabitants. In *The Lion, the Witch, and the Wardrobe* the White Queen is, like Dante's Satan, a cold, bloodless thing turning all those who are good-hearted to stone and the landscape to snow and ice. The imagery of whiteness and cold is especially appropriate as a symbol of all that is opposite to Aslan and his country, with their warmth and refulgence.

In *The Silver Chair* the Green Witch, who in some ways is the antithesis of the Green Lady of *Perelandra*, has an alternate form, that of a serpent. In certain details the imagery of the witch shows the influence of the episode of Eve and the serpent in the Garden of Eden, just as in other ways details in *Perelandra* suggest that same episode. The Green Witch is Queen of the Underworld, which is a dark, dreary warren beneath Narnia with overtones of the Styx and Hades. [42] We have already seen how slyly the witch intermingles reason and falsehood, not to mention magic, as she attempts to bring the children under her control. Like the Devil-possessed Weston in his attempt to beguile the good Green Lady of Venus, the Green Witch tries all possible tricks to persuade the Narnians that her unreality is reality. As her magical charms begin to dull her hearers' minds she plies her evil skills.

"Narnia?" she said. "Narnia? I have often heard your Lordship utter that name in your ravings. Dear Prince, you are very sick. There is no land called Narnia."

"Yes there is though, Ma'am," said Puddleglum. "You see, I happen to have lived there all my life."

"Indeed," said the Witch. "Tell me, I pray you, where that country is."

"Up there," said Puddleglum, stoutly, pointing overhead. "I—I don't know exactly where."

"How?" said the Queen, with a kind, soft, musical laugh. "Is there a country up among the stones and mortar of the roof?"

"No," said Puddleglum, struggling a little to get his breath. "It's in Overworld."

"And what, or where, pray is this . . . how do you call it *Overworld*?"

"Oh don't be so silly," said Scrubb, who was fighting hard against the enchantment of the sweet smell and the thrumming. "As if you didn't know! It's up above, up where you can see the sky and the sun and the stars. Why, you've been there yourself. We met you there."

"I cry you mercy, little brother," laughed the Witch (you couldn't have hear a lovelier laugh). "I have no memory of that meeting. But we often meet our friends in strange places when we dream. And unless all dreamed alike, you must not ask them to remember it." . . .

Puddleglum was still fighting hard. . . . "You can play that fiddle till your fingers drop off, and still you won't make me forget Narnia; and the whole Overworld too. We'll never see it *again*, I shouldn't wonder. You may have blotted it out and turned it dark like this, for all I know. Nothing more likely. But I know

I was there once. I've seen the sky full of stars. I've seen the sun coming up out of the sea of a morning and sinking behind the mountains at night. And I've seen him up in the midday sky when I couldn't look at him for brightness." [43]

Like the Satan whom she represents, the Witch says much that is true, but she subtly twists the truth to her own ends. This, as we have seen, is just what Lewis believes that the Devil inherently does: He bends the truth, so that his arguments will have the ring of truth without the fullness of it, and thereby cause his victims (like the shackled prisoners in Plato's analogy of the cave) to perceive unreality as reality and to regard reality as nothingness. Lewis delineated Satan's upside-down world at greater length in *The Screwtape Letters*. What many readers take there to be merely clever satire or irony, or perhaps nothing more than didacticism, is in fact as consistent an expression as Lewis could present of his understanding of what evil is, and, by indirection, of the truth of his Christian objectivism.

Worth special note is the ape called Shift in *The Last Battle* who is the instigator of the Narnians' blasphemous worship of an ass. Lewis knew that some of the early church fathers had referred to the Devil as "God's ape," on the ground that he was always imitating God. [44] Shift has most of the characteristics that Lewis attributes to Satan. He is clever, but only in the sense of being deceptive; he argues with a semblance of truth, but his premises are false. He exploits others, like Mr. Sensible in *The Pilgrim's Regress*. [45] He is crude, vain, greedy, silly, cowardly, and basically stupid. He is animalistic in the lower sense of that term, which is actually to say that he is human in the worst way; of truer animalistic qualities he is largely devoid. He is a great deceiver, by asking the inhabitants of Narnia to worship a false god who can give them nothing good. For all the lightness of touch with which he describes Shift and his deeds, Lewis was serious about this character, choosing his words and images with both erudition and care. "Always," he wrote in one of his poems, "evil was an ape." [46]

212

Lewis and the church fathers who used the analogy of the Devil as an ape owed much to Plato, who thought not only of lower levels of reality as imitating higher ones, but also of wrong institutions as perversely mirroring right ones. Just as images are reversed in mirrors, so false structures reversed the proper values, often on a one-to-one basis. This reversal is thus a form of imitation and at the same time a total distortion of reality. Lewis utilized this concept at length in *That Hideous Strength*, where the evil organization N.I.C.E. duplicates in its structure the Company of Logres: it has a director, an institutional headquarters, a membership, a plan of attack, and so forth; yet each of these aspects is a horrible parody of what it should be. The Head of the Company of Logres is the Christ-like Ransom; the Head of the N.I.C.E. is literally a slavering, witless, severed head.[47] The Company of Logres are alert, individuated, loving persons; the members of the N.I.C.E. are brainwashed drones who perform insensitive acts of falsification and cruelty. The very ambiences of the two competing forces differ drastically: St. Anne's, where the Company of Logres is centered, is bathed in light, whereas the vale in which the N.I.C.E. headquarters lies is constantly shrouded in fog. In these and various other ways the N.I.C.E. constitutes a form of depraved, inverted imitation of the good.

When all of Lewis's fictional representations of evil are taken together, it may be thought that the picture is more dualistic than Lewis's overt theology could readily tolerate. After all, are not both the Narnian stories and the novels of Deep Heaven alike structured around the mighty conflict between good and evil? The similarities to ancient Zoroastrian and Gnostic world views, as well as to Jewish and Christian apocalyptic literature, might seem to support such a view. Yet we must remember that one staple of all fiction is some kind of conflict among the protagonists. A literary convention should not necessarily be taken as a theological viewpoint. Furthermore, one does not read far into Lewis's novels without realizing that the conflict is inherently out of balance. The forces of evil are never more than momentarily strong; the outcome is never seriously in doubt. By the end of each novel of conflict, evil has faded away like some insubstantial specter of a disturbed sleep. Once again monism has triumphed.

To some readers Lewis's philosophy of religion may have overtones of pantheism, the view that God is to be found in all things, both those we call good and those we call evil. Certainly extreme monism can lead in this direction, and Lewis's writings did occasionally take on a slight pantheistic tinge—as, for instance, when he described God as being "above me and within me and below me and all about me," or when he had one of the creatures of Malacandra say of Maleldil, "He is not that sort that has to live anywhere." [48] Yet one must put such statements in the larger context of Lewis's thought. Repeatedly in his writings Lewis rejected pantheism on the basic ground that reality—God—is good,[49] and therefore cannot partake of anything that is evil. Furthermore, pantheism is much too vague about the nature and functioning of the deity, and has no place for a personal, creating God. "In Pantheism the universe is never something that God made. It is an emanation, something that oozes out of Him, or an appearance, something He looks like to us but really is not, or even an attack of incurable schizophrenia from which He is unaccountably suffering. . . . Pantheism always [is], in the long run, hostility to nature." [50] Lewis's most detailed discussion of pantheism appears in chapter 11 of *Miracles*, where he made a special point of refuting the "fatal picture" that shows God equally present in both evil and good and therefore indifferent to both.

Anyone who has followed Lewis's Christian objectivism thus far may be inclined to wonder why it is that relatively few persons, not only in our world but in Lewis's fictional realms, have a proper insight into reality. The problem falls generally within the discussion of evil in the world. It is particularly acute because the supernaturalist insists that only those who enter, in some measure at least, into the presence of the ultimate can experience joy and self-fulfillment. One may invert the old Aristotelian question and ask, Is it conceivable that human beings are created with a potential fulfillment for which there is no corresponding desire on the part of many of them? One answer is to insist that the desire is indeed there. Lewis could agree with Augustine that our hearts are restless until they rest in God. In many persons, however, that desire is not sufficiently focused; consequently, living within an environment in which evil is rampant, they seek to fulfill that desire in ways that are futile. Lewis would also hold that we have neither the means nor the right to judge the extent to which another person may be approaching God, for, as Aslan says (somewhat ungrammatically) in *The Horse and His Boy*, "No-one is told any story but their own" (p. 194). Most important of all, perhaps, he would point to the Christian gospel as providing a means of insight into reality for those who have not the ability or inclination for philosophical inquiry. On a minimal level, if one comes to know and accept the picture of Christ in the Gospels, one has some idea, however faintly developed it may be, of what God is like; that, in the mercy of God, may make possible a greater spiritual journey, whether in this life or the next. Beyond that, what can anyone say about the ancient fact that the thyrsus-bearers are many and the bacchants are few?

Just as with virtues, Lewis was inclined to resort to fairly traditional lists of vices. All of those things that Satan champions he could readily reject: lust, cruelty, willfulness, and all the rest. The greatest sin, both of Satan and of mortals, is, traditionally enough, pride, or self-conceit.[51] Lewis was sufficiently pietistic and biblically oriented to condemn sins of the heart as well as those of deed; particularly detailed discussions of these can be found in *The Screwtape Letters* and *Letters to Malcolm*, but there are other treatments scattered throughout his essays.

In the matter of social evils Lewis was considerably more individualistic and provocative. Although basically not a political person in any practical way, he was quite prepared to inveigh against certain societal arrangements that he considered wrong, for to the extent that they were so they partook of evil. One of these was theocracy. He wrote only briefly on this subject, but with his customary verve. In part he said, "Theocracy is the worst of all governments. If we must have a tyrant a robber baron is far better than an inquisitor. The baron's cruelty may

215

sometimes sleep, his cupidity at some point be sated; and since he dimly knows he is doing wrong he may possibly repent. But the inquisitor who mistakes his own cruelty and lust of power and fear for the voice of Heaven will torment us infinitely because he torments us with the approval of his own conscience and his better impulses appear to him as temptations." [52] He also expressed, in the same essay, distrust of any government based upon a particular metaphysic; this rubric would include not only theocracy but most political "isms," such as Marxism or fascism. "A metaphysic, held by the rulers with the force of a religion, is a bad sign. It forbids them, like the inquisitor, to admit any grain of truth or good in their opponents, it abrogates the ordinary rules of morality, and it gives a seemingly high, super-personal sanction to all the very ordinary human passions by which, like other men, the rulers will frequently be actuated. In a word, it forbids wholesome doubt. A political programme can never in reality be more than probably right. We never know all the facts about the present and we can only guess the future." [53] Noble as these sentiments are, it can hardly be said that they flow naturally from Lewis's Christian objectivism, the whole tenor of which is that there is one, and only one, right way for things to be. It would perhaps not be entirely amiss to suggest that Lewis held his relatively liberal theory in spite of his philosophy of religion.

We have already had occasion to see something of another major social evil that Lewis identified, that which he called "scientism." Lewis argued against some of the cluster of attitudes that this term represented for him in his *Abolition of Man*, in his fictional character Weston in *Out of the Silent Planet* and *Perelandra*, and in his imaginary institution called the N.I.C.E. in *That Hideous Strength*. Lewis insisted that he was not attempting to undercut science itself, but only the abuse of science by political manipulators. As narrator, he summarizes in *That Hideous Strength* recent historical events leading up to the time when the story takes place:

> The physical sciences, good and innocent in
> themselves, had already, even in Ransom's own time,

begun to be warped, and had been subtly manoeuvred in a certain direction. Despair of objective truth had been increasingly insinuated into the scientists; indifference to it, and a concentration upon mere power, had been the result. Babble about the *élan vital* and flirtations with panpsychism were bidding fair to restore the *Anima Mundi* of the magicians. Dreams of the far future destiny of man were dragging up from its shallow and unquiet grave the old dream of Man as God. The very experiences of the dissecting room and the pathological laboratory were breeding a conviction that the stifling of all deep-set repugnances was the first essential for progress. (P. 203)

He then put in a good word for true scientists, materialists through they were: "You could not have done it with Nineteenth-Century scientists. Their firm objective materialism would have excluded it from their minds; and even if they could have been made to believe, their inherited morality would have kept them from touching dirt." Lewis carried on a running debate with J. B. S. Haldane concerning man's best social arrangements, both in the present and in the future. In clarifying his own views, which he believed that Haldane had misunderstood, he declared that he was attacking, first, a subjective attitude toward values; second, a desire for power that causes men to inflict misery upon their fellow human beings; and third, a tendency of tyrants to disguise the enslavement of others behind the otherwise respectable façade of scientific social planning. He thus saw the greatest present danger not as that of rampant individualism subverting society, but as that of tyranny arising on the ruins of objectivism and individualism.[54]

What will be the ultimate fate of evil in the universe? If one asserts that evil is basically nothingness, it is awkward to try to envision a time in the future when that nothingness will become nothingness. Yet that is what Lewis did. Although philosophically he found it satisfying to think of evil as nothingness, in practice he knew that evil is far too troublesome to be treated as insignificant; hence it must be destroyed in the end. Thus he

217

provided a place in his thought for eschatology. Indeed, his dualistic tendencies sometimes prompted him to write in near panic about the present world's ills and the approach of divine judgment and retribution.[55] Speaking as narrator of *Out of the Silent Planet*, yet at the same time in good measure as himself, he declared that the time of an impending cosmic confrontation between good and evil was imminent: "We are being daily confirmed in our belief that the *oyarses* of Mars was right when it said that the present 'celestial year' was to be a revolutionary one, that the long isolation of our own planet is nearing its end, and that great doings are on foot. . . . And we have also evidence—increasingly almost daily—that 'Weston,' or the force or forces behind 'Weston,' will play a very important part in the events of the next few centuries, and, unless we prevent them, a very disastrous one" (p. 153). Part of such talk is, of course, to set the stage for more planetary romances, but the theme was a serious one for Lewis. Influenced without doubt by the eschatological pictures in the New Testament, he was profoundly concerned for the people of his own twentieth century. In his mind the final great confrontation of God and Satan was being hastened by the rapid collapse of traditional Western concepts and practices. "I look upon the immediate future," he observed, "with great apprehension." [56] All modern trends seemed to him to be pushing mankind toward crisis: wars, technology, sexual permissiveness, and the loss of contact with Old Western Culture itself.

Although a secularist would perhaps describe these as normal human patterns of behavior, or attempt to explain them in terms of societal forces, Lewis discerned in them a diabolical plot. For one who declared, "My primary field is the past. I travel with my back to the engine, and that makes it difficult when you try to steer," [57] he had some definite ideas about the impending eschatological cataclysm. He reflects his anxious concerns in some of the plots and characters in his novels. We have often had occasion to mention the apocalyptic final episodes in *The Last Battle*. So long as the inhabitants of Narnia remain good-hearted and obedient to Aslan, their righteous leaders are able to maintain harmony within the land. But when a majority of them, behaving in a quite human manner, become vulnerable to the beguiling falsehoods of demonic powers, Aslan must destroy the whole of the old order. His heavenly kingdom manifests itself and is discovered to embrace all that was good in the old Narnia, while all that is evil disappears forever into the formless night. There are no heavenly hosts who wreak divine vengeance upon evildoers, nor presumably do the sinful, unredeemed creatures go to a place of eternal punishment; the ultimate punishment is separation from Aslan and annihilation of the self.

In the planetary romances eschatology looms far larger. It commences before the end of *Out of the Silent Planet*, reappears in *Perelandra*, and bursts forth powerfully in *That Hideous Strength*, where the great onslaught of satanic forces against the vulnerable Earth and human society is described. In the first two books, Weston is the primary vehicle for Satan's surge of activity; in the third, the N.I.C.E., with its assorted lurid characters, intensifies the assault, this time with Earth as the battleground.

> The time was ripe. From the point of view which is accepted in Hell, the whole history of our Earth had led up to this moment. There was now at last a real chance for fallen Man to shake off that limitation of his powers which mercy had imposed on him as a protection from the full results of his fall. If this succeeded, Hell would be at last incarnate. Bad men, while still in the body, still crawling on this little globe, would enter that state which, heretofore, they had entered only after death, and would have the diuturnity and power of evil spirits. Nature, all over the globe of Tellus, would become their slave; and of that dominion no end, before the end of time itself, could be certainly foreseen. (Pp. 203–4)

The outcome of this hellish success would be that Satan would reign without impediment over the Earth; God would be defeated. Generally speaking, this scenario owed more to Scripture than to Plato, yet some Platonic details enrich the apocalyptic materials. As the novel moves toward its climax the good celestial intelligences give special powers to the followers of Maleldil, and the N.I.C.E. comes to a catastrophic end. Lewis narrated that fate in a scene that is as grisly as the ancient Canaanite myth of the goddess Anath's slaughter of Mot's henchmen, and in no whit inferior to the woes that the Book of Revelation foresees for the wicked. The language of the banqueting N.I.C.E. members becomes gibberish—a device by which Lewis intended to show the depravity and absurdity of the pseudo-scientific and pseudo-humanitarian pratings of the N.I.C.E. leaders by recalling the biblical story of the tower of Babel. The episode also has a strong Platonic component: The N.I.C.E. is rapidly descending into lower levels of being, in which reality is less and less present. The humorous nonsense that the banqueters utter when they attempt to express themselves seriously suggests the motif of the Devil as an ape. Of course, what is transpiring is but a manifestation of the absurdity that has been inherent in the N.I.C.E. all along. Divinely enraged beasts then plunge into the banquet hall at the special behest of Merlin, whose power over nature is being put to God's use; they maul and slay the N.I.C.E. personnel mercilessly. Whether or not the reader finds this gory scene an appealing aspect of Christian objectivism would hardly matter to Lewis, who was quite sure that the conflict he was describing was a just war, even as was the fierce combat between the loyal Narnians and the apostates in *The Last Battle*.

To a greater or lesser extent Lewis's novels end happily. At the end of *That Hideous Strength* the dark eldils that have instigated the conflict are still on Earth, but the immediate threat has passed and joy can reign. That joy, so much a part of Lewis's thought (just as it figures large in Revelation), manifests itself in the ecstatic, visionary experiences of the band of the faithful. Lewis would probably have liked to show the Earth permanently transformed or redeemed, as he did with Narnia and Perelandra, but he could not claim something that obviously had not yet happened.

When once challenged because of the uniformly happy endings of his planetary romances, Lewis replied, "In my romances the 'good' characters are in fact rewarded. This is because I consider a happy ending appropriate to the light, holiday kind of fiction I was attempting." [58] He grossly understates his concerns here. He could better have pointed out that a happy ending for good persons is requisite in his philosophy of religion, as it has always been in both Platonic and Christian traditions; in the latter two traditions, however, an ultimate reckoning-up must sometimes wait until the future, whereas in Lewis's stories the reckoning comes promptly for the sake of tidying up the book. But we should not think that for Lewis all rewards and punishments are delayed until the end of the story; on the contrary, he makes it amply clear that the very thoughts and actions of day-to-day life contain, in part, their own rewards. The trappings of lakes of fire and heavenly flowers alike are ultimately but images; the doorway to Aslan's country is not somewhere "out there" but is really another dimension that can be reached through innumerable potential doorways in our own world, some well-charted and some as unpredictable as a chance meeting of lovers.

Still there remains the matter of the ultimate metaphysical outcome of all the writhings of this present universe. Only rarely did Lewis attempt to see that far into the future, but his ventures are consistent with the whole of his pattern of thought. The most notable instance is in *Perelandra*. Although Ransom's Christ-like efforts have saved the planet from evil, there is a remote future of which Maleldil has revealed the outlines to the new king of Perelandra. Tor prophesies:

> "When the time is ripe for it and the ten thousand circlings are nearly at an end, we will tear the sky curtain and Deep Heaven shall become familiar to the eyes of our sons as the trees and the waves to ours."
>
> "And what after this, Tor-Oyarsa?" said Malacandra.
>
> "Then it is Maleldil's purpose to make us free of Deep Heaven. Our bodies will be changed, but not all changed. We shall be as the eldila, but not all as eldila. And so will all our sons and daughters be changed in the time of ripeness, until the number is made up

which Maleldil read in his Father's mind before times flowed." (Pp. 211–12)

But this is not the end; Lewis liked to postulate something beyond, a kind of infinity opening up that far exceeds these visions. "About that time," the young king continues, "we shall be not far from the beginning of all things." It is not clear whether Lewis meant something new and greater or a cyclical return of the universe to commence everything again, but it would seem likely that he was thinking of a beginning of all things that puts existence on a higher plane than in this present universe. That kind of distant view would also seem to be implied in the last paragraph of *The Last Battle*. Lewis's inclinations prevent him from ever being willing to say, "This is all there is; there is no more." Always there had to be some remoter reality and greater delight beyond the horizon.

Lewis in Perspective

C. S. LEWIS died in 1963, at the relatively early age of sixty-four. We live too near his time to be able to appraise his thought with any expectation of full impartiality or lofty historical view; another generation or two, or perhaps a longer time, must pass before his contribution to the stream of human endeavor can be assessed comprehensively. If eventually his writings are read only by a few scholars, that fact itself will constitute a judgment of sorts, though not necessarily an objective one. But that is hardly likely to happen. Lewis is still much read today, decades after his heyday, and is holding his own. He was simply too good a writer, and his world view too intriguing, for him to fade into obscurity in the near future.

Lewis must be credited with making one of the most sophisticated, consistent, and elegant explications of supernaturalism in the twentieth century. He devised his Christian objectivism brilliantly and presented it in the most diverse and delightful array of garments imaginable. That philosophy of religion appears not only in his apologetic writings but in virtually all of his other works as well, including his respected studies of English literature, over a span of more than thirty years. His intellect was one of the keenest of his day; his capacity for reading, absorbing, and critically evaluating what he read was enormous, and in addition he was gifted with an extraordinary ability to think logically and rapidly and to write skillfully. All of these qualities he put to the fullest use. He has, nevertheless, often been misjudged, as we suggested at the outset. Some readers have erroneously attributed to him more inventiveness in metaphysics than circumstances warrant, largely because they have failed to recognize the sources from which he borrowed; others have assumed that because, by his own admission, he did not intentionally contravene traditional Christian doctrine, there can be nothing new, and therefore nothing meritorious, in his works. Either assumption is unfair to Lewis, who was highly inventive within the limits that he carefully prescribed for himself. Still, by insisting that his philosophical stance was nothing more than an elaboration of Christianity, he tended to divert attention from the greatest single achievement of his active mind: the refurbishing of the Platonist-Christian world view that had dominated Western culture throughout most of its history.

As a writer he was not without weaknesses. The poetry upon which he lavished much care, though incisive, rich in vocabulary, and occasionally moving, tends to be didactic and relatively uninventive. He achieved far greater success with his novels, particularly in his descriptive passages. The plots of his stories, however, often lack sophistication; usually they are either too linear (*Out of the Silent Planet*) or too cluttered (*That Hideous Strength*), and he displayed only moderate competence in the writing of dialogue. He reached the zenith of his literary skill in his essays; at his best he wrote vigorously, cogently, and wittily, with an erudition and unpredictability that endlessly stimulate the mind.[1] To be sure, his essays sometimes degenerated into philippics in which he virtually bullied those with whom he disagreed, a practice for which his Oxford donship had prepared him all too well. Yet even when his prose was shrill he wrote informatively and charmingly.

As a philosopher of religion Lewis was also not without flaws. He can justly be charged with oversimplifying some philosophical and theological issues; few naturalists, monists, or progressives, for instance, would be likely to agree with his statements of their positions. He sometimes succumbed to the temptation to erect straw figures to demolish. His rigid, if sometimes novel, descriptions of good and evil are so schematically neat that when he attempted to have characters in his stories embody those qualities he often churned out cardboard figures. He occasionally compartmentalized his thought: He rejected monism, yet his thought was heavily monistic; he denied that he was inclined toward sentiment, yet he was obliged to confess that he had a strong streak of romanticism; he wrote loyally of the church in his essays, yet he largely ignored institutional religion in his fiction and occasionally admitted that he found much difficulty with mainstream movements and with corporate activities such as worship. Yet it was all but inevitable that a philosophy of religion as encompassing as his occasionally display loose ends.

Some of Lewis's most acute philosophical problems arose from inherent conflicts between Platonism and Christianity, or from unresolved problems within Platonism or Christianity separately. Many of the issues that gave Lewis trouble were not of his own making, but stood unresolved in Western thought during the long centuries when Platonist Christianity was in the process of development. Among these was the understanding of God, for Platonism had its relatively impersonal absolute and Christianity its more immanent deity. Particularly acute was the problem posed by evil; Lewis was torn between the Platonic view of evil as nothingness and the Christian picture of evil as a mighty power, real and personal, threatening the very order of the universe. A similar problem existed with regard to eschatology: Plato had a weak sense of eschatology, Christianity a full-blown one. In all of these competing viewpoints Lewis could find values; he stressed now this, now some other aspect of the truths contained within the two systems.

We have noted more than once that when Platonism and Christianity came into irreconcilable conflict it was Platonism that had to give way in Lewis's conscious rational processes, even though it might linger to reappear in unguarded moments in his fiction. There is no clearer instance of this dominance than in the exclusivist claims of Christianity. With his Platonic view of a single universal reality in which all persons can, and invariably in some measure do, participate, Lewis had ample raw material for a nonexclusivistic view of religion. Like Plato, he could have held that the truth can be perceived, so far as any human being can apprehend the absolute, by sensitive, persistent inquiry, not

225

by special revelation. Yet he maintained his loyalty to the particularistic claims of Christianity, and above all to the Christian insistence upon salvation through Jesus Christ. Repeatedly in his writings, chiefly in his fiction, he leaned subtly in the direction of universalism, only to pull back at crucial moments into the mainstream of Christian particularism.

With some justification the reader of Lewis's works may conclude that Lewis came close to holding a two-tiered philosophy of religion: an orthodox Christianity that met the needs of his piety and upon occasion served as a refuge from insoluble intellectual problems, and a near-Platonic mystical religion that he shared with a handful of aesthetic and spiritual adepts. To be sure, he tried diligently to deny to himself that any such dichotomy existed in his thought. Often, partly because of the immense effort that had been put into the formulation of the Platonist-Christian theological position in Western culture through the centuries, he could hold the two together; but the signs of internal strain are sometimes too evident to be ignored. The dual aspects of his thought manifested themselves in his own personality. He reveled in his role as the self-appointed mystagogue of a *disciplina arcana*, yet he also cherished his image as a prosaic, middle-of-the-road, unadventuresome English churchman. He was at once a complex blending of the secretive and the overt. In seeking to justify to himself this combination of traits he fell back upon a safe, respectable explanation, and one that in its way was true enough: He was in the twentieth century without being a part of it. His self-description as one of the last dinosaurs [2] is perhaps even more appropriate than he realized, for it has overtones of a dark, primeval world where the monstrous lurks amid the swaying ferns. That, too, was a part of the *disciplina arcana*; alongside the rational clarity of Platonism, the grandeur of the Neoplatonic ascent to the ultimate and the profundity of the Christian myth lay a descent into the world of Merlin, and beneath that the unfathomable realm of Ungit.

It is plausible to suppose that some of the concepts that Lewis took to be concomitants of his Christian objectivism were largely reflections of his own upbringing prior to World War I. Particularly notable are his views on proper place of women in society, the just war, the correctness of certain English social conventions or national traditions, and democracy.[3] However much he might argue that his outlook was based upon his philosophy of religion, he served as a spokesman for many of the presuppositions of his boyhood Edwardian England and Ireland; and, inasmuch as Edwardian life and thought itself contained little that had not been developed in the nineteenth century, he thereby became also a spokesman in some measure for Victorian attitudes on a variety of social and moral issues. Even in his opposition to concepts of evolution and progress he was by no means in disagreement with conservative English thought of Edwardian times. When he asserted that he was largely out of step with his times, he was alluding not so much to the upper-middle-class milieu of his boyhood as to the climate of secularism among intellectuals in the years following the World War.

Some elements in Lewis's thought can be traced to very personal matters of temperament, such as the lifelong yearning for what lies beyond the horizon, delight in landscape, and fascination with the occult. The last-mentioned of these was, Lewis admitted, a particularly persistent thorn in his flesh. The occult was "a spiritual lust," he wrote in *Suprised by Joy*, "and like the lust of the body it has the fatal power of making everything else in the world seem uninteresting while it lasts. It is probably this passion, more even than the desire for power, which makes magicians" (p. 60). He struggled with this "ravenous, quasi-prurient desire" (p. 175) in the years before his acceptance of Christianity, alternately attracted and repelled. If, he mused later in his life, "there had been in the neighborhood some elder person who dabbled in dirt of the Magical kind . . . I might now be a Satanist or a maniac" (p. 176). His interest in other planets was a partial reflection of this preoccupation, for to him a planet was never the lifeless mass of rock and gasses that scientists know, but a place of supernatural activities. When he averred that the planetary romances were "not so much the gratification of that fierce curiosity as its exorcism" (p. 36), his memory was perhaps rather self-serving; for he did not think of Perelandra as a succubus but as a friend to be embraced with delight; neither

227

did he write of Merlin as a demon to be repulsed but as a true, if primitive, hierophant of the mysteries of God. He never quite decided whether to regard magic as "a romantic addition of my own" [4] to his novels or as a logical extension of supernaturalism. In his apologetic works and devotional literature he usually skirted the issue entirely, though in *Miracles* he came close to offering (somewhat unwittingly) a possible rationale for the belief in magic, even though he there confined himself to the accounts of Jesus' miracles as instances of divine intervention into the natural world. In dabbling with the occult he danced perilously close to heterodoxy, yet each time he judiciously retreated to the haven of orthodoxy rather than taking the final bold step.

His interest in the occult had significant ramifications for other aspects of Lewis's thought, above all for the understanding of God himself. Lewis's conviction that when one believes in God one lets oneself in for anything quickly comes into conflict with the belief in God as both rational and good, a concept which was a cornerstone of his Christian objectivism. The Platonic view of reality had no place for an unpredictable, much less a terrifying ultimate reality. The Jewish and Christian traditions come much closer to allowing that God may upon occasion be perceived by mortals to be so absolutely "other" that he is not only awesome but even monstrous at times. Interestingly enough, Lewis himself recognized the implications of his understanding of the supernatural. "Reality," he declared in one of his late works, "looked at steadily, is unbearable." [5] Much earlier, in *Perelandra*, he had given voice to essentially the same thought within the fictional context of his encounter with an eldil:

> I felt sure that the creature was what we call "good,"
> but I wasn't sure whether I liked "goodness" so much
> as I had supposed. This is a very terrible experience. As
> long as what you are afraid of is something evil, you
> may still hope that the good will come to your rescue.
> But suppose you struggle through to the good and find
> that it also is dreadful? How if food itself turns out to be
> the very thing you can't eat, and home the very place

you can't live, and your very comforter the person who makes you uncomfortable? Then, indeed, there is no rescue possible: the last card has been played. . . . Here at last was a bit of that world from beyond the world, which I had always supposed that I loved and desired, breaking through and appearing to my senses: and I didn't like it, I wanted it to go away. I wanted every possible distance, gulf, curtain, blanket, and barrier to be placed between it and me. (P. 19)

Having made this confession of his emotions, he promptly dismissed his anguished ruminations with these words: "But I did not fall quite into the gulf. Oddly enough my very sense of helplessness saved me and steadied me. For now I was quite obviously 'drawn in.' The struggle was over. The next decision did not lie with me." Thereupon he entered into the adventures of Ransom with gusto. The eerie fascination of other worlds and the supernatural has swept away all doubts about the desirability or tolerability of Maleldil's universe. To anyone who might be repulsed by the picture of reality that he envisions, Lewis would doubtless respond that, whether or not one likes it or wants it, that is the way reality is. Being unable to expunge the awesome supernatural, one must take the only viable course, that of embracing it.

So far as his cosmology generally is concerned, Lewis opened himself to the charge that the universe as he sees it is thoroughly stultifying. He admitted cheerfully that he saw reality as essentially static. The phenomenal world displays change: Persons are born and die, the seasons change, and nations rise and fall, but such things are, in his Christian objectivism, relatively insignificant in the light of the unchanging verities. To readers reared on concepts of evolution and progress this static quality of reality may be acutely distressing. Lewis managed, however, to go a long way toward meeting this objection by projecting infinite levels in the cosmic hierarchy—an endless metaphysical ladder by which the self ascends toward God. Thus by lengthening the spiritual journey toward the absolute, and indeed by implying that it may continue in the afterlife, he introduced into his static system a large element of change, discovery, movement, and progress. However unsettling the concept of flux was to him as a characteristic of reality, he was prepared to find movement at all those stages of ascent that are accessible to the human mind. The only static universe that he would find dull would be one in which God was not sufficiently elevated to remain forever beyond man's total grasp; for a God who was too small would be one whom a person could easily patronize and finally discard. If one's God is infinite enough, he insisted, existence will never be boring. He wrote at the end of *The Last Battle*, after he had gotten his band of the saved into the heavenly Narnia: "The things that began to happen after that were so great and beautiful that I cannot write them. And for us this is the end of all the stories, and we can most truly say that they all lived happily ever after. But for them it was only the beginning of the real story. All their life in this world and all their adventures in Narnia had only been the cover and the title page: now at last they were beginning Chapter One of the Great Story, which no one on earth has read: which goes on for ever: in which every chapter is better than the one before" (pp. 183–84). The idea is provocative, and likely to have special appeal for the person with aesthetic or mystical tendencies.

One who has followed Lewis's concept of God and his cosmology closely may be inclined to suspect that, somewhat like the romantic who is in love with love rather than with a person, Lewis was infatuated with the idea of the absolute rather than with the absolute itself. The distinction is important, for if he was indeed captivated by the idea of the absolute, and that alone, there may be no referent for that concept, and, like many a daydream, it may eventually lose its vitality. In quiet moments a dark fear of an empty, cold, and meaningless universe did grip him; as he wrote in one of his poems,

> This is the end, the stratosphere,
> The rim of the world where all life dies,
> The vertigo of space, the fear
> Of nothingness; before me lies

Blank silence, distances untold
Of unimaginable cold. [6]

There is some reason to suspect that in his later years Lewis
continued to have some doubts about his world view. [7] *Till We
Have Faces* is far subtler, more probing and less self-confident
that most of his other fiction, and it leaves the reader with some
uncertainty as to just what Orual has indeed learned by the end
of her life. Even more pronounced is the note of deep despair in
the early pages of *A Grief Observed*, written in the days following
the death of his wife Joy. When he suspected that his Christian
objectivism might be but "a house of cards," he made a full
circle back to a sentiment that he had expressed in a youthful
pre-Christian work: "Our own hearts / Have made a phantom
called the Good, while a few years have sped / Over a little
planet." [8] Yet every moment of doubt about the truth of his
world view was but a passing cloud that was burned away in the
clear light of morning. He was perhaps thinking, in part, of
himself when he wrote a bit of dialogue for *Prince Caspian*:

> "You can search through all the nooks and wild
> places of the land to see if any Fauns or Talking Beasts
> or Dwarfs are perhaps still alive in hiding."
> "Do you think there are any?" asked Caspian
> eagerly.
> "I don't know—I don't know," said the Doctor with
> a deep sigh. "Sometimes I am afraid that there can't be.
> I have been looking for traces of them all my life.
> Sometimes I have thought I heard a dwarf-drum in the
> mountains. Sometimes at night, in the woods, I
> thought I had caught a glimpse of fauns and satyrs
> dancing a long way off; but when I came to the place,
> there was never anything there. I have often despaired;
> but something always happens to start me hoping
> again." (Pp. 49–50)

The romantic hope for fauns and talking beasts, though itself
trivial, is emblematic of the persistent conviction that Lewis held

of the existence of a realm of the absolute that was of inestimable importance.[9]

As a practitioner of rationalism Lewis must surely be accorded high marks. His employment of reason is not, however, entirely unflawed. By adopting the distinction between *ratio* and *intellectus* and declaring that the latter assumes the lead where the former can go no further, he had the best of two worlds: He could assert the absolute validity of both logical thinking and supralogical thinking. Yet to say, as he did, that God acts rationally and then to assert that God's rationality is on a level beyond that of *ratio* is special pleading. With regard to his utilization of logic in his apologetic writings still other difficulties arise. One will recall, for instance, how in several of his most important works—*Mere Christianity*, *The Problem of Pain*, *Miracles*—he abruptly shifted from reasoned arguments for theism to bald assertions of the rightness of Christian doctrines and traditions, above all those pertaining to Christ. In the passages in which he did engage in logical argumentation he was generally a careful thinker. The chief weaknesses in his reasoning, when they do occur, are not so much in his deductions as in his premises; and if a premise is wrong, then the conclusion will not necessarily be correct.[10] Lewis was particularly tempted to chop logic when writing about viewpoints that he found detestable, and he delighted in demolishing the positions of his perceived enemies as efficiently as possible. Furthermore, it may be noticed that he sometimes advanced, in different places in his works, two arguments which, though individually plausible, tend to negate one another.[11] But these questionable uses of reason, taken all together, constitute but a small part of the totality of Lewis's practice of rationalism.

What can be said of Lewis's conviction that there is a basic universal morality? That argument is possibly less convincing today than when Lewis advanced it. In the years that have elapsed the scientific study of ancient religions and primitive societies has not given much new support for his belief, and there may be increasing evidence that a society can be structured around any number of combinations of cultural traits, including those which prize selfishness, suspicion, hostility, and dishonesty. Further, many anthropologists and historians of religion have more recently questioned the validity of the study of religious beliefs and practices apart from their cultural contexts. It should be noted, however, that Lewis never insisted that all cultures and all individuals had an equal awareness of natural law, that all cultures were essentially the same, or that some exceptions would disprove the rule. In his favor is the fact that no culture has yet been shown to be able to exist entirely without those values that he set forth in *The Abolition of Man*.

In other matters, one's evaluation of Lewis's thought will depend upon one's own philosophical or religious orientation. Such is the case with Lewis's eschatological conviction that history is rapidly coming to a focal point in which either the traditional values of the Old Western Culture will reassert themselves, or civilization will fall permanently under satanic despotism and ultimately all values will disappear. Such is also the case with his emphasis upon social betterment through individual Christian conduct rather than through new institutions or the reshaping of the structure of society. Some readers will inevitably say that because of his lack of concern for the systematic restructuring of society Lewis is less universal a man than Plato was. There is little doubt about the fact that Lewis had, in spite of his jovial personality, an introversive tendency. Although his keen mind kept him abreast of many contemporary events in his world, he was essentially a man of ideas rather than of action. Until drawn into the stream of public life to a modest extent by World War II and his own growing fame, he was largely an academician who preferred the constructs of the mind to the rough-and-tumble imprecision of the marketplace and the arena.[12] The rebel within him was an armchair rebel. Curiously enough, the same strain of intellectualism and pietism that fed his introversion also worked to prevent him from slipping into an extreme rejection of wordly concerns; on more than one occasion his Christianity and his reason served to anchor him to his environment when he might otherwise have drifted hopelessly into romanticism, the occult, or even, by his own admission, a life of self-centered indolence.

It would be erroneous to conclude from these evaluative observations that Lewis's philosophy of religion was fatally flawed. No world view has yet been devised that satisfactorily embraces all of the rational and empirical considerations that have pressed themselves upon human attention. The remarkable thing about Lewis is that he succeeded so well in devising a comprehensive objectivist world view for his century—a world view that brought together not only the two great supernaturalist positions of Christianity and Platonism but much of Western culture as well. His philosophy of religion embraced a cosmology, an ethics, an aesthetics, an anthropology, and an eschatology. Other thinkers of his time attempted to formulate world views, some of them with notable success, but none excelled him in the comprehensiveness and beauty of the completed product. Even those personal whims and prejudices that crept into his system took on modified shape and became a part of the totality of his Christian objectivism. He would have expunged them, no doubt, had he perceived them to be the product of personality and environment rather than of rationality; but to us, even from our limited perspective in time and space, the idiosyncrasies and peccadilloes became a part of the totality of Lewis as thinker and person.

Of his sincerity there can be no doubt. If at times Lewis patronized his readers, there is no reason to suppose that he lacked conviction about the truth of what he was saying. Even in his moments of understandable human doubt he was forthright and honest. He was fully aware that the landscape of Malacandra and the person of Wormwood were the products of his imagination, even as the medieval Model was the product of human minds and not a literal description of reality; but he would not have his readers dismiss such imagery as being of no consequence. As much as any thinker who has ever lived, he wanted to bring them into an encounter with the absolute. "Awake, awake! See what is before your very eyes! Press on toward God," he urged. Like Plato's philosopher, he returned to the dark cave to urge his fellow human beings to cast off their bonds of ignorance and be drawn forever by light into light.

Notes

Books and articles for which no author is listed are by Lewis. Articles are cited according to the collection of Lewis's essays in which they most conveniently appear rather than according to the original journal in which they were published.

Preface

1. "On the Reading of Old Books," in *God in the Dock*, p. 200.

Chapter 1: Lewis's Christian Objectivism

1. See "The Idea of an English School," in *Rehabilitations and Other Essays*, p. 64.
2. See "Religion without Dogma?" in *God in the Dock*, p. 132.
3. See, for example, *Surprised by Joy*, p. 213; "Christianity and Culture," in *Christian Reflections*, p. 15; "Religion without Dogma?" in *God in the Dock*, p. 141.
4. See Walter Hooper, "To the Martlets," in *C. S. Lewis: Speaker and Teacher*, ed. Carolyn Keefe (Grand Rapids, Michigan: Zondervan Publishing House, 1971), p. 52.
5. *Surprised by Joy*, p. 225.
6. Quoted in Roger Lancelyn Green and Walter Hooper, *C. S. Lewis: A Biography* (New York: Harcourt Brace Jovanovich, 1974), p. 111.
7. Plato *Symposium* 211A–B, my translation.
8. See *Surprised by Joy*, p. 213.
9. Reported by George Bailey, "In the University," in *C. S. Lewis: Speaker and Teacher*, pp. 82–83.
10. "On the Reading of Old Books," in *God in the Dock*, p. 200.
11. Lewis was scathing in his denunciation of those "erudite limpets . . . who write histories of philosophy and give lectures on comparative religion, and who have never had any vision of their own" (*Miracles*, p. 91).
12. See "Transposition," in *The Weight of Glory and Other Addresses*, p. 24.
13. Lewis did, however, give passing assent to the Platonic system of pedagogy

when he had the youthful humanoid Tor in *Perelandra* (p. 210) declare that the first stage in the education he received from Maleldil consisted of geometry.

14. See, for instance, chapter 6 of *Christian Behaviour* (in *Mere Christianity*); Lewis's attitude crops out in various other ways, as, for instance, in his reference to "the master touch—the rough, male taste of reality" in *The Problem of Pain*, p. 25. See further in chapter 7.

15. Lewis's most specific commendation of the doctrine of the forms appears in *Letters to Malcolm*, a work in which Lewis alluded to Plato by name with some affection. "The terrible and the lovely," he wrote there, "are older and solider than terrible and lovely things. If a musical phrase could be translated into words at all it would become an adjective. A great lyric is very like a long, utterly adequate adjective. Plato was not so silly as the Moderns think when he elevated abstract nouns—that is, adjectives disguised as nouns—into the supreme realities—the Forms" (p. 86).

16. *Letters of C. S. Lewis*, p. 162.

17. See "Shelley, Dryden and Mr Eliot" in *Selected Literary Essays*, p. 203. Also see chapter 6.

18. "Religion without Dogma?" in *God in the Dock*, pp. 139–40. Cf. Lewis's linking of the New Testament and Platonism in a passing comment in "What Are We to Make of Jesus Christ?" in *God in the Dock*, p. 159.

19. *Reflections on the Psalms*, pp. 79–80; cf. p. 82.

20. See *Surprised by Joy*, pp. 60, 176.

21. *Mere Christianity*, p. 137.

22. "Answers to Questions on Christianity," in *God in the Dock*, p. 60.

23. "The Poison of Subjectivism," in *Christian Reflections*, p. 81.

24. *Surprised by Joy*, p. 168.

25. See "The Laws of Nature," in *God in the Dock*, p. 79.

26. In *Mere Christianity* Lewis referred to this philosophical position simply as the religious view, inasmuch as it is based upon the belief that "what is behind the universe is more like a mind than anything else we know" (pp. 31–32).

27. See "The Poison of Subjectivism," in *Christian Reflections*.

28. *The Great Divorce*, pp. 77–78, 79.

29. *The Personal Heresy in Criticism*, pp. 15, 21.

30. In a youthful description of an unsuccessful attempt to write an autobiography Lewis denied that he intended to write an apologetic work. (See Green and Hooper, *C. S. Lewis*, p. 113.) It is significant, however, that the possibility of writing a *vade mecum* for the spiritual pilgrim, as distinct from a straightforward autobiography, had occurred to him. His various attempts to write poetic autobiographies, as well as the prose *Pilgrim's Regress* of 1933, also suggest that he intended a didactic and inspirational purpose to the story of his journey to God. See further in Green and Hooper, pp. 126–30.

31. As a source of factual information about Lewis's early life *Surprised by Joy* must be used with considerable caution; for, as Green and Hooper point out

in their definitive biography, Lewis's memory occasionally played him false. Lewis may even have inadvertently oversimplified the stages in his spiritual pilgrimage. It would appear that he may have been more of a crypto-Christian during his early manhood than he later recalled. In *Dymer*, published three years before he became a theist and five years before he became a Christian, we find a number of adumbrations of his subsequent Christian thought. One gets to some extent the impression that at that time Lewis was not so much a hardened atheist as a theist engaged in a lover's quarrel with God.

32. "The Idea of an English School," in *Rehabilitations and Other Essays*, p. 64.

33. *The Great Divorce*, p. 1.

34. "Psycho-analysis and Literary Criticism," in *Selected Literary Essays*, p. 290. It is in this same sense that Lewis speaks of his having gone through a phase of "popular realism" in his young manhood; see the preface to *The Pilgrim's Regress*, 3rd ed., p. 5; cf. *Surprised by Joy*, pp. 208–9.

35. See further in "Man or Rabbit?" in *God in the Dock*.

36. *Miracles*, p. 14.

37. See "Vivisection," in *God in the Dock*; Lewis also mentions his opposition to vivisection through his character Ransom in *Out of the Silent Planet*, p. 27.

38. See "The Funeral of a Great Myth" and "De Futilitate," in *Christian Reflections*; "The World's Last Night," in *The World's Last Night and Other Essays*, pp. 100–104; and "Dogma and the Universe," in *God in the Dock*. Also note Lewis's "Evolutionary Hymn," in *Poems*, pp. 55–56.

39. "Is Theology Poetry?" in *They Asked for a Paper: Papers and Addresses*, p. 163.

40. "Two Lectures," in *God in the Dock*, pp. 210–11.

41. "Horrid Red Things," in *God in the Dock*, p. 69.

42. The lengthiest parade of heresies appears in Lewis's early work *The Pilgrim's Regress*.

43. On Kirkpatrick, see *Surprised by Joy*, chapter 9.

44. The same dichotomizing tendency appeared when Lewis thought mythologically. In his autobiography he spoke of "those great contrasts which have bitten deeply into my mind—Niflheim and Asgard, Britain and Logres, Handramit and Harandra, air and ether, the low world and the high" (*Surprised by Joy*, p. 154).

45. Characteristic of Lewis's eschatological fervor is the statement that "the modern literary world is divided into two camps, that of the positive and militant Christians and that of the convinced materialists" ("William Morris," in *Selected Literary Essays*, pp. 229–30).

46. Note also Lewis's collection of literary essays, *Studies in Words*. It is noteworthy that the words Lewis explicates (*nature, sad, free, simple*, etc.) are ones that would not generally be considered technical. As his comments show, such words have wide and subtle ranges of meaning, not the narrow and sharp ones that technical terms must have. Occasionally, as in his preface to *George MacDonald: An Anthology*, p. 20, Lewis drops scholarly terms into his essays, but he generally does so with a touch of whimsey, scorning pedan-

try in its grosser manifestations. See further in "Before We Can Communicate," in *God in the Dock*.

47. At one point Lewis spoke of the word *joy* as being "in my technical sense" (*Surprised by Joy*, p. 35).

48. See *Surprised by Joy*, pp. 209–11. Also see "The Decline of Religion," in *God in the Dock*, p. 222.

49. *Letters of C. S. Lewis*, p. 38.

50. *Surprised by Joy*, pp. 209–10, 210–11. Cf. Lewis's comment in his essay *The Personal Heresy in Criticism* to the effect that opposite materialism there is "something like Theism or Platonism or Absolute Idealism," all of which assert that "the universe is not blind or mechanical," that "all is designed, all is significant" (p. 28).

51. See the preface to *Dymer* that Lewis wrote for the second edition in 1950 (available in *C. S. Lewis: Narrative Poems*, ed. Walter Hooper [New York: Harcourt Brace Jovanovich, 1969], pp. 3–6).

52. *Surprised by Joy*, pp. 217–18.

53. On Kierkegaard, see *Letters of C. S. Lewis*, pp. 297–98, where Lewis also commented on the view of another existentialist, Sartre (see also "Cross-examination," in *God in the Dock*, p. 264). In this latter work Lewis also confessed that he had read very little written by twentieth-century novelists, specifically Ernest Hemingway and Samuel Beckett. Note also Nevill Coghill's comments in "The Approach to English," in *Light on C. S. Lewis*, ed. Jocelyn Gibb (New York: Harcourt, Brace and World, 1965), p. 60. As one might expect, however, Lewis was favorably inclined toward the "I-Thou" concept of Jewish theologian Martin Buber (see *The Abolition of Man*, p. 49).

54. To the extent that the orthodox revival rejected the validity of reason as a path to God and insisted on divine revelation as the sole means of knowing the will of God, it rejected not only liberal Christian tradition but the Platonic viewpoint as well.

Chapter 2: The Old Western Model of Reality

1. "God in the Dock," in *God in the Dock*, p. 241.

2. See *Surprised by Joy*, p. 225. At various places in his writings Lewis listed writers who stood in this Platonic-Christian tradition, or at least in the tradition of "Christian classics"; see in particular "On the Reading of Old Books," in *God in the Dock*. Notably absent from such lists is the name of Shakespeare. The chief reason for this omission is perhaps to be found in Lewis's statement that "in all Shakespeare's works the conception of good . . . seems to be purely worldly" ("Christianity and Culture," in *Christian Reflections*, p. 16). Lewis occasionally wrote about Shakespeare, as in his "Variation in Shakespeare and Others," in *Rehabilitations and Other Essays*, and in his limited discussion of the poems of Shakespeare in his *English*

Literature in the Sixteenth Century Excluding Drama (see particularly pages 498–509), but his comments are confined almost entirely to detailed scholarly observations rather than consideration of Shakespeare's world view, for which he had little affinity.

3. See *Surprised by Joy*, pp. 206–8.
4. See *The Discarded Image*, chapter 3.
5. For example: "Apart from bits of the Platonic dialogues, there are no conversations that I know of in ancient literature like the Fourth Gospel." ("What Are We to Make of Jesus Christ?" in *God in the Dock*, p. 159.)
6. Note, for instance, Lewis's implied distaste for "neo-Platonic mysticism" in *The Four Loves*, p. 168.
7. See *The Discarded Image*, chapter 4.
8. Although he discussed him occasionally elsewhere, Lewis did not include Augustine in his history of the development of the Model, since Augustine showed little interest in the kind of cosmological speculations that are the focal point of the Model. Augustine was important, however, in the broader history of Platonism in Christianity.
9. See *The Discarded Image*, p. 43.
10. See "The Idea of an 'English School,' " in *Rehabilitations and Other Essays*, p. 65.
11. On Bernardus Silvestris's Platonism and the school of Chartres, see *The Allegory of Love*, pp. 87–111.
12. See *The Discarded Image*, pp. 10–12 and chapter 5.
13. See ibid., pp. 14–18.
14. Ibid., pp. 17–18.
15. Ibid., pp. 18–19.
16. "Dante's Similes," in *Studies in Medieval and Renaissance Literature*, p. 74.
17. See *"De Descriptione Temporum,"* in *Selected Literary Essays*.
18. This is the "seething mass" of theosophy which is one form of medieval and Renaissance Platonism, alongside Christianized Platonism and courtly, erotic Platonism; see Lewis's comments on Ellrodt's study of Spenser in Lewis's long book review, "Neoplatonism in the Poetry of Spenser," in *Studies in Medieval and Renaissance Literature*, pp. 149ff.
19. *Poems*, p. 70.
20. See *Spenser's Images of Life*, pp. 8ff.
21. In this regard Spenser differed sharply from the self-conscious Platonists of the Italian Renaissance. See "Neoplatonism in the Poetry of Spenser," in *Studies in Medieval and Renaissance Literature*.
22. See *Spenser's Images of Life*, p. 59.
23. See *A Preface to Paradise Lost*, p. 112, and elsewhere in the work.
24. See ibid., chapter 10.
25. "Christian Apologetics," in *God in the Dock*, p. 102. Lewis did not actually discuss the Old Testament in his address, but he did so in various other writings, such as *Reflections on the Psalms* and *Letters to Malcolm*.
26. *"De Descriptione Temporum,"* in *Selected Literary Essays*, p. 7.

27. See "On the Reading of Old Books," in *God in the Dock*, pp. 202–4.
28. *English Literature in the Sixteenth Century Excluding Drama*, pp. 3–4.
29. See *Surprised by Joy*, p. 5.
30. See *The Pilgrim's Regress*, p. 7; cf. pp. 5–11. Here Lewis discusses many facets of romanticism as well as his own use of the term.
31. See *English Literature in the Sixteenth Century Excluding Drama*, p. 4.
32. "*De Descriptione Temporum*," in *Selected Literary Essays*, pp. 13–14.
33. *The Discarded Image*, p. 218.
34. See "On Ethics," in *Christian Reflections*, p. 52.

Chapter 3: Reality and God

1. Lewis sometimes refers to this figure as the "Emperor-over-sea" (e.g., in *The Last Battle*, p. 133). There is no significance to the variant; both terms are presumably influenced by the medieval practice of referring to the Holy Land as *ultramare* because of its location at the eastern end of the Mediterranean Sea.
2. For Otto, see *The Problem of Pain*, pp. 16ff. George MacDonald is discussed in *Surprised by Joy*, pp. 179–81 and the preface Lewis wrote to *George Mac-Donald: An Anthology*; note also *The Great Divorce*, chapters 9–14. Lewis was deeply impressed by his reading of Bevan's *Symbolism and Belief* (1938), particularly by the chapters on height, time, and light as symbols of divine reality. Bevan's introductory chapter is so much in accord with Lewis's way of viewing religious phenomenology that Lewis himself might almost have written it.
3. *That Hideous Strength*, pp. 326–27.
4. *Perelandra*, pp. 197–98.
5. See *Surprised by Joy*, pp. 171, 228. At the age of eighteen, long before he became a Christian, Lewis wrote to his friend Arthur Greeves, "I am quite content to live without believing in a bogey who is prepared to torture me forever . . . a spirit more cruel and barbarous than any man" (quoted in Douglas Gilbert and Clyde S. Kilby, *C. S. Lewis: Images of His World* [Grand Rapids, Michigan: William B. Eerdmans Publishing Company, 1973], p. 17). Cf. the episode that Walter Hooper relates in his preface to Lewis's *Christian Reflections*, p. xi.
6. *Miracles*, p. 96.
7. Ibid., p. 97. Cf. Jane Studdock's thought once she grants that the supernatural may really exist (*That Hideous Strength*, pp. 142–43, 234).
8. There are, of course, some passages in the Bible in which the monstrous aspect of the deity appears. The visions of the prophet Ezekiel (Ezek. 1, 10) are a case in point. It is interesting to note that Lewis's description of the celestial intelligences in *Perelandra*, cited previously, seems to be influenced by the imagery in the Book of Ezekiel. Lewis seems to imply that the

prophet's vision was not solipsistic and psychological but a reflection of cosmic reality, a genuine visitation by supernatural powers. Although he doubtless did not expect his readers to take him literally, he was trying seriously to link Ezekiel's mystical experiences with the mainstream of supernaturalism through the centuries.

9. See further in chapter 8.
10. Note Lewis's views on "thick" and "clear" religions in chapter 5. Although a primitive goddess who demands gory sacrifices and who dwells in filth, Ungit represents some important values in religion, and with these Orual must eventually come to terms. It ultimately appears that even though Ungit has been wrongly worshipped by people, and certainly does not represent what God is, she is still to be preferred to the Fox's worship of no god at all.
11. *The Voyage of the Dawn Treader,* p. 212.
12. *The Last Battle,* pp. 172–73.
13. *The Silver Chair,* p. 9.
14. *Surprised by Joy,* p. 152. The way in which his imagination heightened his actual observances is attested in a letter that he wrote a short while after the completion of a motor trip in southern England: "The real value of such a holiday is still to come, in the images and ideas which we have put down to mature in the cellarage of our brains, thence to come up with a continually improving bouquet. Already the hills are getting higher, the grass greener, and the sea bluer than they really were; and thanks to the deceptive working of a happy memory our poorest stopping places will become haunts of impossible pleasure and Epicurean repast" (*Letters of C. S. Lewis,* pp. 71–72).
15. W. H. Lewis, "Memoir of C. S. Lewis," in *Letters of C. S. Lewis,* p. 16.
16. See further in chapter 6.
17. "To Roy Campbell," in *Poems,* p. 66.
18. While touring historic towns and their buildings in Britain during his early manhood, Lewis attempted some architectural criticism (e.g., *Letters of C. S. Lewis,* pp. 52, 66, 96, 99–100), but he had nothing particularly incisive to say. He went through a youthful phase in which he was attracted by finely bound books (see Green and Hooper, *C. S. Lewis* p. 144), but outgrew the interest and henceforth used inexpensive editions whenever they were available (see *Surprised by Joy,* p. 164; and *Letters of C. S. Lewis,* p. 259; as well as his brother's comments in his "Memoir of C. S. Lewis" in ibid., p. 16). He appreciated finely carved woodwork at Oxford (ibid., p. 34) and knew about the ugliness of "the worst Victorian period" (ibid., p. 44). He was indifferent to his dress. He had some interest in the music of Chopin (see ibid., p. 28) and some other composers, but in general had little musical competence.
19. "William Morris," in *Selected Literary Essays,* p. 221.
20. Ibid., p. 227.
21. *The Last Battle,* pp. 136–37.
22. Indicative of his proclivities was Lewis's experience as a boy: "When I was

taken to the theatre as a small boy what interested me most of all was the stage scenery" ("Behind the Scenes," in *God in the Dock*, p. 245).

23. *Perelandra*, p. 219.
24. *The Last Battle*, p. 183.
25. *The Great Divorce*, pp. 18–19.
26. Ibid., p. vii. But Lewis's fellow student (and later colleague) at Oxford, Nevill Coghill, records an episode in a seminar on literature which both he and Lewis attended in 1922. Lewis read a paper on *The Faerie Queene* in which, among other things, he described with deep personal insight how the faerie forest and plain "were carpeted with a grass greener than the common stuff of ordinary blades." Coghill continues his summary of Lewis's presentation: 'This was the *reality* of grass, only to be apprehended in poetry: the world of the imagination was nearer to the truth than the world of the senses, notwithstanding its palpable fictions, and Spenser had transcended sensuality by making use of it, giving us the very sheen of grass—no! (he corrected himself), *sheen* was too feeble a word; he needed the Greek word γάνος to express the radiance of the reality of the greenness of Spenser's groves and glades, lawns, hills, and forests. It was like the Platonic idea of greenness, a spiritual reality." ("The Approach to English," in *Light on C. S. Lewis*, p. 52.)
27. See *Out of the Silent Planet*, p. 95.
28. *Perelandra*, pp. 45, 202; cf. pp. 205–6.
29. *Miracles*, pp. 94–95. Lewis was writing this work at about the same time as *The Great Divorce*, hence perhaps the similarity of statements about the solidity of reality in the two works.
30. Ibid., pp. 93–94.
31. *The Great Divorce*, pp. 17–18.
32. *The Last Battle*, p. 180.
33. *The Discarded Image*, p. 116.
34. *The Last Battle*, pp. 144–45.
35. In *Perelandra* Lewis uses the imagery of an inky black hole to represent self-imposed blindness, or Hell, in describing Weston's plight; see chapter 8.
36. "Dante's Similes," in *Studies in Medieval and Renaissance Literature*, p. 71.
37. Ibid.
38. *The Four Loves*, p. 175.
39. Characteristically, Lewis has Ransom speculate on how much greater than the sun the absolute must be (see *Out of the Silent Planet*, p. 40).
40. *That Hideous Strength*, p. 138.
41. See, for instance, *The Lion, the Witch, and the Wardrobe*, pp. 76, 180; *The Voyage of the Dawn Treader*, p. 138; *The Last Battle*, p. 24. Lewis made some interesting observations on awesomeness as an inherent trait of lions in *The Problem of Pain*, pp. 142–43. Aslan's wildness is related to Lewis's conviction that if one grants that God does indeed exist, then one may be in for anything.
42. See *Perelandra*, p. 219; *Miracles*, pp. 95–96.
43. "On Stories," in *Of Other Worlds*, pp. 20–21.

44. So Lewis describes the matter in *Reflections on the Psalms,* pp. 104–5, 135.
45. *Perelandra,* p. 215; see also p. 217; and *Out of the Silent Planet,* pp. 121, 142, etc.
46. *Perelandra,* p. 210.
47. See *The Magician's Nephew,* chapters 8–10.
48. He rises in his former lion form. Lewis allowed, however, that he also had a supernatural form; see *The Last Battle,* p. 183.
49. On Jesus's fierceness, see *The Four Loves,* p. 171.
50. See *The Voyage of the Dawn Treader,* p. 133.
51. Regarding Jadis's involvement in the story of the creation of Narnia, see *The Magician's Nephew,* chapters 8–10.
52. Ransom thus exemplifies Lewis's stated principle of characterization in space fiction. See further in chapter 6.
53. *Perelandra,* p. 147.
54. *Letters of C. S. Lewis,* p. 274.
55. See, among other things, *Beyond Personality* (in *Mere Christianity*); "The Grand Miracle" and "What Are We to Make of Jesus Christ?" in *God in the Dock.*
56. Note, however, Lewis's frequent use of the *aut Deus aut homo malus* argument; see chapter 9.
57. See *Surprised by Joy,* pp. 224, 233.
58. *Letters to Malcolm,* p. 68.
59. *The Case for Christianity,* in *Mere Christianity,* pp. 52–53.
60. The most anthropomorphic picture of all is to be found in *The Screwtape Letters,* but there Lewis was writing so satirically and homiletically that it would be unjustified to take his statements about God literally.

Chapter 4: Cosmology

1. *Surprised by Joy,* pp. 35–36.
2. *English Literature in the Sixteenth Century Excluding Drama,* p. 4.
3. *Out of the Silent Planet,* p. 40.
4. See *The Discarded Image,* chapter 5.
5. *The Discarded Image,* pp. 116–17.
6. Lewis did not refer to *Empyrean* here, but the term is a convenient one for which there is ample medieval warrant, and he does use it elsewhere in his writings.
7. See *The Discarded Image,* pp. 14–15.
8. Writers who stood within the tradition of the Model differed on various details, but were in broad agreement in their cosmology. Lewis's comments on the angelology of Pseudo-Dionysius (see *The Discarded Image,* pp. 70–75) are largely appropriate for the Model in general.
9. Note Lewis's learned comments on ancient, medieval, and Renaissance

opinions concerning the bodies of angels in his *A Preface to Paradise Lost*, chapter 15.

10. *The Discarded Image*, pp. 98–99.
11. See ibid., pp. 95–96.
12. See ibid., chapter 6.
13. Lewis did not discuss the material in this and the following paragraph in *The Discarded Image*, although he touched on aspects of it elsewhere in his works.
14. On Lewis's championing of democracy, see, inter alia, "A Reply to Professor Haldane," in *Of Other Worlds*, p. 81; and "Membership," in *The Weight of Glory and Other Addresses*, pp. 36–37. In the Narnian tales the ideal government is a benevolent monarchy. In the planetary romances the government might appropriately be called a theocracy so long as the planets are governed by celestial intelligences, and (in *Perelandra*) a benevolent monarchy after Tor and Tinidril assume rule over the planet. In his essays, where he had in mind earthly governments, Lewis denounced theocracy as the worst of all governments; see chapter 4.
15. The term *Deep Heaven* was presumably adapted by Lewis from late versions of the Model, such as Milton's *Paradise Lost*. There, in the creation of the world, Christ commands that the Deep become separated into Heaven and Earth; hence Lewis conceives of Deep Heaven as the region of the moon and all spheres beyond, and therefore lying beyond the earth's influence. For Ransom's experience see *Out of the Silent Planet*, p. 28; see also pp. 29–31.
16. Ibid., p. 32.
17. *Out of the Silent Planet*, pp. 37–38. The way in which the absoluteness of the light of the sun (i.e., reality) is described in this passage has overtones of Plato's description of the Good in the passage which we have earlier cited from the *Symposium*.
18. See *Out of the Silent Planet*, p. 152. When Ransom examines a diagram of the planetary orbits on the sacred island of Meldilorn, he sees an oyarsa-figure riding on each of the circles that represent the planets. "In the first and smallest of these was pictured a little ball, on which rode a winged figure . . . holding what appeared to be a trumpet" (ibid., p. 111); this proves to be Mercury, and other slightly different figures represent the other planets. Lewis borrowed directly here from the Platonic concept of the planets as having tutelary intelligences.
19. See *That Hideous Strength*, p. 202. Ransom's audience with the Oyarsa of Malacandra makes the same point in *Out of the Silent Planet* (see chapters 18–21).
20. Pp. 94–95; cf. pp. 119–20. Concerning the way that human beings perceive eldils, see especially *Perelandra*, pp. 17–18.
21. Lewis's representation of eldils also has affinities with certain theosophical notions about supernatural adepts who have astral, rather than physical, bodies, and whose appearance is utterly different from that of human beings.

22. Lewis once took up the conundrum of the Chinese philosopher who slept and dreamed that he was a butterfly, only to awaken and thereafter wonder whether he was a man who had dreamed that he was a butterfly or a butterfly who was now dreaming that he was a man. He easily decides that the state of greater reality is that of the man rather than the butterfly, on the simple ground that as a man he could fit the dream of the butterfly into his world, whereas he could not fit the world of man into his dream of being a butterfly.

23. See *Perelandra*, pp. 9, 12, 23; and *Out of the Silent Planet*, pp. 95, 157.

24. On God's quarantine of Earth, see "Religion and Rocketry," in *The World's Last Night and Other Essays*, p. 91.

25. *English Literature in the Sixteenth Century Excluding Drama*, p. 3. Lewis was quoting Montaigne.

26. See *The Discarded Image*, p. 116.

27. *Out of the Silent Planet*, p. 160. (Cf. also p. 95, in a somewhat different context.) Lewis seemed to imply here that Jupiter is the center of his fictional universe. He appears occasionally to have some inconsistencies in his fictional cosmology. When Ransom studies a diagram of the Deep Heaven while on the sacred island Meldilorn, for instance, he notes that the planets orbit the sun, as they do (except for the moon) in modern astronomy (ibid., pp. 111–12). In still other passages, where he is most influenced by the Model, he tends to imply that the Earth is at the center. These small inconsistencies—if indeed that is what they are—may stem in part from Lewis's attempt to adapt the cosmology of the Model to modern scientific cosmology.

28. *That Hideous Strength*, p. 229.

29. See *That Hideous Strength*, chapter 16, which we shall subsequently have occasion to discuss in several connections.

30. Note, for example, the disunity that occasionally threatens the band of loyalists in *Prince Caspian*.

31. Such reconciliation can be found in Botticelli's paintings and in Spenser's poetry; see *Spenser's Images of Life*, especially pp. 20, 78, and 104. Although his Malacandra (Mars) was scarcely martial, Lewis did suggest that its landscape was far sterner, on the whole, than that of Perelandra (Venus). By comparison with the latter, Malacandra appears to Ransom to be a "cold, archaic world" (*Perelandra*, p. 45). What Lewis emphasized was that the Oyarsa of Malacandra was profoundly masculine, whereas the Oyarsa of Perelandra was utterly feminine (see ibid., pp. 200–201).

32. See *Perelandra*, pp. 214–19. Lewis explained his linking of dance and game in *Letters to Malcolm*, and at the same time clarified both. He wrote playfully, yet with serious intent:

> I know that my tendency to use images like play and dance for the highest things is a stumbling-block to you. . . . But I still think you don't see the real point. I do *not* think that the life of Heaven bears any

analogy to play or dance in respect of frivolity. I do think that while we are in this "valley of tears" . . . certain qualities that must belong to the celestial condition have no chance to get through, can project no image of themselves, except in activities which, for us here and now, are frivolous. . . . Dance and game *are* frivolous, unimportant down here; for "down here" is not their natural place. . . . But in this world everything is upside down. That which, if it could be prolonged here, would be a truancy, is likest that which in a better country is the End of ends. Joy is the serious business of Heaven. (Pp. 92–93)

Thus the dance and the game belong to the imagery by which one may, upon occasion, appropriately attempt to describe heavenly reality. See further in chapter 7.

33. *Longaevi* appear in *That Hideous Strength;* see particularly p. 285. In all essentials, Merlin, as Lewis fictionally describes him, is also to be reckoned among the *longaevi.* For those found in Narnia, see the partial list in *Prince Caspian*, p. 47. Lewis introduced new *longaevi* into the various stories as need arose. There are partial lists of demonic creatures in *The Lion, the Witch, and the Wardrobe*, pp. 132, 148; the story of Eustace as a dragon is told in *The Voyage of the Dawn Treader*, chapter 6–7.

34. See *The Discarded Image*, pp. 146–52.

35. *The Voyage of the Dawn Treader*, pp. 179–80.

36. Ibid., p. 180.

37. See *The Magician's Nephew*, chapters 8–10.

38. Ibid., pp. 98–99.

39. Discounting the fact that two different worlds are involved in the story, the reader may be inclined to suspect that by this device Lewis introduced circularity into his picture of human origins: The London cabbie and his wife give rise to the human race, which ultimately produces the London cabbie and his wife, and so forth ad infinitum. There is indeed circularity in this scheme, but it accords with Lewis's insistence upon the essentially atemporal nature of reality. What appears to human beings as sequence in time is, in fact, but an aspect of the eternal, the timeless; hence all that Lewis was saying here was that humans exist. To speak of man's origins in time is, in that sense, meaningless. The view is quite Platonic and cannot be fully reconciled with the Christian emphasis upon the reality of the historical process. Lewis uses the same kind of circular or atemporal argument in this work in describing the origin of evil.

40. See *The Silver Chair*, p. 21.

41. *The Last Battle*, pp. 167–70. Lewis is misleading when he attributes all of the description of Aslan's country to Plato. The cosmography is broadly Platonic, but it is an offshoot of Platonism that was developed by Charles Williams in novels such as *All Hallow's Eve*.

42. *The Last Battle*, pp. 180–81.

43. Ibid., pp. 181–82.

44. "The Alliterative Meter," in *Selected Literary Essays*, p. 24.

45. "Priestesses in the Church," in *God in the Dock*, p. 239.
46. *The Discarded Image*, p. 222.
47. See "On Stories," in *Of Other Worlds*, p. 15.
48. See chapter 6.

Chapter 5: Universal Truths

1. *The Problem of Pain*, pp. 38–39. Cf. "De Futilitate" in *Christian Reflections*, pp. 66–67.
2. *Mere Christianity*, p. 45. Lewis uses the same idea fictionally in *That Hideous Strength*. After being subjected to surrealistic, scatological experiences calculated to kill all that was truly human in his reactions and thus to make him more like the demons themselves, Mark Studdock has an opposite reaction: "The built and painted perversity of this room had the effect of making him aware, as he had never been aware before, of this room's opposite. . . . There rose up against this background of the sour and the crooked some kind of vision of the sweet and the straight. Something else—something he vaguely called the 'Normal'—apparently existed. He had never thought about it before. But there it was—solid, massive, with a shape of its own. . . . He was not thinking in moral terms at all; or else . . . he was having his first deeply moral experience. He was choosing a side: the Normal" (p. 299).
3. Lewis also deals with this matter in *Studies in Words*, chapter 12.
4. *The Abolition of Man*, p. 2.
5. Ibid., pp. 9–10.
6. Ibid., p. 12.
7. In *That Hideous Strength* Lewis attributes Mark Studdock's lack of "one rag of noble thought" to the fact that he had been brought up as neither a Christian nor a pagan (p. 185). Still, Studdock retains his divinely given, inalienable ability to distinguish right from wrong. He eventually responds to a variety of tutors (Hingest, Dimble, etc.) and begins to gain proper knowledge of reality. The quotation is from *The Abolition of Man*, p. 10.
8. "Work and Prayer," in *God in the Dock*, p. 104.
9. *The Last Battle*, p. 171.
10. See "On Ethics," in *Christian Reflections*, p. 55.
11. *Miracles*, p. 110.
12. See *The Four Loves*, p. 15.
13. Arguments for the existence of God will be found, inter alia, in "Christian Apologetics," in *God in the Dock*, pp. 100–101; "Is Theism Important?" in ibid., especially p. 173; Part I of *Mere Christianity*; chapter 1 of *The Problem of Pain*; and chapters 1–4 of *Miracles*.
14. *Perelandra*, p. 169.
15. See "Is Theology Poetry?" in *They Asked for a Paper and Other Essays*, p. 162; also see *Miracles*, chapters 3–4, especially pp. 19–20; and *A Preface to Paradise*

Lost, p. 11. The quotation is from "De Futilitate," in *Christian Reflections*, pp. 63ff.

16. See *Miracles*, chapters 2–5. Lewis expressed his conviction of the untenability of the doctrine of total depravity, inter alia, in *The Problem of Pain*, pp. 37–38, 66–67. See further in chapter 7.

17. *That Hideous Strength*, p. 184. On Kirkpatrick, see *Surprised by Joy*, chapter 9. Note also Lewis's letter to his father upon learning of Kirkpatrick's death: "I owe him in the intellectual sphere as much as one human being can owe another. . . . It was an atmosphere of unrelenting clearness and rigid honesty of thought that one breathed from living with him—and this I shall be the better for as long as I live" (*Letters of C. S. Lewis*, p. 54).

18. *That Hideous Strength*, p. 72. The statement is placed on the lips of Hingest, whom Lewis obviously intended to be a person of sound judgment.

19. *Miracles*, p. 28.

20. Ibid.

21. *The Voyage of the Dawn Treader*, p. 135.

22. "Christian Apologetics," in *God in the Dock*, p. 102. See *The Problem of Pain*, p. 28.

23. See *The Problem of Pain*, p. 39.

24. *That Hideous Strength*, p. 368.

25. Ibid.

26. One of Lewis's clearest statements on rationality in Christianity is in *Mere Christianity*, p. 123. It may be noted that when Lewis makes such assertions one cannot be sure of precisely what he means, since he includes within reason a wide range of mental activities, commencing with logic but going beyond logic to higher truths; see the discussion of *ratio* and *intellectus* in our next chapter. See also "Bulverism," in *God in the Dock*. A particularly incisive rebuttal of scholarly errors in logic appears in *A Preface to Paradise Lost*, pp. 9–12, where Lewis attacks T. S. Eliot's dictum that the only acceptable critics of poetry are those who are the best practicing poets.

27. See *Christian Behaviour*, chapters 11–12 (in *Mere Christianity*). In the second of these chapters Lewis presents a particularly, though not uniquely, Protestant interpretation of faith.

28. "Is Theism Important?" in *God in the Dock*, p. 175.

29. See "Religion: Reality or Substitute?" in *Christian Reflections*, pp. 42–43.

30. See *Mere Christianity*, pp. 21, 24–25. Upon occasion Lewis refers to this aspect of reality by yet other terms. In "Christian Apologetics," in *God in the Dock*, for instance, Lewis calls it an "enlightened universalist ethic" (p. 103). His casualness of expression reflects his relatively slight interest in technical terminology, noted earlier.

31. *Miracles*, p. 38. In *The Problem of Pain*, pp. 100ff., Lewis insisted that God does not command things arbitrarily but because they are right; he could not command otherwise. Thus in one sense God is subject to absolute moral law, although in another, and equally valid sense, he and his moral imperatives are inseparable elements of a single reality.

32. *That Hideous Strength*, p. 370.
33. *Mere Christianity*, p. 19. Regarding the essential agreement of the world's great religous teachers concerning proper conduct, see also *The Problem of Pain*, p. 63.
34. Lewis granted that not every person seems to display this innate moral sense. In *Mere Christianity* he wrote: "You might . . . find an odd individual here and there who did not know it, just as you might find a few people who are colour-blind or who have no ear for a tune. But taking the race as a whole, they [premodern thinkers] thought that the human idea of decent behaviour was obvious to every one. And I believe they were right" (p. 18).
35. *Mere Christianity*, p. 25.
36. See further in chapter 7.
37. *Mere Christianity*, p. 24.
38. *The Discarded Image*, p. 160.
39. See Green and Hooper, *C. S. Lewis*, p. 218.
40. Lewis gathers passages under these rubrics in an appendix called "Illustrations of the *Tao*," in *The Abolition of Man* (pp. 51–61). He also discusses some of the universal moral principles in "On Ethics," in *Christian Reflections* and in Part III of *Mere Christianity*. Note also the brief list of principles in *Out of the Silent Planet*, p. 138.
41. "On Ethics," in *Christian Reflections*, pp. 53, 55–56.
42. *Mere Christianity*, p. 78.
43. "The Poison of Subjectivism," in *Christian Reflections*, p. 73. See also "We Have No Right to Happiness," in *God in the Dock*, p. 318.
44. *Mere Christianity*, pp. 130–31.
45. *The Last Battle*, p. 137.
46. *Perelandra*, pp. 42–43.
47. Ibid., p. 48.
48. *The Last Battle*, p. 164.
49. The priest of the monstrous goddess Ungit speaks on behalf of primitive religion when he says, "I . . . have dealt with the gods for three generations of men, and I know that they dazzle our eyes and flow in and out of one another like eddies on a river, and nothing that is said clearly can be said truly about them. Holy places are dark places. It is life and strength, not knowledge and words, that we get in them. Holy wisdom is not clear and thin like water, but thick and dark like blood" (*Till We Have Faces*, p. 50). On Lewis's distinction between "thick" and "clear" religions, see also "Christian Apologetics," in *God in the Dock*, pp. 102–3; also note the poem "Reason," in *Poems*, p. 81.
50. See *Surprised by Joy*, p. 213. Also see "Revival or Decay?" and "The Decline of Religion," in *God in the Dock*, particularly p. 219. Lewis speaks of "the rich Platonic or Vergilian *penumbra* of the Faith" in his essay "On the Transmission of Christianity," in *God in the Dock*, p. 118.
51. *Reflections on the Psalms*, pp. 106–7.
52. Ibid., p. 108.

53. Ibid.
54. "Is Theism Important?" in *God in the Dock*, p. 172.
55. *Spenser's Images of Life*, p. 129. The words that Wind quoted are those of Pico della Mirandola.
56. Lewis discussed the two Venuses in *Spenser's Images of Life*, pp. 50–51 and occasionally elsewhere in the work.
57. See *That Hideous Strength*, pp. 316–17.
58. *Perelandra*, pp. 201–2.
59. See *That Hideous Strength*, pp. 304–5; cf. pp. 316–17, and chapter 15, especially pp. 322–24.
60. "Religion Without Dogma?" in *God in the Dock*, p. 132. See the very similar statements in "Answers to Questions on Christianity," in *God in the Dock*, p. 54; and in *The Problem of Pain*, p. 24.
61. See *Mere Christianity*, p. 54.
62. "Religion Without Dogma?" in *God in the Dock*, p. 144.
63. *The Four Loves*, p. 147; *Letters of C. S. Lewis*, p. 258. "I have," said Lewis in *The Problem of Pain*," deepest respect even for Pagan myths, still more for myths in Holy Scripture" (p. 71).
64. *Prince Caspian*, pp. 151–54; see also p. 205.

Chapter 6: Imagination and the Mystical Ascent

1. "Bluspels and Flalansferes," in *Selected Literary Essays*, p. 265.
2. *Letters of C. S. Lewis*, p. 260.
3. Recall Lewis's views on the importance of mythology, discussed in the previous chapter.
4. "The Language of Religion," in *Christian Reflections*, p. 134.
5. "The thing we are talking about," said Lewis, referring to the absolute, or God, "can never appear in the discussion at all" ("The Language of Religion," in *Christian Reflections*, p. 136.
6. "Reason," in *Poems*, p. 81.
7. Ibid.
8. "Christianity and Literature," in *Christian Reflections*, p. 7.
9. *Letters to Malcolm*, p. 73.
10. *Letters of C. S. Lewis*, p. 203. Cf. similar comments in *Miracles*, pp. 41–42.
11. "Christianity and Literature," in *Christian Reflections*, pp. 6–7.
12. Ibid., pp. 8–9. Note Lewis's reference to Phemius in the *Odyssey*, who asserts, "I am self-taught; a god has inspired me with all manner of songs" (ibid., p. 8). Lewis comments: "How can he be self-taught if the god has taught him all he knows? Doubtless because the god's instruction is given internally, not through the senses, and is therefore regarded as part of the Self, to be contrasted with such external aids as, say, the example of other poets."
13. "It All Began with a Picture," in *Of Other Worlds*, p. 42.

14. *Mere Christianity,* p. 121.
15. See *The Voyage of the Dawn Treader,* p. 133. Lucy reads in an ancient book a story about "a cup and a sword and a tree and a green hill" which she senses as being the "loveliest story I've ever read or shall read in my whole life." She does not understand the story, which is of course that of the passion of Jesus as narrated in the Gospels, but Aslan reassures her that he "will tell it to you for years and years" (p. 136)—but in Lucy's proper world rather than in Narnia.
16. "On Three Ways of Writing for Children," in *Of Other Worlds,* pp. 32–33.
17. "Unreal Estates," in *Of Other Worlds,* p. 87.
18. "On Criticism," in *Of Other Worlds,* p. 51.
19. "Sometimes Fairy Stories May Say Best What's To Be Said," in *Of Other Worlds,* p. 36. See also "On Three Ways of Writing for Children," in *Of Other Worlds.*
20. "Unreal Estates," in *Of Other Worlds,* p. 88.
21. "On Three Ways of Writing for Children," in *Of Other Worlds,* pp. 33, 34.
22. *Letters of C. S. Lewis,* p. 182.
23. "Bluspels and Flalansferes," in *Selected Literary Essays,* pp. 264–65.
24. In *Mere Christianity,* p. 22.
25. "The Language of Religion," in *Christian Reflections,* p. 140.
26. *The Pilgrim's Regress,* p. 171. Cf. Lewis's statement in *Perelandra,* p. 202, previously cited, as well as that in *Miracles,* p. 139. Myth is "a real though unfocussed gleam of divine truth falling on human imagination."
27. *Out of the Silent Planet,* pp. 144–45. In *The Problem of Pain* Lewis denied that myth should be understood as being simply the symbolical representation of nonhistorical truth—though it can be that—and insisted that "in the Socratic sense" a myth is "a not unlikely tale" (p. 77), an account of what may be (though it need not be) historical fact.
28. *Letters of C. S. Lewis,* p. 143. Cf. "Christian Apologetics," in *God in the Dock,* p. 101.
29. "Myth Became Fact," in *God in the Dock,* pp. 66, 64–65.
30. This passage is quoted in Green and Hooper, *C. S. Lewis,* pp. 117–18. The letter was written on 11 October 1931, less than two weeks after Lewis passed from a belief in theism to an acceptance of Christianity.
31. Regarding the relationship of Christian theology to poetry and myth, see "Is Theology Poetry?" in *They Asked for a Paper: Papers and Addresses.*
32. In "The Language of Religion," in *Christian Reflections,* Lewis stressed the differences between poetry and myth. Myth has no beauty of itself, whereas poetry does have beauty. Both kinds of writing communicate important things about reality, but not in the same way.
33. "This is the most remarkable of the powers of Poetic language," said Lewis, "to convey to us the quality of experiences which we have not had, or perhaps can never have, to use factors within our experience so that they become pointers to something outside our experience—as two or more roads on a map show us where a town that is off the map must lie" (ibid., p. 133).

34. "Dante's Similes," in *Studies in Medieval and Renaissance Literature*, pp. 76–77.
35. "What they now call 'demythologising' Christianity can easily be a 're-mythologising' it—and substituting a poorer mythology for a richer," wrote Lewis in *Letters to Malcolm*, p. 52. See also "Modern Theology and Biblical Criticism," in *Christian Reflections*.
36. "Horrid Red Things," in *God in the Dock*, pp. 70–71; cf. *Miracles*, chapter 10.
37. Lewis's preface to *George MacDonald: An Anthology*, pp. 14–15.
38. See "On Science Fiction," in *Of Other Worlds*, pp. 64, 65.
39. "On Three Ways of Writing for Children," in *Of Other Worlds*, pp. 29, 23.
40. *That Hideous Strength*, p. 359. Cf. "On Three Ways of Writing for Children," in *Of Other Worlds*, p. 25.
41. "From Christianity itself," Lewis asserted, "we learn that there is a level—in the long run the only level of importance—on which the learned and the adult have no advantage at all over the simple and the child" (*The Problem of Pain*, p. 79).
42. *Surprised by Joy*, p. 221.
43. *Letters to Malcolm*, p. 65. In *The Four Loves* (p. 168) Lewis also spoke with implied disapproval of Neoplatonic mysticism.
44. *Letters to Malcolm*, pp. 64–65.
45. Ibid., p. 65.
46. At least, that is what Lewis knew intellectually to be true. His own predilections sometimes told him otherwise. No matter how important the goal, it was the journey that was most worth the having. Lewis came close to admitting this psychological commonplace when he wrote in the preface to the third edition of *The Pilgrim's Regress*: "Once you grant your fairy, your enchanted forest, your satyr, faun, wood-nymph and well of immortality [to be] *real*, and amidst all the scientific, social and practical interest which the discovery would awake, the Sweet Desire would have disappeared, would have shifted its ground, like the cuckoo's voice or the rainbow's end, and be now calling us from beyond a *further* hill. . . . The human soul was made to enjoy some object that is never fully given—nay, cannot even be imagined as given—in our present mode of subjective and spatio-temporal experience" (pp. 9–10). He came close to suggesting much the same thing in *The Last Battle*, where, as we have observed, the upward journey toward God continues even within the heavenly Narnia, and again in *That Hideous Strength*, where innumerable levels of reality are posited as lying beyond anything conceivable by the human mind (see *That Hideous Strength*, p. 327).
47. See further in the next chapter.
48. *A Grief Observed*, p. 59.
49. Whether or not the Neoplatonic *via negativa* was indeed austere and void, Lewis tended to think of it as such.
50. *The Four Loves*, p. 14.
51. See *The Lion, the Witch, and the Wardrobe*, p. 62.
52. *The Voyage of the Dawn Treader*, p. 163.
53. Ibid., p. 177.
54. Ibid., p. 189.

55. Ibid., p. 199.
56. Ibid.
57. Ibid., pp. 206–7.
58. Ibid., p. 211.
59. Ibid., p. 212.
60. *Mere Christianity,* p. 131.
61. *The Voyage of the Dawn Treader,* pp. 215–16.
62. See *The Last Battle,* pp. 154 and often thereafter. We have noted that this theme appears briefly in the first of the Narnian stories. It is not, however, limited to the Narnian tales, being at least implied in all of Lewis's novels. It appears as "upwards and inwards" in Ransom's walk up the mammary hill of Oyarsa's island in *Out of the Silent Planet* (see p. 110). Each of the Heavenly Spirits in *The Great Divorce* "lives only to journey further and further into the mountains" (p. 69). The influence of George MacDonald is doubtless present in this theme.
63. Cf. Hyoi's description of a mystical encounter with Maleldil at the pool of Balki in *Out of the Silent Planet,* p. 75.
64. *Prince Caspian,* pp. 135–36. Cf. the romp described in *The Lion, the Witch, and the Wardrobe,* pp. 160–61.
65. *Perelandra,* pp. 34–35. Cf. Ransom's first experience with eating on the planet (p. 42).
66. See *That Hideous Strength,* p. 369.
67. "Dogma and the Universe," in *God in the Dock,* p. 47.
68. *The Four Loves,* p. 15.

Chapter 7: The Self

1. *Mere Christianity,* p. 139. Cf. the statement of the Oyarsa of Malacandra to Ransom: "Do not think [you and I] are utterly unlike. We are both copies of Maleldil" (*Out of the Silent Planet,* p. 120).
2. See "Priestesses in the Church?" in *God in the Dock,* pp. 237–39; *Miracles,* p. 63; *Mere Christianity,* pp. 102–3. Note that although Lewis perceived males to be dominant in the sense that they take many roles of leadership intended for them by God, he did not regard them as spiritually superior to women. He looked upon the human soul as having no sexuality (although it might be regarded, as he suggested in *Miracles,* pp. 165–66, as possessing "transsexuality"); still, he believed that maleness and femaleness were expressions of a deep metaphysical reality. See also our chapter 4.
3. *Surprised by Joy,* pp. 221–22.
4. See *The Magician's Nephew,* pp. 136–40. Centuries later, when Narnia is devoid of human beings and evil reigns, the thrones at the capital, Cair Paravel, are still awaiting human beings as their rightful occupants (see *The Lion, the Witch, and the Wardrobe,* pp. 76 et passim). Note also Lewis's comments on man's lordship over animals in *The Problem of Pain,* p. 78.

5. See *Perelandra*, chapters 16-17. In a remarkable passage, even the celestial intelligences bow before the new humanoid king and queen of the planet (p. 204). In referring to the divinely ordained lordship of man over nature, Lewis said that nature is, in one sense, "displaced by the advent of imperial man, yet, in some other sense, not displaced at all." What he means by "displaced" he did not precisely say, but he asserted that nature is "a thing in her own right" (p. 160). Tor and Tinidril can be so exalted because they have not defied Maleldil and sinned. In *A Preface to Paradise Lost* Lewis pointed out that Milton's Adam and Eve prior to their fall are noble and majestic, reflecting their divine maker far more than they do after the fall. Adam's kingly manner is but an outward expression of his supernatural kingship over the earth and his wisdom; and Eve, even in her inferior status to Adam, is queenly (see especially chapter 16 of that work). It should be noted, however, that Lewis's ultimate justification for the exaltation of human beings was not the story of Adam and Eve but the Incarnation. He had the Green Lady say in *Perelandra*, "In your world Maleldil first took Himself this form, the form of your race and mine. . . . Since our Beloved became a man, how should Reason in any world take on another form?" (p. 62).
6. "On Being Human," in *Poems*, pp. 34–35.
7. See the previous chapter.
8. Regarding the idea of the pre-existence of the soul, see *The Four Loves*, p. 153.
9. *The Discarded Image*, pp. 152ff.
10. The *Problem of Pain*, p. 125; cf. p. 81 and elsewhere in that work.
11. The *Abolition of Man*, pp. 15–16.
12. One strain of Christian thought, the Calvinist, held that by the fall in Eden man became totally depraved, to the extent that even the ability of the mind to reason became corrupted by sin. Lewis could not accept this doctrine. He held rather that *ratio*, like mathematical principles, had an inherently incorruptible quality, and that reasoning could be done properly by human beings within the limitations of the available data. He was also not inclined to doubt that the *intellectus* could be the vehicle for an ascent toward God, however incomplete the mortal percepttion of reality might necessarily be. See chapter 6. In *Perelandra* Tinidril, the Eve-figure, is tempted by Satan, but with the help of Ransom (that is, Christ) she withstands Satan's wiles. In this story Lewis may have in mind Milton's *Paradise Regained*, in which, as he put it, "the perfect manhood which Adam lost is . . . matured in conflict with Satan; in that sense Eden, or Paradise, is regained" (*A Preface to Paradise Lost*, p. 90). This background may in part explain the origin of the name Perelandra: a Paradise-land; so suggest Green and Hooper, *C. S. Lewis*, pp. 170, 172. In traditional Christian thought the sacrificial death of Christ atones for human sin and restores the proper relationship of God and man—in Platonic terms, restores the self to a perfect state of harmony in which the soul can apprehend God without the alienation of sin. Concerning evil see chapter 8.

13. The quotation is from "Religion and Rocketry," in *The World's Last Night and Other Essays*, p. 85. In *Letters to Malcolm* Lewis quoted with favor the theologian Alec Vidler's statement that man is "a two-fold creature—not only a political creature, but also a spiritual being" (p. 32). He added: "Vidler and you and I (and Plato) think it is a fact."

14. "Christianity and Culture," in *Christian Reflections*, p. 23. Sometimes Lewis stressed the blindness of human beings toward those residual values. In his *Pilgrim's Regress* (pp. 60–66) he depicted persons who are imprisoned by the Spirit of the Age, wailing and refusing to leave their jail even when Reason opens the door, just as the prisoners in Plato's analogy of the cave are reluctant to abandon their familiar illusions. Elsewhere he recalls H. G. Wells's story "Country of the Blind," about a similar situation (see "The Language of Religion," in *Christian Reflections*, pp. 140–41). Lewis did not have in mind, of course, a total depravity. The idea of a residual, innate knowledge of absolute truth in all human beings found expression in his poem "The Prudent Jailer," where the imagery is that of the memory of heavenly truth imprisoned by modern secularism:

> Always the old nostalgia? Yes.
> We still remember times before
> We had learned to wear the prison dress
> Or steel rings rubbed our ankles sore.
> ....
> Still when we hear the trains at night
> We envy the free travellers, whirled
> In how few moments past the sight
> Of the blind wall that bounds our world.
> Our Jailer (well he may) prefers
> Our thoughts should keep a narrower range.
> "The proper study of prisoners
> Is prison," he tells us. . . . (*Poems*, p. 77).

15. *Letters of C. S. Lewis*, p. 167.

16. *The Last Battle*, p. 141. Particularly informative is the episode in *Prince Caspian*, pp. 137–47.

17. See *The Lion, the Witch, and the Wardrobe*, pp. 104–5. At the same time that she receives the vial Lucy is also given a small dagger. Lewis evidently decided that the dagger was not appropriate to Lucy's character, for he never again mentioned it, whereas Lucy is said to use her cordial on several subsequent occasions in the Narnian series.

18. See ibid., chapters 14–15.

19. Lewis never, however, permits Edmund to surpass Lucy in spiritual insight. In *Prince Caspian* Edmund is impetuous and sometimes weak. Particularly instructive is the sequence in that story in which the four children come to perceive Aslan, who is leading them unseen. The first person to see the lion is Lucy; she is followed by Edmund, then Peter, and finally Susan (pp. 144–47).

20. *The Problem of Pain*, p. 104. What man lost in disobeying God in the Fall was the ability of his rational soul fully to control his whole self; and that control was, in fact, the rule of God over the self. The disobedience of Adam meant the rejection of God's authority over him. See further in ibid., chapter 5, particularly p. 81.

21. It should not be thought that Lewis was consciously molding his characters into Platonic categories. But the characterizations flowed easily from his deeply ingrained Platonist-Christian frame of reference.

22. *The Last Battle*, pp. 134–35.

23. Note that Susan is not simply a skeptic; for MacPhee in *That Hideous Strength* and Trumpkin in *Prince Caspian* are that also, yet they participate in the good inner circle. Susan's problem is that she is no longer willing to remain within the inner circle; she has set herself apart. There is room in Lewis's Friends of Narnia or Company of Logres for skeptics if they love their fellow human beings and are willing to sacrifice themselves for others, but not if they have the capacity to love only themselves.

24. See *The Voyage of the Dawn Treader*, chapters 6–7. Lewis actually gives Eustace a much larger stock of undesirable attributes; he is also hateful, vain, imperious, unadventuresome, insensitive to others, obstreperous, gluttonous, devious, pragmatic, unimaginative, and lazy.

25. See *The Pilgrim's Regress*, pp. 191–94. Thereafter follows a chapter on a Southern Dragon.

26. See *The Voyage of the Dawn Treader*, pp. 89–91. As was the case with Edmund, Lewis emphasized (following traditional Christian doctrine) that Eustace cannot redeem himself. He tries repeatedly to pull off his squamous skin, only to find another like it beneath. The pain that Eustace feels as Aslan strips off his dragon's skin is perhaps meant to signify a lingering love of the dragon-self on Eustace's part, present unconsciously even though Eustace consciously wants the skin removed. Cf. the episode of the man with the lizard in *The Great Divorce*. Lewis treated the same subject in *Letters to Malcolm*, where he wrote:

> The saved soul, at the very foot of the throne, begs to be taken away and cleansed. It cannot bear for a moment longer "With its darkness to affront that light." Religion has reclaimed Purgatory. Our souls *demand* Purgatory, don't they? Would it not break the heart if God said to us, "It is true, my son, that your breath smells and your rags drip with mud and slime, but we are charitable here and no one will upbraid you with these things nor draw away from you. Enter into the joy"? Should we not reply, "With submission, sir, and if there is no objection, I'd *rather* be cleansed first." "It may hurt, you know"—"Even so, sir." (Pp. 108–9).

27. Reepicheep figures in the action of *Prince Caspian* and *The Voyage of the Dawn Treader*, and appears briefly at the conclusion of *The Last Battle*.

28. Although one can find in the secondary literature on Lewis the suggestion that the inhabitants of Malacandra represent the three elements of the

Platonic soul (the seroni, reason; the pfifltriggi, will; the hrossa, the appetites), I can see no basis for such an interpretation.

29. Ransom appears to be, in part, Lewis's fantasy of himself adventuresomely participating in a world where reality was just as the Platonic-Christian tradition had described it. Lewis had earlier fictionalized himself to some extent in the person of John in *The Pilgrim's Regress*, and would do so again in some of his later writings—as, for instance, in his picture of Orual. That such was the case has, however, relatively slight bearing upon the understanding of Lewis's thought.

30. The only close approximation of a Platonic philosopher-ruler in the Narnian tales is Professor Digory Kirke, who, by virtue of his study of Plato, comprehends what is transpiring in the final apocalyptic episodes of *The Last Battle*.

31. On one occasion Lewis revised the tripartite Platonic self along somewhat Christianized lines and spoke of a person as consisting of a human self, an animal self, and a diabolical self (see *Mere Christianity*, p. 95). Weston could be said to be one in whom the diabolical self has totally gained control.

32. Concerning Weston, Satan, and the deterioration of the self, see further in chapter 8.

33. *The Great Divorce*, p. 129. Regarding the freedom of a person to disobey God, see *The Problem of Pain*, pp. 34–35, 69–70, 85, and elsewhere in that work.

34. Note, for example, Lewis's statement, "Because Nature, and especially human nature, is fallen, it must be corrected and the evil within it must be mortified" ("Some Thoughts," in *God in the Dock*, p. 148; cf. *The Problem of Pain*, chapter 6, especially p. 92). The use of the traditional term "mortify" suggests the possibility of excessive attempts to discipline the mind and the body. Lewis maintained, however, a fairly rationalisic view of asceticism, concluding, as Luther had centuries earlier, that self-flagellation was a cul-de-sac in spiritual growth, not to mention being psychologically and theologically difficult to justify.

35. *Letters of C. S. Lewis*, p. 268.

36. *Letters to an American Lady*, p. 108.

37. "Scraps," in *God in the Dock*, pp. 216–17.

38. By rejecting repression as an effective means of self-control Lewis had at least a minimal common ground with most modern psychologists. In general, however, he had little concern with psychology. It is possible to find in the tripartite soul rough equivalents to Freud's ego, superego, and id. Lewis knew something of Freudian psychology and respected it, but had disagreement with some of its central hypotheses (see "Psycho-Analysis and Literary Criticism," in *Selected Literary Essays*; *Christian Behaviour*, chapter 4 [in *Mere Christianity*]; *The Pilgrim's Regress*, Book 3, chapter 6). He was much more interested in Jungian psychology, particularly in its postulation of the existence of archetypes; these latter he could integrate to a considerable extent into both the Platonic world view and his own. Behavioral psychology, which usually has no room for supernatural or collective realities at all and tends toward determinism, he could readily dismiss.

NOTES

39. *Letters of C. S. Lewis*, p. 126.
40. See also *The Four Loves*.
41. See *Reflections on the Psalms*, chapter 3. In *The Four Loves* Lewis even permits the "hating" of persons, but softens the meaning of the term to something like rejection of others "when they come between us and our obedience to God" (p. 172).
42. See "The Conditions for a Just War," in *God in the Dock*, pp. 325–27; "Answers to Questions on Christianity," in *God in the Dock*, p. 49; *Mere Christianity*, pp. 106–8.
43. P. 200. See also Ransom's first awakening to the concept that evil might be, and sometimes could only be, defeated through physical combat—violence and, ultimately, killing (*Perelandra*, p. 143). Note also Lewis's comments in *Letters of C. S. Lewis*, pp. 247–48.
44. P. 145. See also *The Magician's Nephew*, p. 18.
45. *The Four Loves*, p. 16.
46. Lewis was doubtless much influenced by the description of the House of Coelia (representing cosmic goodness) in Spenser's *Faerie Queene*. (See *Spenser's Images of Life*, pp. 86–93 and the subsequent section describing Spenser's sense of good and evil.) The good is, among other things, humble, unconscious, spontaneous, naive, superbly vital, and fecund. It leads to dancing, revelry and all sorts of other motion. It may also at times be inarticulate, even clumsy.
47. See Lewis's discussion of "need-love" in *The Four Loves*, especially pp. 12–13. Cf. *That Hideous Strength*, p. 360.
48. As an example of Lewis's conscientious attempt to participate in the community of the faithful, see his comments in "Answers to Questions on Christianity," in *God in the Dock*, pp. 61–62. Lewis's confession of gaucherie is found in *Surprised by Joy*, p. 234. See also the comments of Lewis's brother Warren in *Letters of C. S. Lewis*, p. 19. In *Letters to Malcolm* Lewis noticeably shied away from any pronouncements concerning corporate worship (pp. 3–4 in particular).
49. When, in *The Silver Chair*, the followers of Aslan "kneel and kiss his likeness" (p. 168), the reader is likely to be stunned, even though Lewis probably wrote with the conventions of medieval piety in mind. Cf. mention of an amuletic gold image of Aslan in *The Voyage of the Dawn Treader*, p. 13. On private religious practices see, among other things, *Mere Christianity*, pp. 71ff., 142ff., 145ff.; "Work and Prayer," in *God in the Dock*; "Petitionary Prayer: A Problem without an Answer," in *Christian Reflections*; *Letters to an American Lady*, p. 22; and often in *Letters to Malcolm*. Ransom prays for Weston's soul in *Perelandra* (p. 130). At the end of that work King Tor says that he and his wife will "speak" always to Maleldil about Ransom, and he asks that Ransom do the same for them (p. 222).
50. In *The Silver Chair* (p. 1) Lewis caustically described the progressive school that Scrubb and Pole attend. Note that the issue of subjectively oriented education arises indirectly but often in *That Hideous Strength*, which Lewis

said in his preface "has behind it a serious 'point' which I have tried to make in my *Abolition of Man*" (p. 7).

51. *Out of the Silent Planet,* pp. 39–40, 120.

52. *The Silver Chair,* p. 21. The concept of the descent of the soul into the dark regions of Earth serves as a partial justification to Lewis for his interest in magic. Magic represents the operation of unchanging laws of reality that most people do not comprehend and cannot safely manipulate because, as earthly creatures, they have lost their former knowledge of higher laws. Although evil beings can perform some magic, deeper (that is, profounder) magic can be performed only by celestial intelligences such as Aslan (see *The Lion, the Witch, and the Wardrobe,* chapter 15) and the Magician on the Island of the Voices (see *The Voyage of the Dawn Treader,* chapters 10–11). Merlin, as Lewis fictionalized him, is a survival from an earlier era when human minds were allegedly in closer contract with natural and supernatural processes. This "Atlantean magic" (*That Hideous Strength,* p. 201), always dangerous but potentially good, stands in contrast to black magic (as it were), such as that practiced by the N.I.C.E.

53. "Meditation in a Toolshed," in *God in the Dock,* p. 212.

54. *The Lion, the Witch, and the Wardrobe,* pp. 64–65. Cf. the suggestion of Platonic recollection in *The Magician's Nephew,* where the London cabbie, upon meeting Aslan for the first time, declares, "Yet I feel somehow . . . we've met before" (pp. 136–37).

55. Recollection does not mean that everyone knows Christian truth intuitively. Initially one can only recollect, or intuit, a limited range of truth, such as some basic moral principles or the axioms of reason. Much truth—the most important kind, in fact—comes only by revelation: first of all, by God revealing Himself to man, then by teachers (the Bible and human beings) passing on divine truth. See further in "On the Transmission of Christianity," in *God in the Dock.* Lewis seems to have believed, though he did not discuss the matter in that article, that the person who has been properly taught concerning reality will find other recollections pertaining to the absolute coming to mind; hence education of the right sort aids the self in apprehending an increasing amount of reality in an endless process of learning and insight.

56. *Perelandra,* p. 103. Lewis was, however, relatively favorably inclined toward the Jungian archetypes because of their potential affinities with his Christian objectivism. See his comments on Jung in "Psycho-Analysis and Literary Criticism" in *Selected Literary Essays,* pp. 296–300.

57. *Out of the Silent Planet,* p. 43.

58. *The Four Loves,* p. 15.

59. "The Weight of Glory," in *The Weight of Glory and Other Addresses,* p. 11.

60. *The Problem of Pain,* p. 153.

61. See *Letters to Malcolm,* p. 93. The joy that Lewis speaks so much of, particularly in *Surprised by Joy,* should not be thought of primarily in terms of romanticism (although it involves romantic elements), or of aestheticism in

general, or of intellectualism as such. It is closely related to the kind of joy (*gaudium*) that some of the Christian Platonists of the Renaissance, such as Marsilio Ficino, describe. It is a joy of a mystical sort which comes in its fullness only as one enters the presence of God. For Lewis, as for Ficino, all other joys are but fleeting suggestions of this one absolute joy. Not all Renaissance Platonists shared Ficino's viewpoint; Ficino's pupil, Pico della Mirandola, followed a mystical road that led to the ultimate annihilation of the self as it was absorbed into the totality of God.

62. "Man or Rabbit?" in *God in the Dock*, p. 112.
63. "The Weight of Glory," in *The Weight of Glory and Other Addresses*, pp. 12–13.
64. Ibid., pp. 13–14.
65. All human loves will be transformed; hence Lewis affirmed, with evident regret, that it is unrealistic to expect to renew friendships or meet loved ones in the afterlife. Yet he insisted that all that was good in those relationships would be preserved, and that one would indeed have far vaster joy than was ever possible in earthly relationships. See his comments in *The Four Loves*, pp. 187–92; cf. *A Grief Observed*, p. 23.
66. Thus the reader is cautioned not to suppose that Lewis intended his description of the heavenly Narnia in *The Last Battle* to be taken literally.

Chapter 8: Evil and Eschatology

1. Evil can also be useful in the education of human beings. In *Perelandra* the newly invested king of the planet says to Ransom:

    "We have learned of evil, though not as the Evil One wished us to learn. . . . There is an ignorance of evil that comes from being young: there is a darker ignorance that comes from doing it, as men by sleeping lose the knowledge of sleep. You are more ignorant of evil in Thulcandra now than in the days before your Lord and Lady began to do it. But Maleldil has brought us out of the one ignorance, and we have not entered the other. It was by the Evil One himself that he brought us out of the first. Little did that dark mind know the errand on which he really came to Perelandra!" (p. 209)

2. *Out of the Silent Planet*, p. 75.
3. See *The Problem of Pain*, chapters 6–7.
4. *Letters to Malcolm*, p. 69. "Satan, the leader or dictator of devils," said Lewis in one of his prefaces to *The Screwtape Letters*, "is the opposite, not of God, but of [the archangel] Michael" (p. vii).
5. *Letters of C. S. Lewis*, p. 257. Cf. *An Experiment in Criticism*, p. 21.
6. *The Great Divorce*, p. 127. This conviction caused Lewis to have much difficulty in carrying out his intention in *The Screwtape Letters* of having the satanic Screwtape be the direct antithesis of all that is angelic or good. Lewis later commented that the book was the only one of his that he did not take

pleasure in writing, inasmuch as "making goods 'bad' and bads 'good' gets to be fatiguing" ("Cross-examination," in *God in the Dock*, p. 263). He might have added that the endeavor was, according to his own understanding of the nature of evil, theoretically impossible.

7. *Mere Christianity*, p. 48; cf. his further comment on pp. 50–51.

8. *Mere Christianity*, pp. 49–50. See also "Evil and God," in *God in the Dock*.

9. If one defines monism in its most basic sense as that metaphysical view which emphasizes the unity of reality, then Lewis, like Plato, is certainly a monist. Curiously, and largely unjustifiably, Lewis once attempted to reject monism. He wrote in *Miracles*:

> You must really . . . work hard . . . to eradicate from your mind the whole type of thought . . . called *Monism*; but perhaps the unlearned reader will understand me best if I call it *Everythingism*. I mean by this the belief that "everything," or "the whole show," must be self-existent, must be more important than every particular thing, and must contain all particular things in such a way that they cannot really be very different from one another—and that they must be not merely "at one" but one. Thus the Everythingist, if he starts from God, becomes a Pantheist; there must be nothing that is not God. If he starts from Nature he becomes a Naturalist; there must be nothing that is not Nature. . . . This philosophy I believe to be profoundly untrue. One of the moderns has said that reality is "incorrigibly plural." I think he is right. All things come from One. All things are related—related in different and complicated ways. But all things are not one. (P. 171)

He thus opted in this passage for pluralism as a philosophical stance. That he could seriously claim to be a pluralist borders on the absurd; his entire philosophy of religion denied what is commonly called pluralism. Lewis could dismiss monism because he chose to see it as leading only to pantheism or naturalism, neither of which philosophies he could accept. As was so often the case, however, he was narrowing his definitions to suit his own purposes. Monism obviously need not be linked only with pantheism and naturalism, nor, for that matter, does it need to be thought of as being limited to certain philosophical schools that have appeared in Western thought only in the last several centuries. The quotation is from *Letters of C. S. Lewis*, page 175.

10. *Perelandra*, p. 195.

11. Earth is the silent planet because human beings fell into Satan's power, not because (as one scholar has asserted) they have lost the language that articulates cosmic harmony. The loss of Old Solar is only a by-product of the fall, just as in Genesis the loss of a universal language is an outcome of man's sinfulness and God's judgment.

12. *Out of the Silent Planet*, pp. 120–21.

13. *The Great Divorce*, p. 65; cf. *Miracles*, p. 167.

14. *The Last Battle*, pp. 80–82.

15. Everything depends, of course, upon what substance one has in mind, and at times Lewis referred to eldils as "unsubstantial," but without altering his meaning. Note the contrast between the wraithlike Tash and the richly solid body of Aslan. So lacking in absolute substantiality is Tash that when Aslan appears he simply banishes Tash from existence by a short, simple command (ibid., pp. 132–33).

16. See chapter 13 of that work.

17. *The Magician's Nephew*, p. 174.

18. See also *The Screwtape Letters*, p. ix.

19. *The Last Battle*, pp. 146–47.

20. Ibid., p. 148. Cf. *The Great Divorce*, p. 127: "Good beats upon the damned incessantly as sound waves beat on the ears of the deaf, but they cannot receive it. Their fists are clenched, their teeth are clenched, their eyes fast shut. First they will not, in the end they cannot, open their hands for gifts, or their mouths for food, or their eyes to see."

21. See *Out of the Silent Planet*, p. 138.

22. *Perelandra*, p. 81.

23. See Weston's statements in *Out of the Silent Planet*, pp. 135–37 and *Perelandra*, pp. 89–96 and elsewhere. Lewis was particularly emphatic in his expression of dislike for allegedly scientific projections of "remote futures and universal benefits" (*That Hideous Strength*, p. 259), on the grounds that such lofty aims can be, and are being, used to justify all sorts of amoral and immoral conduct. In Weston he caricatures the views of J. B. S. Haldane as he understood them from Haldane's *Possible Words and Other Essays* (1927). "Professor Haldane pictured a future in which Man, foreseeing that Earth would soon be uninhabitable, adapted himself for migration to Venus by drastically modifying his physiology and abandoning justice, pity, and happiness" ("Is Progress Possible?" in *God in the Dock*, p. 311).

24. *Perelandra*, p. 85.

25. Ibid., p. 96.

26. *The Last Battle*, p. 83. A similar comment is made on p. 142.

27. *Perelandra*, p. 96.

28. Ibid., p. 128.

29. Hence Lewis portrayed those who serve the Devil as being ultimately disorderly in their thought, even when they try to mask their incoherence with lofty words. The incoherence that besets the members of the N.I.C.E. at their banquet (see *That Hideous Strength*, chapter 16) is a dramatic manifestation of the true nature of evil thought. Over against this Lewis set the verbal éclat of the Company of Logres when they are inspired by the celestial intelligences. He had scriptural authority for the former in the story of the tower of Babel in Genesis 11, and for the latter in the episodes of Pentecost described in Acts 2. Inevitably the brilliant banter of the Company of Logres will bring to mind that of Lewis's own small group of fellow Christians at Oxford, the Inklings. "At the Inklings," wrote his brother Warren later, Lewis's own talk "was an outpouring of wit, nonsense, whimsey, dialectical

swordplay, and pungent judgement such as I have rarely heard equalled" (W. H. Lewis, "Memoir of C. S. Lewis" in *Letters of C. S. Lewis*, p. 14).

30. Lewis agreed with Charles Williams's aphorism, "Hell is inaccurate." See *An Arthurian Torso*, p. 106, where he calls it a "great saying." Note the description of satanic behavior in *Perelandra*, pp. 109–11. Also see Lewis's survey of evil's aspects in *The Faerie Queene* (in *Spenser's Images of Life*, especially chapter 4 and pp. 93–97), where one finds evil portrayed as disorderly, pompous, flashy, mentally twisted, indolent, tormented, unloving, lustful, without fecundity, crabbed, and jealous. Beneath Satan's surface lie drabness and emptiness; cf. Withers in *That Hideous Strength*. Lewis's picture of the N.I.C.E. is modeled closely upon this view of evil in the Old Western Culture: the organization is disordered, decayed, chaotic, foolish. See also Lewis's characterization of Milton's Satan in his *A Preface to Paradise Lost*, where he notes, among other things, that Satan displays "a subtle and incessant intellectual activity with an incapacity to understand anything" (p. 99; see the whole of his chapter 13 in that work). Lewis stresses self-centeredness as the heart of the predicament of Milton's Satan: "Satan's monomaniac concern with himself and his supposed rights and wrongs is a necessity of the Satanic predicament. Certainly, he has no choice. He has chosen to have no choice. He has wished to 'be himself,' and to be in himself and for himself, and his wish has been granted. . . . Satan, like Miss Bates, is interesting to read about; but Milton makes plain the blank uninterestingness of *being* Satan. To admire Satan, then, is to give one's vote not only for a world of misery, but also for a world of lies and propaganda, of wishful thinking, of incessant autobiography" (p. 102). That he lies is asserted also in *The Screwtape Letters*, p. 4.

31. *Perelandra*, pp. 129–30.
32. *Mere Christianity*, pp. 53–54.
33. *The Great Divorce*, p. 72.
34. See chapter 7.
35. *Perelandra*, p. 129.
36. *The Great Divorce*, pp. 125–27.
37. See *The Last Battle*, pp. 140–41.
38. *The Problem of Pain*, pp. 128, 127.
39. *The Great Divorce*, p. 69.
40. "The Middle Ages," Lewis once wrote, "knew the devil was an ass" (*Letters of C. S. Lewis*, p. 255). Even Milton's Satan, who has often been admired for his intelligence, activeness and gentlemanliness is, Lewis argued, in some ways a comic figure. "It is a mistake to demand that Satan . . . should be able to rant and posture through the whole universe without sooner or later awakening the comic spirit. . . . We know from his prose works that he [Milton] believed everything detestable to be, in the long run, also ridiculous; and mere Christianity commits every Christian to believing that 'the Devil is (in the long run) an ass' " (*A Preface to Paradise Lost*, p. 95). See *The Magician's Nephew*, chapter 2.

41. See ibid., p. 186.

42. There is also a similarity between the children's experience in the underworld of Narnia and that of the prisoners in Plato's analogy of the cave. In
both of these reality is badly distorted, and that which is of lesser reality is
taken to be absolute. When at long last Jill emerges from the cave into the
overworld of Narnia, she at first has trouble grasping the reality before her
eyes, even as Plato's prisoners do upon emerging from the cave, and when
she turns back to announce the news to her companions who are still in the
cave she is greeted with disbelief. (See *The Silver Chair*, pp. 191–97).

43. *The Silver Chair*, pp. 151–54.

44. See *Reflections on the Psalms*, p. 106.

45. See *The Pilgrim's Regress*, pp. 82–87.

46. "Sweet Desire," in *Poems*, p. 115.

47. The severed head that is the ostensible intelligence behind the N.I.C.E. is
more than a gaucherie, although a number of reviewers of *That Hideous
Strength* took it to be little more than that. It reflects Lewis's belief that Satan
and evil in general are severed from reality, employing the appearance of
intelligence without its substance and being incapable of making right
judgments or having proper insights.

48. *Letters to Malcolm*, p. 21; *Out of the Silent Planet*, p. 68.

49. On pantheism, see "God in the Dock," in *God in the Dock*, p. 241; and *Letters
of C. S. Lewis*, p. 296.

50. "Some Thoughts," in *God in the Dock*, p. 149.

51. See *Christian Behaviour*, chapter 8 (in *Mere Christianity*).

52. "A Reply to Professor Haldane," in *Of Other Worlds*, p. 81.

53. Ibid.

54. See "A Reply to Professor Haldane," in *Of Other Worlds*, pp. 78–80.

55. As a Christian Lewis adhered to the belief in the second coming of Christ,
though he was not greatly interested in speculating about details of that
event, and the subject barely figures in his fiction at all. See further in "The
World's Last Night," in *The World's Last Night and Other Essays*. Lewis's
writings sometimes display an urgency akin to that in some parts of the
New Testament. Note Professor Dimble's eschatological demand that Mark
Studdock decide which side he will serve in the pressing conflict between
good and evil in *That Hideous Strength* (p. 223).

56. "Cross-examination," in *God in the Dock*, p. 265.

57. Ibid., p. 266.

58. "A Reply to Professor Haldane," in *Of Other Worlds*, p. 74.

Chapter 9: Lewis in Perspective

1. Perhaps the most perceptive assessment of Lewis as an essayist is that of
Nevill Coghill in his "Approach to English," in *Light on C. S. Lewis*, pp.
64–66.

2. See *"De Descriptione Temporum,"* in *Selected Literary Essays,* pp. 13–14.

3. Lewis reminded himself with some difficulty, we may assume, through one of his characters in *That Hideous Strength,* that "there's no special privilege for England—no nonsense about a chosen nation" (p. 370). Probably without giving it much thought he made the royal emblem of Narnia a red lion (see, for instance, *The Horse and His Boy,* p. 169) not unlike the heraldic symbol of Britain. His preference for the traditional liturgy of the Church of England is another case in point, though he was prepared to accept serious modern translations of the Bible (see "Modern Translations of the Bible," in *God in the Dock*).

4. *Letters of C. S. Lewis,* p. 207.

5. *A Grief Observed,* p. 25.

6. *"The Salamander,"* in *Poems,* p. 72.

7. Indeed, the feelings may have intensified. Lewis admitted in his autobiography that with passing years romantic loves turned into academicism: "My first delight in Valhalla and Valkyries," he said in *Surprised by Joy,* "began to turn itself imperceptibly into a scholar's interest in them" (p. 165). The phenomenon is one that many intellectuals experience during their maturing years. Lewis tried, of course, to protect himself from the pain of these ravages by denying ultimate validity to romantic sentiments.

8. *A Grief Observed,* p. 31 et passim; *Spirits in Bondage,* p. 25.

9. Lewis would doubtless have wanted his readers to say of him what he said of William Morris in his essay by that name in *Selected Literary Essays:*

> Morris has "faced the facts." This is the paradox of him. He seems to retire far from the real world and to build a world out of his wishes; but when he has finished the result stands out as a picture of experience ineluctably true. No full-grown mind wants optimism or pessimism—philosophies of the nursery where they are not philosophies of the clinic; but to have presented in one vision the ravishing sweetness and the heartbreaking melancholy of our experience, to have shown how the one continually passes over into the other, and to have combined all this with a stirring practical creed, this is to have presented the *datum* which all our adventures, worldly and otherworldly alike, must take into account. (P. 231).

10. Among Lewis's most memorable premises is the *aut Deus aut homo malus* dichotomy. It takes many forms in his writings; typical is his statement that Jesus either was "a raving lunatic of an unusually abominable type, or else He was, and is, precisely what He said" (*The Problem of Pain,* pp. 23–24; see also *Mere Christianity,* p. 56). In "Christian Apologetics" in *God in the Dock* Lewis indicates that he regards this as a stock apologetic argument, and refers the reader to G. K. Chesterton's *The Everlasting Man* for a detailed exposition of the reasoning involved. See also "What Are We to Make of Jesus Christ?" in *God in the Dock;* and *"The Language of Religion,"* in *Christian Reflections,* p. 137.

11. Lewis argued, for example, that if the Christian religion contains something that cannot be found in paganism, that fact shows the superiority of Christianity over paganism. Yet he also argued upon occasion that if Christianity contains concepts that have been anticipated in paganism, that fact demonstrates how God has carefully paved the way within paganism for Christianity. Individually the two arguments simply assert that whatever is in Christianity is superior to paganism; together they prove nothing.

12. When theory and experience suggested different things, Lewis tended to opt for that which was theoretically satisfying to him. He wrote, for instance, learnedly and reassuringly about pain, yet found that actual pain did not fit well into his system. He wrote in one of his letters: "If you are writing a book about pain and then get some actual pain, as I did in my ribs, it does *not* either, as the cynic would expect, blow the doctrine to bits, nor, as a Christian would hope, turn it into practice, but remains quite unconnected and irrelevant, just as any other bit of actual life does when you are reading or writing" (*Letters of C. S. Lewis*, p. 172). Perhaps, however, he does not mean quite what he seems to say, but has in mind the fact that one dare not generalize on the basis of single experiences.

Lewis's Works

The Abolition of Man, or Reflections on Education with Special Reference to the Teaching of English in the Upper Forms of Schools. New York: The Macmillan Company, 1947.

The Allegory of Love: A Study in Medieval Tradition. London: Oxford University Press, 1938 (with corrections).

Arthurian Torso, Containing the Posthumous Fragment of the Figure of Arthur by Charles Williams and a Commentary on the Arthurian Poems of Charles Williams by C. S. Lewis. New York: Oxford University Press, 1948.

Christian Reflections. Edited by Walter Hooper. Grand Rapids, Michigan: William B. Eerdmans Publishing Company, 1967.

The Discarded Image: An Introduction to Medieval and Renaissance Literature. New York: Cambridge University Press, 1964.

Dymer. New edition with preface. New York: The Macmillan Company, 1950.

English Literature in the Sixteenth Century Excluding Drama. Oxford: Oxford University Press, 1954.

An Experiment in Criticism. New York: Cambridge University Press, 1961.

The Four Loves. New York: Harcourt, Brace and World, 1960.

George MacDonald: An Anthology. London: Geoffrey Bles, 1946.

God in the Dock: Essays on Theology and Ethics. Edited by Walter Hooper. Grand Rapids, Michigan: William B. Eerdmans Publishing Company, 1970. (Published in Britain under the title *Undeceptions.*)

The Great Divorce. New York: The Macmillan Company, 1946.

A Grief Observed. New York: Seabury Press, 1961.

The Horse and His Boy. New York: Collier Books, 1970.

The Last Battle. New York: Collier Books, 1970.

Letters of C. S. Lewis. Edited by W. H. Lewis. New York: Harcourt, Brace and World, 1966.

Letters to an American Lady. Edited by Clyde S. Kilby. Grand Rapids, Michigan: William B. Eerdmans Publishing Company, 1967.

Letters to Malcolm: Chiefly on Prayer. New York: Harcourt, Brace and World, 1964.

The Lion, the Witch, and the Wardrobe. New York: Collier Books, 1970.

The Magician's Nephew. New York: Collier Books, 1970.

Mere Christianity. Rev. and enlarged ed., with a new introduction, of three books: *The Case for Christianity, Christian Behaviour,* and *Beyond Personality.* New York: The Macmillan Company, 1960.

Miracles: A Preliminary Study. New York: The Macmillan Company, 1947.

Of Other Worlds: Essays and Stories. Edited by Walter Hooper. New York: Harcourt, Brace and World, 1967.

Out of the Silent Planet. New York: The Macmillan Company, 1965.

Perelandra. New York: The Macmillan Company, 1965.

The Personal Heresy in Criticism. Essays and Studies by Members of the English Association, vol. 19, (1934), pp. 7–28. (Reprinted in 1939 by Oxford University Press as *The Personal Heresy: A Controversy,* by E. M. W. Tillyard and C. S. Lewis.)

The Pilgrim's Regress: An Allegorical Apology for Christianity, Reason, and Romanticism. 3rd ed. Grand Rapids, Michigan: William B. Eerdmans Publishing Company, 1943.

Poems. Edited by Walter Hooper. New York: Harcourt, Brace and World, 1965.

A Preface to "Paradise Lost." New York: Oxford University Press, 1961.

Prince Caspian: The Return to Narnia. New York: Collier Books, 1970.

The Problem of Pain. New York: The Macmillan Company, 1962.

Reflections on the Psalms. New York: Harcourt, Brace and World, 1958.

Rehabilitations and Other Essays. New York: Oxford University Press, 1939.

The Screwtape Letters and Screwtape Proposes a Toast. New York: The Macmillan Company, 1961.

Selected Literary Essays. Edited by Walter Hooper. Cambridge: at the University Press, 1969.

The Silver Chair. New York: Collier Books, 1970.

Spenser's Images of Life. Edited by Alastair Fowler. New York: Cambridge University Press, 1967.

Spirits in Bondage: A Cycle of Lyrics (under the pseudonym Clive Hamilton). London: William Heinemann, 1919.

Studies in Medieval and Renaissance Literature. Collected by Walter Hooper. New York: Cambridge University Press, 1966.

Studies in Words. 2nd ed. Cambridge: at the University Press, 1967.

Surprised by Joy. New York: Harcourt, Brace and World, 1956.

That Hideous Strength: A Modern Fairy-Tale for Grown-Ups. New York: The Macmillan Company, 1965.

They Asked for a Paper: Papers and Addresses. London: Geoffrey Bles, 1962.

Till We Have Faces: A Myth Retold. New York: Harcourt, Brace and Company, 1957.

The Voyage of the Dawn Treader. New York: Collier Books, 1970.

The Weight of Glory and Other Addresses. Grand Rapids, Michigan: William B. Eerdmans Publishing Company, 1965. (Published in Britain under the title of *Transposition and Other Addresses.*)

The World's Last Night and Other Essays. New York: Harcourt Brace Jovanovich, 1973.

Index

Not included in this index are persons and things mentioned only once in the text or notes. Also not indexed are frequently used words such as God, Christ, Christianity, Satan, love, evil, and reason. Likewise generally omitted are imaginative names and terms that appear in Lewis's fiction, such as Narnia, Deep Heaven, Atlantean magic, Ungit, and Old Solar.

DATE DUE